21 DAYS IN AFRICA

A HUNTER'S SAFARI
JOURNAL

21 DAYS IN AFRICA

A HUNTER'S SAFARI JOURNAL

Daniel J. Donarski Jr.

STACKPOLE
BOOKS

Published by
STACKPOLE BOOKS
5067 Ritter Road
Mechanicsburg, PA 17055
www.stackpolebooks.com

Printed in China

First edition

10 9 8 7 6 5 4 3 2 1

Library of Congress Cataloging-in-Publication Data

Donarski, Daniel J.
   21 days in Africa : a hunter's safari journal / Daniel J. Donarski Jr.
     p. cm.
   Includes index.
   ISBN-13: 978-0-8117-0288-1; 978-0-8117-0436-6 (special limited edition)
   ISBN-10: 0-8117-0288-X; 0-8117-0436-X (special limited edition)
  1. Big game hunting—South Africa—Anecdotes. 2. Donarski, Daniel J.—Travel—South Africa. I. Title.

SK251.D66 2008
799.2'60968—dc22
2007023699

*For Mary Jane and Daniel J. Donarski Sr., my parents,
who allowed me to wander.*

Contents

Preface

The first question you should be asking before you read my book is this: Who the hell paid for this trip so I could go along? It's a dirty little secret in the outdoor writers' world that those whiz-bang trips you read about, the gear you hear glowing reports about, are in large part words written about free trips and free gear.

This safari was bought and paid for in full by me from start to finish. (Okay, with a little help from my wife.) No deals were given, nor asked for. I am beholden to no one or to any company. Cabela's did supply three shirts and help with a scope and double rifle case. Remington built a .375 H&H for me at a sale price.

I could have gotten a pile of stuff. I could have gotten freebies. What impressed me about Robert Ruark and his classic, *Horn of the Hunter*, was that he embarked on his safari with his own cash. I wanted to do the same. I did the same.

I believe that for some foolish and sentimental reason Ruark wrote the book at first for himself, and secondarily hoping that somehow his words would touch a reader or two. They certainly touched me. I heard the flare of the notes from the hunting horn. They ripped through me. I heeded their call.

In this section I'm supposed to tell you, the reader, some things you might like to know before getting into the book. Which means that I have to assume some things. That is a dangerous thing for me to do. So, instead of more normal A–Z, I think it best to explain why I wanted to wear my pen on my sleeve.

I have, as you probably have, read numerous books on the how-to and where-to on any number of species we hunt for. These run the gamut from quite good to pure rubbish. There is one style in the hunting genre that has been tragically overlooked, specifically the personal "why" and the narrative. In fact, in the blood-sport world, only the fly-fishing genre still relishes the narrative personal journey.

Think of all the highly successful narrative books centered around fly fishing. These stories warm the heart on a chilly night; they are thoughtful—at least the good ones—and bring a personal perspective to the genre.

Now think of the last time you saw a modern narrative book revolving around hunting, written as the fishing tales are. You can't think of one, can you? That's just wrong. I hope to change that with this book sharing my experiences during a three-week safari to South Africa.

My name is neither Ruark nor Hemingway. Yet I hope I can approach their literary achievements. That is, to tell a story from a single safari that holds the reader's interest and has the reader sitting beside the fire at night with me. It will dive into the thought process of the safari mystique. It will twist and turn with the terrain, bringing the reader along on an amazing journey filled with adventure and strange sights.

Writing about the rules governing South African hunting is dangerous. In the past four months alone, there have been at least three major changes. Yet my writing will provide some idea as to the current regulations. You'll find the latest information on planning a safari to get as much as you can from your trip to Africa.

This information will be offered as brief interruptions to the story in order to more fully illustrate the salient points. Rifle and bullet selection, travel insurance, presafari preparations, including physical fitness and the numerous forms required, clothing, et cetera, are all covered in these brief departures from the main story and are offered by asking the reader to "go around the bend" for a moment.

Too many people believe that Africa is all gone, particularly South Africa. It is not. Through my words and photos I hope to show the reader just how close and wonderful Africa is. From the big city of Johannesburg to the Zulu village of Wasbank, I want you to see and feel this incredible place.

I want you to come to realize that there still is very real adventure in our modern world. That it is up to you to listen to the hunting horn's flare and heed its call. That you, too, have the innate ability to go on an adventure; the only limits are your own imagination and desire.

In its most basic form, what you are reading is a journal, my journal. I didn't plan for it to be anything more than that. Just something I could look upon to relive the experience on brutally cold Michigan nights. Then Diana Rupp at *Sports Afield* asked me to do a story about the bushbuck hunt. Some writers whom I highly regard read the story and asked me to tell them more, and then said they thought there was a book here. Stackpole Books thought so, too. I hope they are right.

I kept in the raw language, though it is tempered some. I kept in my personal opinions as I saw fit. I'm a former Army infantry officer. Arguing with an infantryman is like wrestling with a pig—you both get dirty but the pig likes it. I have opinions; you are going to hear some.

I'm a hunter. I kill things. I have full knowledge and appreciation of what I do. Emotionally I'm a silly sap. I weep at movies. And, I get a bit misty when I stroke the fur or feathers of an animal that has just fallen to my bullet or arrow. I call it hunter's remorse. So sue me, that's who I am. I am also a provider of food for myself and others, a wildlife manager, and a lover of where the wild things are.

Like Ruark's tome did for me, I can only hope that someone out there will be inspired enough to do something as simple as dream. Dream of an adventure. Of fires welcoming you to camp at night. Of hills ablaze in golden grasses and studded with green acacias. Of beautiful animals with funny looking horns. And then do something to realize that dream.

In the end I hope you'll understand that I am only the puppet on the string. Africa is the dancing puppet's master. Africa is the star. She works magic in those strings. I pray she isn't disappointed at my attempt to describe her wonders.

Acknowledgments

There simply wouldn't be a book if it weren't for some writers who encouraged me to write more. Two, in particular, deserve special note: Jim Juntilla, a remarkable fishing scribe, who knows that there is so much more to fishing than the fish; and Jerry Dennis, the finest natural history essayist working today. Both encouraged me to go beyond the brass tacks and lay it out there. Someday I hope to paint the pictures you two do so well with my words. I hope you guys aren't disappointed with this effort.

Kevin Michalowski, my editor, has the patience of Job, and allowed me to let my hair down and simply tell the story as it happened without restraint. That is all too rare in this world. Don Gulbrandsen, the acquisitions editor at Stackpole, told me from the start that this book would be a stretch for Stackpole but was willing to go to bat for the project. He also kept me on track and on schedule, massaging my doubts with personal encouragement.

Pierre van Tonder and Spyker Joubert, Anneli van Tonder, Clinton van Tonder, and Isak, Robert, Cyril, and Moses. You welcomed me into your world as an unknown entity, just another client, and left me bewitched and enchanted, and as a friend.

Tielmann DeVillers and Awie Marais from Moreson, Monte and Nadine Pienaar from Kwaggashoek, Francois and Petra Heynes of Kameelkop—landowners and land managers, who have done more than their share to ensure that the land remains, the animals prosper, and the dreams continue. If only all owners and managers would do the same. . . .

Doug Chester, my friend and coconspirator, who brought me to the edge and then pushed me over, starting my love affair with Africa. Margaret, his wife, and Dave and Mary Westphal, friends all, who invited me to join them and then allowed me to tell our tale.

My wife, Kris, and my children, Karen and Eric. You have put up with my mood swings and dreams, my infinitely "itchy feet," allowing me to reach out for those dreams and scratch that itch. I don't know how you do it, or why. I'm just very lucky that you do. Without you I'd be lost.

Commonly Hunted Game

For all practical purposes, South Africa is an antelope hunting destination. Arguably it is the best country in which to take the most species. Small cats, jackals, and hogs are also favorite game. The following is a list of commonly hunted animals that our group took on safari.

COMMONLY HUNTED ANTELOPE

Black Wildebeest, a.k.a. White-Tailed Gnu

Average size: 365 lbs; shoulder height: 47 inches. A grassland species often seen in big herds, the black wildebeest is known as the "clown of the veldt" due to its seemingly foolish antics when disturbed. Both sexes have horns that sweep down off the fore-head and then back upwards. The males' horns are much heavier and longer. Coat is dark gray. Mane is light sand-colored with black tips.

Blue Wildebeest, a.k.a. Brindled Gnu

Average size: 535 lbs; shoulder height: 47 inches. Often called "the poor man's buffalo," this species inhabits grasslands and thornveldt and is found in small herds. Both sexes have cattlelike horns, and as usual, the males' horns are much heavier. Coat is blue-black with brindled striping.

Bushbuck

Average size: 125 lbs; shoulder height: 31 inches. This member of the spiral horned antelope family has tightly twisted horns and is considered dangerous, particularly when cornered or wounded. It is territorial and inhabits thick river bottoms and dense thorn patches. Bushbuck are quite secretive and solitary in nature. Only the males have horns. Coat is mahogany to chocolate with some spots on the hind.

Common Reedbuck

Average size: 175 lbs; shoulder height: 36 inches. Loves the tall grasslands and marshy areas. Establishes territories, and when startled will often bound away, only to drop into the grass after a short run. Only the male has horns, which curve out toward the ears and then climb up and forward. Coat is tawny like a white-tailed deer.

Eland

Average size: 1,500 lbs; shoulder height: 67 inches. The largest member of the antelope family, the eland is highly adaptable to a variety of habitats and is commonly found in small herds. Both sexes have horns, but the males' are larger. Horns are tightly spiraled or twisted. Coat is tawny with white stripes.

Gemsbok, a.k.a. Oryx

Average size: 520 lbs; shoulder height: 46 inches. Often called "the desert warrior," the gemsbok favors arid, open environments and is found in small herds. Both sexes possess horns, which are generally straight and quite long. In this case, the females' horns are often longer, though the males' horns are thicker. Coat is gray with a dark blaze on the chest extending along the bottom of the body. Face has a distinct mask of black on white.

Impala

Average size: 145 lbs; shoulder height: 36 inches. The impala is a beautiful antelope found in herds from a half dozen to over 100 in the thornveldt to the open grasslands. Only the males have horns, which are swept back in a "saddle" before reaching for the sky. Coat is cinnamon with a noticeable dark stripe on both sides of buttocks.

Kudu

Average size: 500 lbs; shoulder height: 60 inches. Known as "the gray ghost," the kudu is found in loose herds rarely numbering more than ten. It favors open woodlands but isn't afraid to get into the thick stuff. Only the males have horns that majestically spiral upward in a corkscrew fashion. Coat is gray with white stripes. Face shows a white chevron just below the eyes.

Mountain Reedbuck
Average size: 65 lbs; shoulder height: 30 inches.
A small antelope, the mountain reedbuck favors the
habitat implied by its name—mountainous terrain.
Males' horns are rarely longer than eight inches and
curve up and out. The female has no horns. Their
coat is grayish-red in color. Below the ear is a single
black spot.

Nyala
Average size: 240 lbs; shoulder height: 45 inches.
Possibly the prettiest antelope, nyala thrive in thick
cover such as forests of dense woods. They are generally solitary, particularly the males. Only the males
have horns, which are formed in an elegant medium
single spiral and are often tipped with ivory. Coat is
dark gray with white stripes. A long beard extends
from the chin past the front legs. A beautiful white
mane extends along the entire back.

Red Hartebeest
Average size: 150 lbs; shoulder height: 50 inches.
A social animal often found in herds of 50 or more,
red hartebeest prefer open plains and grasslands.
Male horns are much heavier than the females'.
Horns resemble the handlebars of a Harley Davidson
with their sweptback look. Coat is a dusty red color.

Springbok
Average size: 75 lbs; shoulder height: 30 inches.
The springbok is the national animal of South Africa.
Generally found in small herds, this grassland
species is a speedster. Both sexes have horns that
resemble a lyre or a heart. Male horns are much
heavier than female horns. Their coat is light brown
with a dark Nike-like swoosh extending from the front
shoulder to the hind. White is found underneath. A
gorgeous white ruff along the spine is hidden by the
light brown. The face is white with a dark strip from
the eye to the corner of the mouth.

OTHER SPECIES

 **Warthog**

Genet

 **Zebra**

Jackal

 **Baboon**

Other antelope species, particularly sable, roan, and lechwe, are also available but entail a more specialized, pricier safari.

The "Big Five" (lion, leopard, elephant, rhino, and Cape buffalo) are also available but are extremely limited and hunting is aggressively controlled. The same can be said for crocodile and hippo.

Beginnings

orty-some years is a long time for a beginning, but that's how long it took.

Growing up in Green Bay, Wisconsin, was easy. Sure, there were the trials and tribulations of adolescence and puberty. Trials by fire and torment of teenage male hormones raging, the ever-present hated nicknames, trying to fit in. They all sucked. But it was still easy.

From my parents' home it was a short fifteen-minute walk down the street, through a ritzy neighborhood, into abandoned farm fields and finally over the East River Bridge on Hoffman Road. Once over the bridge, we were in the wilds. Technically it was old pastureland, but to us it was wild.

In the summer we carried fishing rods and caught small bullhead and perch. In the fall, after we had turned 14 and passed the hunter's safety course, we carried our shotguns. Yes, shotguns. We carried them in thin vinyl cases, shotshells in our pockets, past the houses, down the road, over the bridge. In full view! Try doing that now.

Squirrels, pheasants, rabbits, and ducks were the goals. Sometimes, but really not that often, my brothers and I and a handful of friends were successful.

I remember the first duck I shot, a drake blue-winged teal. The bird was juking and jiving down the river, came into range, and I shot it. Unfortunately the bird's momentum carried it across the river, and it landed on the other side. Somehow I convinced my brother Mark that since I shot it, and saw where it landed, that it was he who should swim the river and retrieve it.

He did, too. Stripped to his underwear on that chilly October afternoon, he walked into the dirty brown water, grumbled once or twice, and then swam for the other shore. Mark found the bird and brought it back. Not in his teeth, though, which disappointed me just a tad. When Mark told my father what he had done, and why, I was not exactly on dad's "favorite son" list.

A few years later, when I shot my first buck, Mark was with me again. And, scoundrel or clever fellow that I am, I convinced him to gut the thing. God, it was great to be the eldest!

We hunted a lot back then. Fueled by dad's love of the wilds, and his tales of deer camp, we caught the bug hard. Mark, Tom, Paul, and I wanted to be hunters. The youngest in the family, my sister, Jane, along with my mother, cheered us on and hailed a heavy game bag, but neither ever wanted to be personally involved with the collecting of game. As the eldest, I was able to start first.

Sunday mornings, after High Mass at Resurrection Catholic Church, the whole family loaded up the blue Chevy Biscayne station wagon and drove to my grand-parents' house, about ten miles away. There, every Sunday, stale cheese and stale bread, along with real wieners and, sometimes, Polish sausage would be laid out. Flavored pop would be offered if we were exceptionally well mannered.

Behind my grandparents' house was 60 acres of wild country, which they owned. After our lunch my brothers and I would head out, after being warned for the umpteenth time to stay out of the swamp (we never did), and go exploring. Covered by high sand hills and forests of birch, maple, and oak, we pretended we were hunting. Deer were there, as were more than a few pheasants. We climbed Eagle's Peak and scoured the ground for wild asparagus.

When we returned from exploring, if it was late summer or early fall, dad and grandpa would be found talking about the upcoming deer season and the hunting shack. We four boys clung to the outskirts of the conversation, hanging on every word of the magical season, imagining what it must be like. We couldn't wait until we were old enough to join our father and grandfather and our uncles.

It was a rule in our family that at 13 a grandson could join his father at the hunting shack for the opening weekend of deer season. At 14, and if we had passed the hunter's safety course, we could carry a gun if we stayed with our father or an uncle. Fifteen was the magical year that we could go out on our own, if we followed all the rules. I remember each of those first three years at the shack like they were just last week.

On special Sundays, and if grandpa had finished reading them, he would allow us to take his sporting magazines home with us. *Outdoor Life, Sports Afield,* and *Field & Stream* were all there, and we devoured them. I can't say for sure, but I'm relatively certain that the stories centered on the Dark Continent, Africa, were the ones that interested my brothers as much as they did me. So it was with his copies of *National Geographic,* which, of course, we only picked up for the articles, never the pictures of the naked ladies who lived in Africa, or elsewhere.

I pretended I was along as Ruark, Hemingway, and Capstick chased and were chased by lion and Cape buffalo. When a leopard nearly caught O'Connor, I huffed and puffed, and sweat ran down my back and into my eyes from running beside him.

My mind took me to the jungle, where I slashed through vines and struggled over tree roots as big as any maple's trunk. I felt the sticky heat, struggled to see through the dark rain forest for that one splash of gray marking the location of an elephant we had tracked for more than ten miles. Hearing the trumpet blast, then the thunder of monstrous feet and the cracking of trees as the elephant charged, I settled behind the gun. Seeing the elephant's head, ears laid back and trunk thrust forward, the crosshairs settled on that one small sweet spot right between the eyes and just underneath that bony knob found 4 inches high. The elephant shook and buckled under the impact of the .416 Rigby. It fell with its trunk no more than two feet from the end of my barrel. Ninety pounds of bright white ivory on each side, both in perfect arcs and only a one-inch difference in length.

My mind took me to the hills and plains where herds of zebra, wildebeest, impala, and gazelle grazed and lions fed. It's the dry season, and the small river running through the golden grass held water in only the deepest of its holes. We settled into our chairs in front of the fire after dinner. A ceiling of more stars than darkness covered us. We listened to the night come alive. Baboons roared in alarm not far off, near the river bottom. Listening closer we heard the cough of a leopard looking for his supper. A soft breeze carried the long grunts of lions followed by a distinct and chilling roar no more than 100 yards from our tented safari camp.

Tomorrow, maybe tomorrow would be our day. . . .

And so it was with me, and maybe with you, too. We dreamed of things we wished to see, and even with our young eyes, we knew that our chances of realizing those dreams were at best quite poor. No, perhaps this wouldn't be for us. Too much money, not enough time. Too dangerous, not enough of "real" Africa left. All of this reality did nothing to extinguish the dream. You just never know. . . .

Robert Ruark, early on in his classic, *Horn of the Hunter,* said it better than anyone else ever has or ever will, "Dreams are not taxed for young boys, not even the wildest ones."

I continued to dream. Floundering through college with seven documented changes in my major, into an Army career, then marriage and children, guiding fly anglers across Michigan's Upper Peninsula, in Wyoming, and into the Carribean, and writing about fishing and hunting, through all of it I still dreamed. And, through all of it, when the dreams turned to hunting, the dreams turned to Africa.

But they stayed as dreams. There was still too much required, and not enough for it to be realized. I was never old enough, or had enough of (fill in the dream-killing word of your choice).

Through my writing I met Tom, who has become one of my closest friends. He introduced me to Doug, a fiendishly delightful collector of people, who is now just as close. When the three of us get together, we aren't just dangerous, we're terminal. And, this fellow Doug, through a slick twist of fate, brought me together, in South Africa no less, with Pierre and Spyker, two Professional Hunters. (Professional hunter should not technically be capitalized, but they deserve it. They earned it.)

Young men's dreams may not be taxed but, when realized, will serve to pick your pocket. So be it, and let them pick away. For, as I was to find out, I came away from Africa, my dream, with much more than the simple cost of admission allowed. You're invited to come along for the ride.

CHAPTER 1

Michigan to Johannesburg

he very last e-mail I received from Doug Chester before beginning this safari was delivered May 12, 2005. It promised a lot.

Dan,

It's over there, just beyond that tree line. Just past that little hill. Or the next one. Everything we ever wanted.

FFA—fame, fortune, adventure. Beautiful women. Epic journeys with legendary friends. Dappled sunlight. Large, exotic animals. Vultures circling. Strange-looking, exotic people speaking unknown languages. Shimmering hot blue-white sun, and stars close enough to touch with your fingertip. Tiny, glimmering campfires in the black of night.

And all we have to do is walk over there and collect it.

Karibu, Africa! (Welcome to Africa.)

Doug, who is again, as he dreamed, Bwana Kiboko

3 A.M.: Moreson Ranch, Vrede Free State Province, Republic of South Africa

My watch screamed the time, or more properly whined. For the last two hours, I've tossed and turned, fighting for more sleep. "Damn," I muttered as my feet hit the cold tile floor of the chalet. No more sleep.

Then I smiled. This was my first morning outside of any hotel in anywhere South Africa, in the savannahs of Free State.

It was chilly in the chalet. I could hear Doug, at least I hoped it was Doug, snoring from the other bedroom. I turned the light on over the sink, filled a coffee pot with water, and set the heat on.

The door to the chalet creaked as I opened it. The night wasn't black. With the nearly full moon, it was bluish-gray and shiny. It was cold outside, and too dark to really see. I went back to the table and waited for coffee.

1

Just your typical African sunrise in the Free State, taken from the porch of my chalet at Moreson. (You can see tomorrow just beyond the farthest clouds.)

By 4 A.M. I had three cups of coffee in me. At 4:30 I stepped back outside. To the east I could see the silhouette of high distant hills. Their crest now in a bright silver-gray. The moon had set, and where there were no stars just an hour before, the sky was now filled with twinkling lights so close you could throw a rock and hit one. Low grunting came from somewhere in the distance. It was probably a wildebeest. I was told they grunt like that. I was in Africa!

Just after the grunt, a low muffled cough came from beyond the lodge slowly showing itself as shadows. Followed by a long roar just beyond the lodge. I was in *Africa*!

The roars continued off and on as the sun struggled to climb above the distant hills. Wildebeest appeared first as black blobs moving across a gray landscape. Then as individual shadows as the sun continued to climb.

Just before 5:30, the eastern sky transformed from a fading silver glow to a blend of bright yellows and oranges highlighted with red in the east and a spectrum wheel of deep blues and finally purple in the west. Stars disappeared like waves moving across the sky as it brightened. Grunting became more frequent. Birdcalls could be heard in the trees to the north.

It took a bit of strength, but the sun did reach the summit of the hills. When it did, the land erupted in song. Lions roared constantly, and laughing doves kept hitting the repeat button, never ending their song. The wildebeest grunted, providing the percussion.

Now, in the first light of day, I could see the animals. A couple dozen black wildebeest came by to pay a visit at no more than 30 yards. Farther into the grasslands, a herd of blesbok several hundred strong made their way to an inky waterhole. Springbok scampered father out into the plains. Lions continued to roar.

Africa, what a tease. All the books and stories I had read about her had teased me. Africa, in the flesh, in the early light, with the birds, and the sweet scent of the grasses, is the High Priestess of Tease. She ever so slowly disrobes the cloak of night, and when I saw her in the soft light of early morning, that first real morning, my body hummed in delight, in wonder.

And to think that just a few short days ago, I was safely tucked in and secure in my own little everyday world of Sault Ste. Marie, Michigan. In more ways than one, it was a galaxy away.

Getting here was interesting.

"Trust me." Doug had said, during more than one phone call over the past five months.

I did. I did to the point of buying into this fool's journey hook, line, and sinker—or in this case, bullet, scope, and barrel. Bwana Kiboko, a moniker given to Doug by the game trackers on his last safari, sang the Siren's call. I had the simple audacity to believe I could listen, and do so willingly, and not be dashed amongst the rocks.

Kiboko, by the way, is Swahili for hippopotamus. With Doug's unquenchable thirst and large frame, the name fits like a glove.

It should be noted, and remembered throughout, that if it were not for Mr. Douglas Chester, Attorney-At-Law, this little trek to Africa would never have happened. It was he who went on safari in Tanzania with his wife, Margaret. Pierre van Tonder was his professional hunter, or PH. Three buffalo, a pair of topi, and a warthog came home from that trip.

It was Doug who wrote an outstanding short book of his trip, *Moyowasi Stories.* He gave me a copy. Full of excitement and adventure, the book and his stories served as the spark. The fuel came in the form of his announcement of a return trip in 2005, this time for plains game in South Africa. The PH would again be Pierre. No one else would do. "You should come along," he said. "It'll be great," he said.

A kudu morning, I hope. Up on the third step of the climb, we found a group of giraffes munching away on grass at a waterhole. They let us pass at about 25 meters.

IMPORTING GUNS

In order to import guns to South Africa, even temporarily for a hunt, there's a bit of paperwork. First, you need proof of ownership of the firearms you are bringing in. For U.S. citizens this comes in the form of a Declaration of Ownership form you get through any U.S. Customs office. I live in a U.S. Port of Entry town, which means for me it was a quick trip to the border, a quick check of the serial numbers on the two rifles I would be bringing, and then, finally, the heavy thumping of the red stamp saying they were mine was embossed on the form.

The second piece of paper you need is what is called a "letter of invitation." You get this from your professional hunter or your outfitter. It tells the customs officer and the police officer you'll meet in Johannesburg that someone actually invited you. It also tells them the duration of your hunt and generally where you are staying and who is responsible for your lowly ass while there.

Third is something that is called the SAP Form 520. It may still be called that, but you never know. Two months before this trip, the South African government changed the way it did business and altered the form. This one, SAP 520, is a full eight pages long. It must be filled out in black ink. It must not be signed until the police officer screening your papers at the Johannesburg airport says to sign it.

The SAP 520 also asks for a detailed list of all ammunition broken down by caliber or gauge, shot size or grain of bullet, and manufacturer. Hand-loaded rounds are actually a bit easier. As you are the manufacturer, you don't have to go through the gyrations of filling out column three (or was it four?), when you have different grain bullets for the same caliber.

And, like the carnival barker who entices you in with a quick look at the bearded lady, he invited me to once again look at the photos from Tanzania.

The ember glowed hot when my lovely wife, Kris, gave her consent. This was surprisingly easy. I still struggled with the financial questions as well as the "worthiness" issue. The financial one was easiest. Easiest here should in no way be implied to mean easy; only that the financial question was easier than the worthiness. Worthiness, as in: "Am I a good enough shot not to screw the pooch? Am I in good enough shape? Even with the money available, should I spend it?"

With all the questions answered, I found myself patiently awaiting the call to board the flight that would take me from Detroit to Amsterdam, then on to Johannesburg. It was an eight-hour wait. Eight hours is a long time to wait anywhere. The "what if" gremlins struck hard.

What if my guns don't make it due to some luggage monkey taking a shine to the bright, new, aluminum case? What if I miss my connection in Amsterdam? What if the South African customs agents don't like the way I look, or my letter of introduction?

A small herd of red hartebeest works its way through an African grassland.

Many of the "what ifs" no one has any control over. These include mechanics, strikes, sick pilots or flight attendants, weather, migrating birds, deer on the runway, or the death of your third cousin on your mother's side, twice removed. In other words, there are any number of things that will delay or cancel your flight. Anyone who travels more than occasionally has had a flight cancelled or delayed. This was my dream; I was worried. Maybe a better term is anxious. But none of the "what ifs" came to pass.

I tried to watch the in-flight movie. I couldn't. My brain wouldn't let me. Instead a picture of Africa filled my mind's eye. I heard lions roar at night. Kudus barked through the whine of the engines and disappeared into the acacia's silence. A leopard sawed somewhere in the tall grass, stalking a warthog. The scotch served by the staff wasn't placed on a plastic fold-down table. It was placed on the bare earth beside a hunting chair in front of a fire burning a hole in the dark African sky.

My body hummed.

Do you remember when you first saw, in real life, a naked woman's body and realized the delights it could deliver? (Female readers can change that word to male, if they want.) Do you remember how your body tingled, all synapses firing at once and continuing in a constant rhythm? Remember how the intensity increased as your hand drew near her supple skin? How, upon touching this new fruit of sensuality, you were overwhelmed with the electricity of the moment? That sexual electricity, that intensity, is how my body hummed. It continued to hum throughout this journey.

It was Sunday, 6 A.M., when the plane landed in Amsterdam on time. The connection to South Africa was four hours away.

The Amsterdam airport is much like a Greyhound bus station in downtown anywhere Big City, USA. Even with the casino, it is just an overgrown bus station. But still, I was on my way to Africa for a safari.

And what is Africa without missionaries? Honest to God missionaries. Three groups of them waiting for the plane to Johannesburg. My plane. Each group was clad in matching T-shirts: red, lime green, and blue. Each shirt was emblazoned with a slogan, but the one that stood out was on the green shirts. It read "Mission 2005: Enlightenment in Africa." For some reason I thought perhaps that Africans might be offended to be told they need enlightenment.

After nearly 24 hours without sleep and only fitful sleep before that, I wasn't ready for what happened next. One of the leaders approached his group and declared out of the clear blue sky, "Let's sing." He proceeded to belt out a hymn, and was soon joined by his flock. There was applause. And more than one declaration of "Amen."

Not to be outdone, the next group broke into song. I was feeling sick and headed for the bathroom. As I emerged from the lavatory, the third group was warming up. I turned away, walking to nowhere in particular.

Thirty minutes later I returned to a scene of hugging, some applause, and more "Amens." But, the singing had stopped. For now. When the announcement came that boarding would begin soon, the entire group broke into song again.

I prayed. I prayed hard. "Dear Lord, I know these people mean well. But please, Lord, please help to keep them quiet on board this plane." While I do believe in prayer, I do not believe that all prayers are answered. But, for whatever reason, the group didn't sing on the plane. Hallelujah!

I had a plan: I would not fall asleep on the flight to South Africa! Not once. The plane was scheduled to arrive at 9:30 P.M. Staying awake on the plane meant I'd sure need sleep upon arrival. As I was arriving at night, I'd have a full night's sleep to look forward to. That's called a jumpstart on getting over jet lag. It's also called a very good idea.

So I did not sleep. I kept myself occupied by watching the KLM stewardesses. (Yes, I know they are called flight attendants now, but either way the women were beautiful.) And waiting for them to come around with their cart offering doses of scotch at regular intervals. I carried a pocket-sized copy of *The Perfect Shot: Africa* and studied intently. Then there was the scotch—oh yeah, I already mentioned that. I like scotch, I'll mention it again.

The Alps, snow-capped with mountain lakes looking like deep blue gashes between the ridges, stand out in my mind. But what I remember most is the night. It came in an instant somewhere around the equator. One moment it was bright and sunny, the next dark. Black dark.

This was true blackness unlike anything I had ever seen. It wrapped around the plane, the navigation lights disappearing into an oozing empty darkness that swallowed everything and allowed nothing through.

Then, after two sleep-deprived days, countless little worries, and my first brush with real missionaries, the wheels were lowered. Johannesburg spread out like any big city anywhere. The wheels screeched on the tarmac. I was in Africa!

CHAPTER 2

Johannesburg

'm not one who tolerates waiting in line. If there are unmanned lanes in the grocery store, and the line has more than four people, I've been known to put ice cream into the grocery cart and simply leave the cart somewhere in the store as the ice cream melts and I walk out empty-handed.

Immigration at Johannesburg was a lot like those grocery stores. Two lines open for aliens. Three lines open for South African citizens. Guess which one had the longest line. I'm not complaining though. Five minutes into the wait, six other lanes opened up, and less than fifteen minutes later, I was standing in front of a rather formidable black lady with a badge.

"Good evening, ma'am," says I in my best imitation of Eddie Haskel.

A large hand was thrust out and opened in front of me. No words were spoken. I handed her my passport and the incoming visitor declaration form I filled out on the plane. She took the passport and handed back the declaration form without a glance. Still no words were spoken.

She gave my passport the once-over and shot me a quick glance. The stamp came down on my passport with a quick and loud thump. Her hand again thrust itself out toward me, holding my passport. I think the South African immigration folks went through the same training as those in the United States.

"Thank you, ma'am. Have a good night." A grunt, maybe, but certainly a slight smile crossed her lips. She must have been the valedictorian of her class.

Now it's on to baggage and that ultimate of wonder, the baggage bingo game. I wasn't worried, not that much anyhow, about my guns. Packed in an international airline-approved aluminum locked case, I was fairly certain they were on board the plane from Amsterdam. Heck, one of the stewardesses, before we took off from Amsterdam, came up to my seat, addressed me by name, and told me that my guns were on board.

The Dutch government is awful touchy about firearms. At the time of my trip, you needed to inform the sales agent whom you purchased the airline tickets from that you were going to be traveling with guns. They asked for the make and model, as well as the caliber, but not the serial number.

It's a bit tougher now. The Dutch government has outlawed bringing guns into the country even in transit to somewhere else. Even if you never leave the airport, even if your connection is only a 45-minute wait, your guns are not welcome.

You can, however, get a special form that gives you extra special permission to do just that. All you need to do is get the Netherlands Customs Office in Groningen to convince its government that you are a superb member of the human race. It then, if the wind is blowing in the proper direction and the stars are aligned, will issue you a special permit for you and your guns to stay in its airport while waiting for your connecting flight. All this, and only if you get the application to customs in time for its electronic body cavity search. Trouble is, it won't tell you how soon before you fly you need to apply for the form.

Make that two forms. In its infinite wisdom, the Netherlands government does not have a form that works both ways. On your flight to Africa, or anywhere you may be taking guns to, if you touch down in the Netherlands, you are required to have one form, properly approved. On your flight back to the United States or else-where, you'll need the same form, just a new one that says you are flying some-where, again properly approved. And, as your flight dates are required, this is not a form you can fill out, get approved, and then sit on until needed.

(In the summer of 2006, these rules changed once again. Now you need only one form that covers you there and back. Stay tuned, however; these too will change.)

Meanwhile, back on the baggage carousel, I saw my big duffel whirling around, having a grand time. And, directly behind the carousel, a silver door opened up and there, in all its brilliant glory, was my gun case. So were a dozen or more other gun cases. I knew the one I was looking at was mine even though there were three exact copies behind the door. How did I know? Simple, I stuck two Grateful Dead decals, those whimsical dancing teddy bears, on my case. All this has been too simple. The waiting must start now. All those guns. All those forms.

Then out of the blue, and wearing dark blue, smartly pressed trousers and a just as smartly pressed white shirt came Simon. At least that's what his ID badge said. It looked official. His smile was so bright it could break ice. Smilin' Simon. Along with Simon were three others, all similarly dressed and badged.

"Sir, are these your guns?" he asked.

"Yes."

"Do you have all your bags, everything?"

"Yes."

"My name is Simon. Your guns, sir, please follow me. I will help."

Sure you will, I thought. Maybe due to his clean and official appearance, maybe due to his greeting and the well-armed police officer standing five feet away, maybe because I was just tired and willing to be led, I followed.

I followed him up two long flights of stairs. My large duffel and my gun case, though wheeled, bounced along right behind me. Simon could move. I tried to keep up.

"Come, sir, quickly please. You'll be first. That is good." First? Sounded good to me.

After the climb Simon, with me struggling along behind, climbed down two other flights of stairs. We entered a rather narrow hall, lots of doors, small spaces behind those doors, no windows.

"Here we are, sir. Wait for me here," he commanded. Simon then disappeared into one of the doors, then through another, and I heard voices. A close look at the second door showed the crest of the South African Police.

A short while later he came back. "The forms, sir, do you have them?"

"Yes."

"All of them—SAP 520, ownership, invitation letter?"

"Yes."

"Filled out in black ink?"

"Yes."

Simon smiled. "Very good, sir. Very good. One more moment, please." Back through the doors he went. Just as quickly he came back.

"Wait for me here, sir. The lady will call for you when she is ready. Wait for me. I will come back for you, but I must check for others with guns." With that he actually scampered off, leaving me standing out in a dimly lit hallway, which led to another short hallway, which led to the office where "the lady" was.

No more than a minute later, I heard a "Come in, please" from what sounded like a young female voice. It was. She was. Young, not yet 30, and beautiful. High cheekbones, smooth skin, eyes that shined like new velvet, very well formed, picture-perfect. And in the uniform of the South African police.

Standing beside her was a man, roughly the same age, and in the same uniform. Well, not the same, they each had their own.

"Papers?" she asked. I handed them over. "Simon was right, you do have them all filled out, correctly and in black ink. You'd be surprised how few do." I detected a smile.

"Please open the gun case and then your baggage. Serial numbers need to be checked and the ammunition accounted for." The male officer checked the serial numbers of the guns and counted the ammo. He gave a quick nod to the lady. Done and done. She scribbled into her logbook.

"Letter of invitation?"

I handed it over as the male officer came to her side on the opposite side of the old desk.

"Sir!" said the male officer, and then spoke an African dialect to the lady. They spoke back and forth for a sentence or two, quite animated.

"Sir, this is the best place. Very beautiful. You are going to KZN, KwaaZulu Natal. That is where I am from. You have chosen well; you will see much game."

The lady nodded in agreement. "Sir, you will have a very good time. Good luck," she said. "Everything is in order, too. You can go. And please do enjoy your stay." She meant that, too. All this immigration and customs stuff was just way too cool, too easy.

In and out in five minutes. Simon, along with nearly a dozen other passengers with guns, was waiting for me.

"Done?"

"Done."

"Very good, sir, please follow."

I assumed this would take me to customs. These assumptions were correct, sort of.

Simon did, in fact, walk me to customs, and when I started going for a line he grabbed my arm. "Follow, please." He shot me one of those "please-follow-me-you-ignorant-tourist, I'm getting you through without any hassle" sort of glances. He did offer one of the customs officers a quick wave.

Now, I have no idea if my guns, and the necessity of going to the police office inside the airport, served the same purpose as other nongun-toting passengers going through customs. All I know is that the declaration form I filled out on board the airplane was never looked at and I never stood in front of any customs officer. I'm not complaining.

Getting past the customs line, Simon started to beat around the bush. The bush he was beating was about tea, grease, payola.

"I helped you, right, sir? Very nice to be first."

I didn't want the bush to die; I knew what it took. That's why I had five $20 bills in my pants pocket, each folded individually so only one would come out at a time.

"Simon, dear fellow, you helped a lot. More than I could ask for. I'd really like to shake your hand." Which I did, and when he felt that crisp paper his smile lit up the hallway. Twenty dollars seemed quite reasonable for me to go effortlessly through the incoming process.

"Anytime for you, sir, anytime. Can I get you a cab?" I wasn't sure if I needed one or not.

A friend I hadn't yet met was supposed to be picking me up. Three months previously I saw a picture of him. I did go to his Web site and found another photo of him right before I left to remind me of the first. Tall, in good physical shape, dirty blond/light brown hair, beard.

Simon and I made our way into the terminal. It was not busy. One of six money-changing stations was open. No other shops were. Then again, it was well past 10 P.M. On a Sunday night no less.

Pierre van Tonder, the professional hunter I had booked the trip with, told me by e-mail that he would be there to pick me up and take me to the hotel. Finding him was another matter.

No one with a beard. But, as I was looking, I saw someone else looking at each person as they entered. Hmm. Luck was with me. It was Pierre.

"You must be Dan. Welcome to Africa. I'm Pierre."

He sure was. An elephant hair bracelet circled one wrist. On the other hung what looked like well-worn pitted plastic. It was really the toenail from a hippo. Around his neck dangled two white objects that looked very much like claws or teeth. Nope, these were the inner nerve core of elephant tusks. I knew what the elephant hair was, the others I found out about later.

"Thanks, it's good to be here and finally meet you."

"You must be tired. Let's get you to a hotel. Do you have reservations?"

I had. Any night before or after your safari starts is on you. I made reservations with Airport Grand Hotel, which advertised itself as just five minutes from the airport.

"Okay, I'm staying at a hotel near there. Let's get you to yours, have a drink, and then I'll see you tomorrow."

I liked him right away. Friendly, thirsty, and seemingly ready to get down to it.

Just as we were leaving the airport, I heard a loud voice and the sound of heavy feet running on tile.

"Stop! Stop!" It was the male police officer from the gun check. I stopped. I also made sure my hands were in plain view.

A thousand things ran through my mind. Pierre looked at me with an expression of "what the hell?"

You may recall that when you fill out SAP 520, the gun import form, that

Meet Pierre van Tonder and his wife, Anneli. He may be the Great White Hunter, the professional hunter; Anneli, however, has a voice as sweet and lyrical as a flute.

you must not sign it until asked to do so. Well, I hadn't, and wasn't asked, so I didn't sign it.

"Sir," says the officer, "I apologize, but you must sign the form. We forgot to have you sign. I am sorry."

I signed the form then, as I was asked to do. After another round of apologies from the officer, and his wishes for a good trip, we were off.

Johannesburg would have been impossible for me to navigate. Hell, I tried to get in the safari car, a Land Cruiser, on the right side, which is the wrong side. Sleep depravity didn't allow me to catch the joke when Pierre asked me if I wanted to drive upon climbing in. The steering wheel six inches from my chest served as no clue, either.

Hallelujah to the stewardesses. Hallelujah to Smilin' Simon. Hallelujah to Pierre. This was coming together quite nicely. And, a big hallelujah to the bartender at the Airport Grand Hotel for staying open when we walked in.

Tonight was my treat. Pierre, needing to drive to his hotel, only had a couple of cocktails. I, on the other hand, took it upon myself to self-medicate and quickly consumed three triple Dewars and waters, in a tall glass.

Meet Doug Chester. He's the one responsible for getting my sorry self to Africa. For that I will be forever grateful.

Pierre, before he left, told me to expect him tomorrow, mid-morning. Four others, including two close friends of mine, Doug and Margaret Chester, and one slight acquaintance, Dave Westphal, and his wife, Mary, who I had never met, were flying in tomorrow morning at 8 A.M.

Pierre would retrieve them from the airport, swing by to get me, and off we'd go.

I was going to sleep. I was going to sleep for a long time.

After Pierre left I ordered one more, a double. Sometimes a fellow is just too wired to sleep. I was trying to prevent such an unpleasant evening.

Which is exactly what I did. But first I watched a rugby game on the TV, and tossed, then turned. But sleep did come.

CHAPTER 3

On to Moreson

Sleep came and went last night. Just before 7 A.M., light screamed through the hotel room window and forced me awake. Shower, shave, coffee, food. Now.

Breakfast at the hotel consisted of a buffet. Eggs, things that looked like sausages, various pastries and breads, and things that didn't look like anything I'd ever seen before. Even mango juice. I ate but didn't taste. I ate quickly. I ate a lot.

The wait staff served the coffee. I believe they grew a bit tired of my cup being empty, so they left the pot after the fourth or fifth filling. I drained the pot. Then charged my lip with tobacco. My Skoal addiction now fixed, I was content yet anxious for Pierre to return. That would have to wait, however, as my friends' plane was still in the air. The waiter brought another pot.

A dozen different languages could be heard from the tables around me. Afrikaans was dominant, but German, a Swahili dialect, what sounded like Dutch, and other tongues drifted in and out. I alone spoke English, except for the wait staff, who doted on me.

"New York?" one of the waiters asked as to where I lived.

"Michigan," I said. He wasn't impressed.

The busboy asked, "Orlando?"

"Michigan," I replied again. The busboy was equally unimpressed. Good thing I didn't just mention the city's name, Sault Ste. Marie.

At 9 A.M. I checked out of the hotel. Sort of. Yes, the bill was paid, but I didn't leave. Pierre said to be ready at 10:00, and on the off chance that the flight was early and the formalities of getting everything and everybody went as quickly as mine had, I wanted to be ready. As much as I detest waiting in line, I am even more disgusted with myself when someone is forced to wait on me not being ready.

By 9:30 I was wired for sound. Waiting. In the lobby. My gear piled in a rough heap next to an overstuffed chair. At 10, still waiting. I noticed the vending machine had cold drinks. I exchanged some money at the front desk. South African cash and coins are simply beautiful. Animals like Cape buffalo, kudu, rhino, and lions grace the paper stuff. Springbok and others grace the coins.

I chose a cold can of Windhoek Light. Yes, a beer, in a vending machine. Brewed in the city of Windhoek in the neighboring country of Namibia. It tasted much like any standard beer from any U.S. brewery. It was different, though.

On the can you'll find, tucked away near the bottom and adjacent to the brewery name, a small red heart. Alongside the heart you'll find a small white rectangle with black letters, much like our surgeon general's warning on cigarettes. I expected to find some sort of alert to pregnant women or some such warning. This was no warning. This was Africa.

Instead, you'll find these words: "Approved as part of the heart foundation eating plan."

Cool. Ya gotta love a beer that's been approved like that. I bought another. For my heart.

Just after noon, Pierre's tan Land Cruiser pulled up, followed by a blue van. I looked hard into the van while toting my bags and gun case to the curb. Doug and Margaret, Dave and Mary, and the driver were all inside. I dropped my bags, set the gun case down, and threw the door open.

"Karibu, welcome to Africa, Dan!" exclaimed Doug. He had tears in his eyes when I threw my arms around him as we hugged. My sunglasses were on due to the bright midday sun. No tears from me. None that showed, anyway.

Margaret gave me a kiss, Dave shook my hand, and Mary and I introduced ourselves. I liked the kiss best.

"Dan," says Pierre, "this is Spyker, another professional hunter who'll be helping us on our safari." We shook hands, and Spyker moved off to the Land Cruiser and loaded my gear. A black man in well-worn pants and a sweater was sitting on top of the well-loaded safari car. "That's Isak, my number-one man," said Spyker. Isak gave me a quick nod and went to packing the vehicle.

A fine lady, and I mean fine, climbed out of the cruiser. Long black hair with a wave, legs that stretched all the way to the ground and back again, with a smile and eyes that would melt the ice caps. "Hello, Dan," she sang. "I'm Anneli, Pierre's wife. It's nice to finally meet you after all Doug has told me." I shook her hand and I swear I was shaking. Her voice was as soft and clear, as musical and alluring as a flute.

We left the hotel, Land Cruiser in the lead driven by Pierre, blue van following with Spyker driving and Anneli riding shotgun. Isak continued to ride in the back of the Cruiser, blasted by wind. A number of thoughts went through my head. Thoughts like a bit of inequity, seeing as there was plenty of room in the Cruiser next to Pierre.

Ten miles out of the city the Cruiser pulled over. Isak hopped out of the back and into the cab. Turns out that his riding in the back was to discourage any foolhardy fellows from doing a quick grab-and-go of our gear at one of the stoplights.

Doug lit his pipe, a prop he is always in control of. The smoke smelled like friendship, and has ever since I first met him. He then promptly fell asleep, lit pipe clenched in his teeth. He was still in control.

We headed south and a bit east, Spyker telling those of us still awake that we were going to be traveling to the Free State, wherever the hell that was. For the sake of easing the reader's questions as to what the Free State is, was, and will be, consider the Free State like a state in the United States or a province in Canada. Four

lanes of highway, rich black pavement, a high sun, and intermittent groups of something called blesbok and others called eland could be seen far off the highway in
prairie-like golden grass.

At about 1 P.M. I heard Doug's stomach rumble, which brought a chuckle. Margaret, being the faithful and attentive wife she is, said, "Oh-oh, Doug's waking up.
He'll want food."

Doug did wake up, too, in a startled early morning soft rumbling grumble. With
his pipe still clenched in his teeth, he declared, or more properly softly roared, "It's
time to feed the bear!"

Our little caravan pulled off into a U.S.-looking gas/food and rest stop ten minutes later. Bright red neon letters declared the restaurant to be Wimpy's.

"We'll grab a quick bite here and then continue on to the first concession," said
Pierre.

This Wimpy's joint is like any other fast-food emporium you have had the mis-
fortune of dining at while on a road trip. Plastic chairs, plastic tables that are made
to look like wood, institutional at its finest.

They come to take your order at Wimpy's. Quite a change from the automatons
behind the counter at Micky D's. The burgers taste the same, though. They do have
all sorts of extras to choose from, meaning you could get some interesting combina-
tions that would thoroughly confuse the folks at the golden arches. I stayed safe
with the bacon, cheese, and mushrooms. Oh yeah, and onions. We ate and hit the
road. It would be the last institutional food I would have for the duration of my stay.

Just before 3 P.M. we pulled off the highway onto a gravel and dirt road. Fifteen
more minutes and we turned off the first road onto a private drive and crossed under

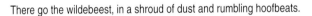
There go the wildebeest, in a shroud of dust and rumbling hoofbeats.

Going on safari doesn't mean roughing it. This is Dave and Mary outside their chalet. Hot and cold running water, real beds, electricity, daily laundry. Roughing it is way overrated.

a gate declaring we were at Moreson. The grasses just outside the window were joined by cosmos, still in flower, providing an almost hallucinogenic color scheme. High rugged hills jumped up through the grass and reached for the sky.

Herds of blesbok and springbok were also just out the window. Black and blue wildebeest careened off one another like drunks at a frat party. A few other animals were close. Lions to be exact.

Forget the notion of tents on this safari. Moreson had chalets waiting for us. Built of heavy stone, with thatched roofs, these were two-story jobs complete with an east-facing deck off the second story. Two bedrooms downstairs, each with a private bath, four more beds upstairs, a large living area, and a wood fireplace/cooking stove rounded out the chalet. Oh yeah, I almost forgot, a heavy wood bar ran most of the width of the main room. Cool.

This certainly would keep our group comfortable, but it got better. We didn't have just one chalet. We had two. Doug and Margaret would share one with me; Pierre and Anneli would share with Dave and Mary. Spyker and the rest of the crew would be staying in the motel-style rooms near the chalets.

The chalet with Pierre, Anneli, Dave, and Mary would also serve as our headquarters. Mary has an issue at times getting around. Pierre, infinitely wise, thought it best for her and Dave to be where all the action would be. Plans would be made, drinks drunk, and meals prepared and served there by the more than capable Moses, Pierre's cook on safari and while at home. The bar was in this chalet as well.

First things first. Our guns needed to be sighted in before we thought of food or drink. All were sighted in before we left the states, but with baggage handlers not

Doug thinks that guns hate gun cases. He's right. For those of you with a bit too much time on your hands, you'll notice all the bolts are up.

Inside one of Moreson's chalets. Wood heat, electrical hurricane lamps, and a heavy wooden bar. Margaret's the one with the map. She's a rocket scientist—honestly. Here she is trying to find South Africa on a map . . . of South Africa.

using kid gloves, we needed to make sure they would shoot where pointed. Light was beginning to fade; we had to hustle if we were going to be ready to hunt the next morning.

I brought two rifles. One was the first rifle I ever owned, a Remington Model 700 BDL chambered in 7mm Remington Magnum. I would be firing Winchester, Partition Gold ammo, pushing 165-grain bullets. With this combination, I had taken some of the biggest game available in North America. Even at thirty years old, it still puts bullets in the sweet spot. It is a rifle in which I have supreme confidence.

My other gun had me in fits. Not the gun itself, but the choice.

Back to Moreson, where we were getting ready to sight in our guns.

Pierre asked each of us what we brought. Doug had his .30-.06 and the .375. Margaret carried a .270 and a .375. Dave brought along one gun, a .300 Winchester Magnum, and I had my two. Mary was along as an observer. Though a true supporter of hunting, she doesn't hunt herself.

Dave started the zeroing process and after just three shots was "Spot on." I went second.

Pierre had told me that at this concession we would be using our light guns, no need for the heavier stuff. I brought the 7mm to the range, leaving the .375 crying and cussing in the chalet. The first two bullets landed side by side, kissing one another exactly 2 inches high of the bull's eye at 100 yards. Perfect, just like at the range back home. With this arrangement the gun would be dead on target at 200, and 7 inches low at 300. In other words, what I shot at I would hit. As long as I did my part on the shot.

CHOOSING GUNS TO TAKE ON SAFARI

The decision on which guns to bring on a safari is as important as finally deciding you are going on safari in the first place. If you hunt deer with anything like a .30-.06, a .308, a .270, or a 7mm Remington Magnum, the first gun will be a no-brainer. Bring the deer gun. It will work. It will work very well with the right loads.

I'm a shotgunner mainly. I can talk about cast-on and cast-off. I can talk about length of pull. Heck, I can almost recite the entire loading table for Winchester loads down to the exact number of pellets found in a 28-gauge loaded with number 9s.

Rifles are different. Not foreign, just different. Africa is both foreign and different. I needed help for my second gun. Help with someone I could talk to, not from a sterile book.

I sent a letter to Doug asking for advice. I was really leaning toward something in the .338 range, nothing heavier. There is one big reason for this: While living in Alaska and hunting brown bears, I owned a .375. It was not pretty. Shots off the range bench were painful to the extreme.

I received Doug's reply a day later by e-mail.

Brother Dan,

The .375 is the minimum for dangerous game in all of Africa. In Boddington's *Safari Rifles*, the vast majority of professional hunters polled answered the question, "If a client can only bring one rifle, which one?" with ".375 H&H." John "Pondoro" Taylor gives the .375 its own chapter in his book *Big Game Rifles*. He has killed more animals than you've had hot meals.

[We were not, it should be duly noted, going to South Africa for anything considered to be dangerous game. But, as Doug points out below, you just never know.]

In Africa you just don't know what's in the brush 20 yards away from you. The buffalo with a sore leg from a poacher's snare doesn't know that you don't have a license when he smells you from 30 yards away. He's pissed, and you smell like what pissed him off. He now wants to come and remonstrate with you regarding the illegal hunting habits of your fellow humans. You have four seconds to deliver two shots. You really, really want enough gun. Even in South Africa, buffalo are common, as are lions and other large animals that may be in a foul mood. Just because you're hunting a light-phase Lady Grey's Gemsbontebok doesn't mean you'll actually encounter one, nor does it mean that you won't encounter something else, first.

Ammo for the .375 is available everywhere in Africa. .338 ammo is another story.

Recoil from newer guns is not what you remember from the Alaskan Beast you told me about. .375s shoot relatively flat at ranges we will encounter. Hit something with a .338 and it is probably down. Hit it with a .375 and it *is* down.

A man needs to own, ought to own, at least one true dangerous-game rifle, not a weasel-wimp compromise caliber because he's afraid of a little push in the shoulder.

Buy yourself a gun you can be proud of. This gun is going to be in your gun cabinet for years. You'll take it out on winter evenings and put it to your shoulder and it will speak to you. A .375 H&H whispers in your ear, "We've been to Africa together, and we're going back." The .338 says, "You read a magazine article."

Besides, I'm going back to Tanzania in 2007, if not before, to chase buffalo and lion. If you want to come, and you do, you will, you will have to have a .375. You may as well buy it now.

Sincerely,

Doug, the once and future Bwana Kiboko

As I've mentioned previously, Doug Chester is a benevolent, fiendish, delightful elf. I chose the .375 H&H.

A call to the fine folks at Remington was made. As my trusted 7mm Rem. Mag. was a Model 700, that is what I wanted in the .375. I wanted the new gun to operate exactly like the old gun. Why? Ever go quickly from a pump shotgun to an over and under or vice-versa? Ever then try to pump the over and under, or just pull the trigger for a second shot without pumping the pump gun? I've done both. More than once.

The safety, in my mind, must be in the same place and operate the same way as my other rifle. Why? Ever go from a safety just in front of the trigger guard to another gun where the safety is at the end of the receiver? Ever push and push on the front of the trigger guard instead of the thumb safety? I have. Again, more than once.

These mistakes cost birds and other game. They could also cost you your life. My advice—if you like the gun you currently own, then continue to buy guns in the same make and model. There will be no unfortunate mistakes caused by brain cramps in any excitement.

The phone call brought a bit of bad news. Remington doesn't make a .375 H&H in an off-the-shelf model. The gunmaker does produce its own .375 Rem.

CHOOSING GUNS TO TAKE ON SAFARI

Mag., but the availability of bullets could be an issue with this one in a foreign land.

The good news is that Remington's custom shop would be glad to custom-make a .375 H&H for me, at a cost. I chose the African Plains Edition and sent them the cash.

This particular model comes with a laminated stock. I hate these. Who wants to carry around a gun with an orange, yellow, green, and black tiger-striped stock? But, at least it was Model 700, and it was a .375 H&H.

Imagine my complete delight, when, after a time, the gun was delivered. I had called Cabela's and had them send out to Remington a 3X9 Premium Alaskan Guide Series Scope so the custom shop could mount it. This particular scope, through rigorous field tests, had stood up to the elements and punishment. It gathers light well. You won't find a better scope at twice, maybe three times the money.

The barrel was black, satin-finished, as was the scope. As for that laminated stock, my impressions of what it would look like were completely off kilter. This laminated stock looks and feels like honey oak. The laminate "grain" appears as fire-hardened wood. There are no strange colors. It is, in a word, beautiful.

I let Doug know in a quick phone call that it had arrived, I told him about how it looked, and that I was in love. I received an e-mail the next day.

Bwana Dan,
[This was the first time anyone called me Bwana. Cool.]
I couldn't be more pleased by your phone call Friday night. This is all fantastic.
First, the rifle sounds wonderful. Just what you needed for this trip, and *will* need again. I say this with confidence; we are too much alike, thee and me. Africa bit me and hasn't let go. I think it will sink its hooks as deeply in your soul as they're set in mine.
When you first shoot it, let the gun ride up when it goes off. Don't fight it, just let it rise, and take your time pulling it down for the next

Doug and Margaret followed. Doug, with both guns, was "spot on." The gremlins attacked Margaret. Her .270 was as perfect as when she packed it. The .375 took a half box of shells to get back to that most cherished of phrases, "spot on." Thankfully it didn't take more as the fading light had all but disappeared. Time for dinner.

Back at the chalet Moses laid out some kudu biltong, a jerkylike product. My first taste of this critter turned to handfuls of the stuff. When the dried sticks of kudu shot. After awhile it'll just seem normal and you'll find the gun rises less and less. And your .270/7mm-/.30-.06 guns will seem like the pussy guns they are.

If there is a single "all-around" rifle, one that will actually do for the high end and the low end of the hunting spectrum, the .375 H&H is it. It is *the* "Classic African Calibre." Calibre spelled 're,' not 'er,' when discussing the African classics. One must adhere to the British usage.

This is the gun with all the magic. There is a testosterone joy in shooting a .375 H&H that can't be achieved in any other gun, bigger or smaller. The bigger ones hurt and the smaller ones don't quite do it.

Damn all of those "super-improved-short-stroke-magnums." Twenty-five years from now, the ammo for these much-touted short-mags will be collector's items. The guns themselves are already flooding the second-hand market. People are discovering that they don't really do anything better than the guns they already had.

You've got the gun and you can't let it gather dust. It needs to walk in the noonday sun. The stock needs to be scratched by thorns and stained with sweat.

This will be a fabulous trip and much good will come of it. The three weeks of this trip will rebound and reverberate, bringing good fortune with every bounce.

This is like being 21 years old, in Paris, and on the front steps of Madame Claude's with your old man's American Express card in your pocket. You don't know exactly what's going to happen when you ring the bell, but you know that it'll be something good.

Come, ring the bell with me.

Bwana Kiboko

and gemsbok sausage were added, I was in heaven. Drinks were poured and delivered by Pierre and Spykr. Anneli, as women all over the world are wont to do, supervised.

From outside the chalet, coming from the plains below, but not that far below, a lion roared, loudly. Very loudly. This roar was followed by another, somewhat farther away. A series of low, drawn-out guttural grunts joined the roars. The lions

Meet Moses, chef extraordinaire. What he does can only be described as genius with food. Even impala liver.

were restless. Or complaining about the chill coming with the night. Or something.

You have heard lions roar before. On TV. Maybe at a circus or in a zoo. It's not the same. It's not even close. Live and in person, and from somewhere in the darkness, a lion's roar, or its grunting, will cause you to shiver, shake a bit maybe, and definitely will give you cause to pause. These beautiful creatures eat people. You are a people. You are in Africa. No, unless you've been to Africa and heard the lions roar, you have never heard it. It is, in a word, magnificent.

Dinner was incredible, as all of them would prove to be. Prawns á la Moses with trimmings that I can't remember. The onset of jet lag being the primary culprit here, but I'm sure the scotch (I did have three), or the wine (two glasses), had something to do with what happened next.

Out of nowhere, a mule appeared on top of the table. It was facing north and I was looking at the beast's south end. The damn thing, for no reason whatsoever, reared back and planted both rear hooves directly into my forehead. One moment I was fine. The next, well, not so fine. I left the table, making a quick exit, with a feeble excuse.

Stumbling back to the chalet, I slipped on a rock and fell. Thankfully the ground came up to catch me. Once in the chalet I planted myself in bed. I don't know when Doug and Margaret returned.

I don't even remember turning off the light.

I do remember the lions continuing with their displeasure. Maybe it was in contentment. Maybe. But, hell, I was in Africa, by God!

CHAPTER 4

I Think I Want to Try

hree A.M. is awful early, but it was nine back home, 9 P.M. My body said it was not time for bed and wouldn't take no for an answer. Why? Who knows. It just was. So be it. I tossed and tried to force a couple more hours of sleep. Success came in the form of a brief 15-minute nap. At 5 A.M., I cried uncle and got out of bed.

I enjoy my sleep. When at home, or at some other place that is very familiar in surroundings to my home, I like to sleep in. Rising at 8:30 isn't unusual, 9:30 isn't out of the question. You miss nothing except for the insipid morning news shows.

In places unfamiliar, where there is a promise of something particularly fine at dawn, I like—I demand—to see the sunrise. This, being Africa, was obviously such a place.

Instant coffee was on the counter of my chalet. After more than a few choice words figuring out how the South African appliances worked, I had hot water so I wouldn't have to just eat the coffee.

Sunrise, the exact rising of the sun up to and above the horizon, was still a half hour or so away. Gray sky to the east and a deep purple overhead, so deep the stars were still dancing directly above, showed a smooth but broken horizon across a miles-wide valley. Moreson anchored the western hills, and to the east her sisters were being warmed and tickled on their backsides.

The lions also knew day was approaching. The concert of roars and grunts started anew and built with each minute as the sun slowly climbed its way up the backside of the distant hills. From my seat on the patio of the chalet, I saw a herd of wildebeest no more than 25 yards away slowly saunter by on their way to a water hole. They grunted to one another softly to hurry it up. Dark spots in the grasses below moved slowly across the plain. Blesbok and springbok most likely, maybe a hartebeest thrown in as well.

It was getting brighter. The stars all but vanished overhead. Color was coming back to the world. Brown and yellow grass poked through the gray flannel of bad light. Blue sky could be seen above the hills in the east if you looked closely. You needed to look closely in order to see the blue because the sun was putting on a

The grasslands and rolling hills of Free State Province go on forever. You can see tomorrow in the sunrise, yesterday in the sunset.

particularly fine show with its yellow, orange, and red. The few clouds in the sky above were lit up like Christmas tree bulbs.

When the first true rays showed themselves, the trees around Moreson erupted like the first movement of a symphony. Birds sang, but were unseen. Wildebeest grunted. Lions growled. Of all the animals and birds welcoming the day, it was the laughing dove, all four or five ounces of him, that outshone the rest. I can't describe it to you any better than its name does. When you are in Africa at daylight, or anytime I came to find out, and you hear a bird singing like a warbling castrati, it's the laughing dove.

Footsteps behind me became Pierre, coming round to wake us and get the hunting started.

"You're up. Very good. What happened last night?" he asked.

"I have no idea, one moment I was fine, and in another moment I was kicked by a mule."

"Well, Dan, my boy, it is time to get at it. Let Doug and Margaret know."

"Uh, Pierre?" I asked. "You've hunted with those two. You know what it's like to get them up. You, dear sir, are the professional, the one being paid. I am the payer. While I am quite willing to go toe to toe with just about anything, waking those two is something I figure I'm paying you to do. Sorry, Pierre, this one's on you. Get to work."

Pierre, I believe, called me something similar to the droppings of a barnyard chicken. He said it in Afrikaans, so I'm not quite sure, but sure enough. That's okay; I am such when it comes to waking those two. What I am certain of is this—that when he poked his head in the door and told them to wake up, he was greeted with words most haven't heard. Only his promise of coffee being ready brought a reprieve to the tirade.

"Good call on that one, Dan. Come on up to the other chalet. Real coffee's ready and something light to eat before we head out."

Anneli was waiting for me with a cup of coffee in hand. "This will be better than that instant Pierre left for you." She didn't say those words, she played them on that flutelike voice of hers. Simply incredible that one can be so pleasant at such an early hour.

After I thanked her, she responded simply with a musical, "Pleasure," as in, "It's my pleasure" but shortened so as not to waste any voice with unnecessary words. It sure was. A pleasure, that is.

The light prehunt food consisted of something called rusks. Think biscotti but with corn meal and you have rusks. Nice and light, nothing that would weigh a body down is served before the morning hunt is over.

When we were all together, Pierre told us the game plan. Doug and Margaret would join him. Tielman DeVillers, one of Moreson's owners, would join them in one of Moreson's hunting cars. Dave, Mary, and I, along with Spyker, would meet Awie (pronounced Harvey without the "H") Marais, the other owner of the concession. We'd be in another Moreson hunting car.

"While here, we should see some good blesbok, springbok, and hartebeest. This country is perfect for them. Wildebeest, too. You'll see eland probably and a few oryx. (These are also called gemsbok—the desert warrior.) You must make sure of your shot," instructed Pierre. "These are herd animals; there will most likely be a lot of them very close together. We need to be talking about the same animal. Please, do not shoot until we tell you, until we are sure."

All of us quickly gathered up our gear.

There's something to be said for being the client. Food magically appears. Dirty plates disappear. You will never have better service than in a well-run safari camp. Everything is done with "pleasure."

PACKAGE DEALS OR Á LA CARTE?

There are a number of ways to hunt in South Africa. You can go on a package deal. Or, you could go á la carte.

Chances are you've seen ads to hunt here showcasing a set price for a set number of days with a set number of animals in specific species. These are called packages, and, in my mind, they're a sucker's bet.

Say you sign the big check for a packaged hunt. Let's say that it's for seven days and includes five animals. Those five being oryx, impala, warthog, blesbok, and springbok. You'll be told that you are free to shoot other animals but at "trophy fee costs."

Now, say you don't come upon an oryx. Do you get any money back? Nope. Say that the oryx you do come upon are not exactly noteworthy. Do you shoot it anyway because you already "paid" for it? That question is one only you can answer.

The other problem with packages is that the hunts will most often take place on a single concession. Only God knows how many other groups have gone there before you, and only He knows just what is left, and of what quality. If something seems simply too good to be true, *it is*! Unless you'll settle for an oyrx with 12-inch horns or an impala that barely measures above the ears. Heck, the ad guaranteed the animal; they didn't say of what size.

And think about the pressure on a reputable professional hunter. Any PH worth his salt is going to try to get you a very good animal. As time dwindles and you still haven't shot your Lady Macbethrhebokala, and you have already paid for it, what is that PH going to do? He certainly doesn't want to explain why he isn't giving your money back; he's going to get you "the biggest one he's seen all year," even if it isn't much more than a puppy.

"Dan, where is your rifle?" asked Pierre, who, as the lead professional hunter and responsible for everything, was watching the loading process. I had left it in the chalet, on purpose.

"Just cameras this first day, Pierre. There is so much to soak in. Besides I need photos as much or more than animals for any story a foolish editor may buy from me after all this is over."

While it is true that I did, or hopefully would, need photos for a story or stories, there was another reason.

Heading out, we stopped at a series of smaller cabins. Two young black men, dressed in coveralls, came out of one. These were our trackers, our scouts. One would ride in each hunting car.

Up and over the hill behind the main compound. A hill noteworthy for its steepness. Noteworthy for its cement tracks, two of them, no wider than 8 inches. Why the tracks? Because on either side and in between them, there were deep gullies that could swallow a horse. It's best to ride the tracks even with your heart,

Going á la carte, in my mind, makes the most sense. Africa can be a benevolent lover or she can be a dominatrix—often times she's both in the same moment. Going á la carte also comes with a serious need for self-control. You are going to see a lot of animals, magnificently beautiful animals with funny-looking horns; you are going to want them. They will cost you money. Some will cost you a lot of money.

In my planning for this trip I had e-mailed Pierre a number of times. I had let him know that kudu, oryx (or gemsbok, if you recall), impala, and zebra were on my "want" list. No guarantees were desired; none would have been taken. These four, however, were the four that I'd like to hunt. These four were based on my dreams. And on cash. Pierre always replied with something like, "That shouldn't be too difficult."

This trip was not a junket paid for by manufacturers of guns or bullets, by the government wishing for good press, nor was any "writer's special" rate given to me by the PH or the booking agent. This trip was paid for at the retail rate, compliments of Danny Boy and my most benevolent wife, Kris. Ruark had done his first safari that way, and I respected him for that. If I was lucky enough to get something printed from this trip, I hoped that knowing it was paid for at retail would make it all the more "real."

So, while definitely feeling the pain of the almighty dollar, I wanted to do one thing: I wanted to report the real story, not fluffed up, not prettied up, and without any inclination that my writing couldn't be brutally honest, no matter the outcome. I have done, am doing, just that. Yes, I certainly hoped for a magazine story or two to come of it to help ease the pinch, but even this little bit of help was not guaranteed. (If you've dreamed of becoming a freelance

intestines, and colon up in your throat. The alternative would be a very long, very steep walk.

Once on top, eyes searched for an animal for Dave. Herds of blesbok and springbok could be seen in the distance, but they were spooky. Whenever we got within 100 yards or so, a good spot to start a stalk, the antelope would dash off over the next hill, leaving a dust trail in their wake.

Just before 9 A.M. Awie brought the car to an abrupt halt. "Spyker, springdeboker!" Or something that sounded like that. Awie and Spyker spoke to one another excitedly, in Afrikaans. Now, Afrikaans is a language like no other. A confusing mix of Dutch, maybe a little German, and maybe just a touch of a Slavic tongue. It is full of consonants, burred r's, hard k's, and more than a little spittle. It sounds a bit gruff, like the clearing of one's throat. (Except when Anneli spoke it. Then it sounded, well, like a flute.)

At any rate, they talked excitedly. Seems a springbok, a rather nice one from their gestures, was on the horizon. This horizon was a good 800 yards away. Eight

PACKAGE DEALS OR Á LA CARTE?

writer and getting the big bucks, well, I want some of that stuff you're definitely smoking.)

Money was an issue. The four animals I hoped for would come to exactly $3,400. That was my self-imposed limit in trophy fees. Hunting a blesbok or a springbok, though very cool, just wasn't in my wallet.

Pierre van Tonder Safaris does not offer any package in South Africa. Specialized buffalo hunts in his Tanzanian big-game concession can be packaged. Pierre fully believes, and said so emphatically in a number of e-mails to me (I was probably a royal pain in his backside for the two months leading up to this hunt) that, "you should not squander opportunities," that "you should let Africa decide." Spyker, whose real name is Leon Joubert, feels the same way and operates the same way when on his hunts.

The hunting fee is unlike the standard U.S. hunting license. In the United States you get a license to kill an animal, and you pay a guide/outfitter when needed. There is no refund if the animal is not taken. If the animal is wounded but not recovered, the lowest of the low feeling a hunter may ever have, you can still, if your heart allows, go out and try on another one on the same license.

In South Africa, as well as in most countries in Africa, you pay a daily rate to hunt. Then, when you take an animal, a certain amount of money is added

hundred yards of waist-high golden grass. Grass that, almost as if by magic, is as tall, and as golden, as an adult ram springbok. Through my binoculars only the whimsical, lyrelike horns could be seen. And these appeared as not much more than sticks.

Dave and Spyker leapt out of the truck and started the stalk. Crouching in what Army guys call a kim-chee squat, they slowly made their way closer. Wind would be an issue. It was right on their backs most of the time, and blowing at a good clip. The only saving grace was it would gust and then immediately do a swirl. It was possible that the swirling would allow them to get into decent range.

At 300 yards the shooting sticks were brought out. Dave got into a kneeling position and settled behind the rifle. No shot came. He switched to the sitting position. And back to kneeling. Five minutes behind the gun, the springbok broadside and statue-still, no shot. Spyker pointing at the springbok, telling him to shoot. Then Dave stood, shaking his head.

When they got back to the truck, Dave didn't wait for a question. "It's the first day, it was a long shot, and it is windy. I just wasn't comfortable with it."

Good for Dave. Great for Dave! I am thankful that I left my gun behind and I wasn't up first on the first animal of the first day. I don't know if I would have turned the shot down. It certainly was the right thing to do. I'm just not that sure I would have done the right thing.

to your bill. There is no license per se. Heck, if the wallet is flush, you can, with the PH's and concession owner's approval, take multiple numbers of the same species. Each at that species-specific trophy fee.

One thing a hunter must remember is to be quite sure of his shot. If an animal is nicked in the slightest way, if a single hair cut by a bullet is found or the smallest of blood drops found, then you just paid for that animal. In full. Even if that animal is not recovered. No questions asked. Just simply, and rather humbly, pay the man.

One way I was able to go along on this safari, which for me was scheduled for two weeks—for the others, three weeks—and still stay in range, or at least in sight of the final total costs, was to simply "observe" on a number of days. Half of the days, to be exact. At least that was my plan. Plans suck.

When you bring along the gun, there is one price per day. When you just bring the cameras, simply to "observe," there is a different price. These observer days are roughly one-half of the daily hunting rate. This can add up to real savings and can, if used, extend your trip. And the enjoyment.

If you choose to go—and you should—go á la carte. Go hunting, not simply collecting.

"Okay, let's try to find one a bit closer." Spyker sounded slightly perplexed. The animal had been broadside after all. Still, it was the right decision. And, by all appearances, we were in the middle of a springbok convention.

We continued to drive the dusty two-track looking for a good head. Small rolling hills blocked our forward view more than a few times. It was always with the expectation of a kid on Christmas morning that we came on top, waiting to see what was on the other side. In the distance mixed herds could be seen. On we continued.

The track took us toward a rather abrupt small hill and then skirted around it. Awie was quick on the brakes.

"Hartebeest. One's a monster!" This time in perfect English. "Foc, he is beeg." Not so perfect English here, but the meaning was lost on no one. The "beeg" one was traveling with a small herd of smaller rams and a fair number of females.

"Dave," says Spyker. "This one is in the book. I have not seen many bigger anywhere. Do you want him?"

"He's not on my list."

"Dave, are you sure? He's a monster. You'll never see a bigger one."

Dave thought about it as the herd walked toward a small dry river. "No, it's not on my list. Let's go, we'll stick to the game plan." Seems the wallet was on Dave's mind as much as it was on mine.

Antelope species often mix together in a form of joint guard duty. Red hartebeest in the foreground, blue wildebeest in the center, with impala as the backdrop.

Spyker looked at Awie, then at me and then back to Awie. "Let's go, no hartebeest for us today." Now it was Awie's turn to look more than a little perplexed. He just shook his head and looked back at the hartebeest disappearing into a dry riverbed.

The engine of the hunting car turned over. Then, before we started to move forward, a little voice, a female voice, from the front said softly and simply, "I think I might want to try."

"Really?" asked Spyker.

"Yes."

God bless Mary.

Mary never had the pleasure of squeezing the trigger on a rifle before. Not even a little .22. Her only time with a gun was about ten years before when her son took her to a pistol range and they popped some caps. She had never looked down the barrel of any type of gun at an animal that was in risk of losing its life. And, God love her, she says, "I think I'd like to try."

Mary had come along to be here in Africa to see her husband, Dave, fulfill a lifelong fantasy of hunting Africa and to fulfill her fantasy of seeing the amazing continent. Years ago she would have probably stepped right up to the plate and batted the hartebeest. Not now. Or so we thought.

You see, Mary has M.S., multiple sclerosis, a cruel and satanic mistress. She walks with a worried cane, each step carefully planned. She tires easily and at times has tremors.

And this sweet woman, this woman who steadfastly refuses to throw in the towel, Mary, who most likely has never said a disparaging word in her life, laughed right in the face of this burden, ordering it to go straight back to hell with that one simple phrase, "I think I might want to try."

Well, let me tell you! Awie put the truck in reverse and rammed the gas pedal down speeding us back behind the hill, out of sight of the hartebeest. "Are you sure, Mary?" asked Spyker. He knew about Mary.

She giggled a nervous laugh, "Yes, I think so."

"Love? Uh, I don't think this is such a good idea," said Dave in a voice loud enough for everyone to hear. Everyone pretended not to.

Spyker grabbed Dave's rifle from the gun rack and emptied the magazine. Then, with me, Awie, and Spyker all giving advice and direction on the gun's operation and where to place the crosshairs, we coached her. Spyker had her get behind the gun, sighting in on a distant rock with the scope's crosshairs. "Now Mary, there is no bullet in the gun. Just slowly squeeze the trigger, keeping the crosshairs on that rock." The rifle didn't move at all at the trigger's break.

Yes, we all know that letting the firing pin fall on an empty chamber can, heavy on the "can," damage the mechanism. "Can" is not "will." This was Mary's first shot, for God's sake.

Forget what might happen.

"OK, that was good. Let's do it again."

The second time was just as good. Smooth squeeze, no movement of the muzzle off the target.

"What about the kick?" Oops. Potential downfall.

"Love," said Dave, using the pet name he uses when he wants to ensure being heard, "I don't know if this is such a good idea." Mary was looking at him the whole time he was talking. If she heard him, she pretended not to. Temporary blindness, mixed with a touch of selective hearing, must be two of the MS symptoms I hadn't heard of.

"Yes, Mary, there will be recoil. You will feel it. It won't be too bad as you will be too excited when you shoot. Just remember, nice and smooth on the trigger, hold the gun steady. You can do it," Spyker encouraged. Awie and I said something similar. We were geeked. This would be so cool.

Dave again mentioned something about the idea and its worth, but he went unanswered, unheard, and thoroughly ignored. Spyker loaded the gun, put the safety on, and handed the gun to Mary.

We got Mary back around the hill. The hartebeest were still in the dry riverbed. Only their backs and heads could be seen. The big ram was trailing the rest and was clearly the best of the bunch. Even my virgin eyes could tell he was much bigger than the others.

The hartebeest is an ungainly beautiful animal. One would be wrong to call him delicately featured. Swept back onyx-black horns with deeply ringed ridges. His butt has white cheeks that abruptly change to a chestnut-red cape. There's a black flash on the muzzle, then that chestnut red between the eyes, and a black forehead. The ears are oxlike. His body size comes in right between a huge mule deer and a cow elk.

They were moving slowly in front of us, in the riverbed, from left to right. They may have known we were there or they may not have. They just continued to move slowly, grazing on some small green patches on the sides of the dry bed.

We watched for a full ten minutes, maybe longer, when the big boy jumped up on our side of the bank. Broadside.

Mary took her place, and the gun went on the rest. "Okay, Mary," Spyker whispered. "Put the crosshairs just behind his shoulder. The one on the far left. See him."

"Yes."

"Are you sure, Mary? Be sure."

"Yes. Crosshairs just behind the shoulders. They're there."

Spyker started whispering the play-by-play, again ensuring Mary was on the same animal he was. "Okay, now he's turning left . . . watch him . . . damn! He's turning again, watch him . . . Now turning back right . . . he's broadside, Mary." Mary gave a slight nod and soft affirming answers to Spyker's commentary.

"With your thumb, take the safety off."

"Okay."

"Now hold the gun firmly, breathe easy, and when the crosshairs settle back down, squeeze the trigger just like we practiced." My binoculars were focused on the hartebeest.

Whether the gun was held firm or not, whether Mary's breathing was easy or not, I can't say. As soon as Spyker finished talking, the gun went off. Through my binoculars I watched the hartebeest being knocked flat on his back as if hit by an uppercut. Its legs went straight into the air, and then very slowly gravity took over, settling its insides, rolling it to its side. It didn't even twitch. Never had an animal been shot deader.

"Mary! You got him!" Spyker hugged her.

"Well done," from Awie, who had a Cheshire cat smile.

"Way to go," from me.

"Did I get him? Oh I hope I did, and he isn't wounded."

"Mary, that hartebeest is dead-dead. You really clocked him."

I walked with her up to the hartebeest. She was shaking, the shake of adrenaline rushing through her, hunter's tremors.

She whispered to me, "Dan, I'm shaking. I'm really shaking. Don't tell Dave. Should I be—is it normal?"

"It sure is, Mary. It happens every time I shoot something. Don't be worried."

Mary took her time at the animal. Gingerly she bent down and stroked its back softly, murmuring to it. Her hands wrapped around the horns, slowly moving from the base to the tips, feeling every ridge. She spoke quietly, barely above a whisper, "My God, he's huge. He's beautiful. I can't believe I just did that." Her eyes were wet, her heart raced. Her emotions on rapid-fire from joy to wonder to a touch of remorse and back to joy and wonder. Her soul heard, and heeded, the hunter's horn. Its music now and forever sounding in her.

Over the course of the next fifteen minutes, when an album's worth of photos were taken, she continued to shake. Not constantly, intermittently. When she asked,

Mary Westphal, a fine lady who never shot a rifle, thought she'd like to try. Results? The first animal taken on the safari and a record book red hartebeest at that! Her husband, Dave, didn't think it was a good idea. Dave was obviously wrong.

I again told her that it was normal and that it was to be enjoyed, not worried about. She giggled, giddy as a schoolgirl.

"Mary," said Spyker, "this one is huge. His horns are Harley-Davidsons (referring to their swept-back form, like the handlebars of the motorcycle), and he's well in the book."

The book he's referring to is the record book. Make that *the* record book. Not the SCI book. There's nothing wrong with Safari Club International and their record keeping; in fact there are a lot of things that are right with that tally sheet. But, when a PH says something is "in the book," he is referring to that most fancy of dancers, Mr. Rowland Ward's itself. *The* book, the Rowland Ward book, is the time-tested, most respected in the world.

Dave hugged her more than once. He asked her more than once if she was all right. He also shot Spyker, Awie, and me with a few glances that came with a "not-such-a-good-idea" expression. Dave and Mary both had tears in their eyes. I still had sunglasses on.

God bless Mary! This was way too cool.

There is still magic in the world. I was there, I saw it.

All this before breakfast, which we now desperately wanted.

CHAPTER 5

37th From the Right

e dropped off Mary's magnificent red hartebeest at the skinning shed. The boys were already working on another, smaller animal. Seems Margaret took a nice blesbok earlier in the morning. They whistled in approval at the beast's horns and grunted the grunt of heft as they lifted it out of the car.

Doug and Margaret were diving headfirst into breakfast when we walked in. Breakfast was served in Moreson's dining room by a waitress who knew as much English as I did Afrikaans. Moses, our fully capable and bright-smiling cook, was being held in reserve for the evening's duties. Eggs to order, hot and cold cereals, fruit, sausages, and bacon and patties of one sort or another, potatoes (I think they were potatoes anyway), fresh squeezed juice, toast, and coffee and tea and milk and pop. I was hungry. I don't remember how it all tasted. But my plate was returned empty. And I didn't die.

The tale of Mary's hartebeest was told an even dozen times. Doug and Margaret couldn't believe she actually shot a rifle. At an animal. And killed it dead, no less. More hugs, more kisses. Then Pierre had to be told all about it. As did anyone else within radio hailing or telephonic distance. Anneli came in last, and the tale was told again. Mary was beaming. It seemed that Dave was through with his not-such-a-good-idea thought.

Moreson, besides operating as a hunting concession, also has a captive breeding program with lions. Its goal is to be able to release more and more of these animals into the concession so the land returns to the full glory it once was. That's not to say it isn't glorious now: it most certainly is, but more cats would make it more like it once was before white settlement.

Just two months before we arrived, one of the lionesses gave birth. The cubs like to play. You can, if you are careful, play with them.

One thing you do not want to do is turn your back on them. These cats may be cubs, but they are also predators. Turning your back is an open invitation for them to pounce, throwing their paws, claws extended, around your head and toward your throat, and an invitation to sink their teeth into the back of your neck. Needle sharp teeth.

Margaret with her first critter, a dandy blesbok. You'd be smiling that wide, too, if it were yours.

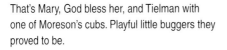

That's Mary, God bless her, and Tielman with one of Moreson's cubs. Playful little buggers they proved to be.

Yes, these cubs are cute and cuddly. Yes, it is very cool to hold them. As long as you hold them like their mama does, by the scruff of the neck. It's way too sappy to say this, but it did feel a bit like the movie *Born Free* playing with them. As long as you keep in mind not to turn your back to them.

Doug took a seat on a small rock. One of the cute little cubs snuck around behind him.

"Careful, Doug," I cautioned.

"Ahh, I'm fine, they're fine." He chuckled at the antics of another at his feet.

The chuckle didn't last too long. Seems the sneaky little cub has the pounce down pat at such a young age. It wrapped Doug's head up in his arms, paws with extended claws digging into his forehead. The cub's mouth was wide open and full of the hair on the back of Doug's neck.

Doug laughed. Initially. "Damn it, these hurt. Fuck you, cub!" He was still chuckling, sort of. Chuckling in a this-isn't-that-funny-anymore chuckle. Slowly he pried the cub off of him. Very slowly—as the claws and teeth, though not breaking skin, were close to it.

I thought of Ruark's passage in his *Horn of the Hunter*: "Sometimes you eat the lion, sometimes the lion eats you." When I got the photos back—yes, I took photos the whole time Doug was being eaten by the cub—they became priceless. I also took photos of Doug chewing on the cub's neck. He reports they taste "a bit dusty."

After visiting the cubs, it was time for something else.

As Doug found out, lion cubs are also predators and even at this young age are quite versed in the power of the claw.

As I said before, Doug and Margaret like their sleep. That's not to say that they don't run hard when the time comes, they just like their sleep. This also includes naps. Mary tires easily, too. After the adrenaline rush of the hartebeest and the crushing fall that always follows the rush, she needed a rest.

And it was the heat of the day. The animals wouldn't be all that active. The 40-degree temperature in the morning had climbed into the 70s, the sun shone brightly, and a slight breeze was fluffing the curtains. In other words, perfect napping conditions. We agreed to sally forth again at 2 P.M.

Now, I'm not a napping kind of guy. I love them, but they don't like me. Years ago I learned that if I take a nap, I am less than worthless for the rest of the day. My brain and body never want anything more to do. It's a struggle to make it through the day after a nap.

Back at the chalet, I kept myself occupied glassing the herds of springbok, blesbok, and wildebeest a good mile or so away on the plain. They were moving slowly; even the wildebeest were only bumping into each other in a half-hearted state. I listened to the doves. I wrote some in my journal. I watched my watch. Two would not come soon enough. I was antsy.

Around about 1 P.M. I got restless to the point of absurdity. Time to check out the upstairs loft of the chalet. I remember thinking that the view from the top deck would probably be better than the one at ground level.

Two steps out onto the deck, I found myself sitting. Sort of. My left leg spread crooked out to the side. My hands spread out in front. My right leg was unseen. It had gone through a section of dry-rotted decking. Angry white slashes of wood stuck out of the broken board and pressed against the leg of my trousers and my skin. A quick check around me showed a distinct possibility that if I moved I'd crash through to the hard tile and cement below. I didn't move.

Doug came racing out the bedroom. I could see him through the small slit openings between the boards. Found out he's a Fruit of the Loom man. "Shit! Dan, you okay?"

"Umm, I think so."

"Can you move?"

"Don't know if I should. Do ya see any more rotten boards next to me?"

"Not really."

Margaret came out just then. "Dan—what happened?"

"I fell through, sort of."

"Dan, be careful."

"Yes, Margaret, I'll try." It was almost funny. I could have used that advice a few minutes ago.

"Margaret," says Doug, "we've got it covered. It's okay. I'll just catch him if he falls."

There's a happy thought.

Slowly, and I mean slowly, I moved my hands to either side, gradually applying more and more weight. Upon lifting my butt off the boards, I leaned back, but the right leg didn't want to move. Slowly I again let myself settle back down on the boards. More than a few wood slivers had snagged on my pants and my skin. I broke these off and tried again. But not before seeing a rather angry and mean rusted nail that sent a crisp red streak up my pants leg from my knee to my right nut, where it rested ever so gently. The tingling sensation was not the one you would associate with, or want, in that area. No blood, mind you, but if it went down even one-half inch farther I'd get a discount at the vasectomy clinic. Again slowly, after removing the splinters and being mindful of that nail, I rose up off my butt and leaned back. This time the leg came, too, and after rolling back inside I could breath again.

"That was interesting," I said to Doug upon getting downstairs.

"Apparently. That could have been trouble."

"Yup, could have been."

A few red welts came up where the splinters dug into the leg, but none broke skin. Neither did the nail. Outside of a few stretched muscles I was fine. I checked again though just to make sure. Righty, I was just fine.

I didn't go back out on that deck. I'm Polish, not stupid. Not even on the other chalet's deck. Not even the next day after the camp staff had replaced the entire deck with new wood. Not that I'm a chicken. It just doesn't make sense to take an unnecessary chance and screw up a trip.

Ten minutes later it was time to hunt.

Mary stayed back at camp. Seems the adrenaline rush and the subsequent crash had her exhausted. I have a feeling that Anneli's promise of a jacuzzi soak also had something to do with it. Other than Mary, the game plan remained the same. Except for the fact that Pierre and Spyker ganged up on me and convinced me to bring along my 7mm.

Back on the thin two tracks of concrete, to the top of the hill we went. Dave still had the honors. Blesbok and springbok were on his list. They didn't disappoint.

We found a group of blessies not long into the hunt. These were closer than the morning's springbok. Dave set up nicely for the shot, took it, and missed. A few words were muttered by Dave. Dave is not one to remonstrate, not one to cuss much if any, and generally keeps his emotions quite closely buttoned. I can't say he swore, but I bet he did.

With the shot the herd took off, as you would guess, and we followed, again as you probably guessed. We found them after a time, over a series of small kopjes, small hills, and still a bit agitated. With Spyker's and Awie's help, he picked out the best one.

How these guys know which one is best, at a half-mile or more, in a group of 100 or more, is beyond me. They just do. Show them a herd off in the distance, and within seconds they will have picked the best head, the one with the best-horned ornamentation. Lucky for Dave, the herd was rather widely scattered.

Dave set up for the shot and made it. The blessie took the bullet well but ran. Up over another hill went the herd and down into a valley. We did the same. Spyker and Awie immediately picked out the animal, now wounded, and Dave set up again. Other animals were milling about Dave's blesbok. "Don't shoot until he's clear of the others. We don't want two."

Through the binoculars I watched the event unfold. Other blessies went back and forth, Dave's slowly moving right to left. Through the binos, I saw the others clear. Dave was given the okay to shoot. He did. The blesbok went down.

So did the other one that had positioned itself directly and perfectly behind Dave's. Dave's bullet went through "his" and continued into the other. This one got back up, and with the herd it ran off. Just before cresting the hill, it fell, dead. Dave got a two-fer. He also was given the supreme pleasure of paying for two.

You got two, Dave! The smaller blesbok was standing directly behind the larger. We didn't see him, but the bullet sure did.

We, actually the tracker and Spyker and Awie, loaded the blessies into the vehicle. "Dave, let's get you a springbok, too." I said. I wasn't being gracious. Do not for a moment accuse me of that. Rather, I didn't have these on my list. I was watching my wallet. I had other plans.

We did just that, too. No more than five minutes into the search, a dandy little springbok graced us with its presence no more than 300 meters away. In short grass.

The ram was alone, which was rather odd, as springbok are gregarious little fellows much like our pronghorns. They like to travel in groups, or more properly herds, that are in most cases headed up by one boss ram.

This guy was approaching boss status. There is a very good chance that not long before he was in a herd. There is an equally good chance that this fellow, not long ago, was feeling his oats and tried something with one of the ladies. The boss would not like that. So, here was this fellow, looking to join another party, when our party came along.

There was no wind this time. There were no other animals to worry about, male or female. When Spyker said to take him, there was no doubt which "him" he was talking about.

Dave, though rather unemotional, does have a sense of humor. Dave saw the animal hunch up and begin taking a crap. Spyker and I started to laugh watching the small pellets fall. Dave didn't laugh. Mid-crap, Dave pulled the trigger, and the springbok fell. Dead.

We could have been nice about it, seeing as this was an excellent shot, one where the animal died then and there without any company. We could have. But nooo . . .

Instead I started. "Jesus Christ, Dave. You could have given the little bugger a bit of time to finish up with his duties before blasting him. How rude."

That was Spyker's invitation to start in on him, too. Which he did mercilessly. Awie came dangerously close to rolling out of the vehicle, he was laughing so hard. Dave maintained his composure, but a Cheshire grin betrayed his enjoyment of the extra special attention he was getting.

It's an interesting relationship, guide and client. I know. I've been a guide. There's a courtship of sorts that goes on when a guide and client first meet. Neither knows the other. True, reputations precede notable guides. Referrals of a guide by a trusted friend help to build confidence. The same sort of confidence you get when saying yes to a buddy about going on a blind date with his true love's special friend. It's called raw courage. Often stupidity.

Guides, the good ones, let the client decide when the tide ebbs and when it flows. Certainly the guide will do his best to get you into the right spot at the right time, but whether you get your sorry butt out of bed or not is really on you. A guide, again a good one, goes along for the ride, while still trying his best to get you into a position where all your hopes and dreams are realized.

Guides also let the client decide on the seriousness of the conversation. Clients also pick the level of cursing—either none, mild, wild, or world-class. Guides need to be able to sing Hymn No. 457 or recite There Once Was a Man From Nantucket, with equal enthusiasm.

This was, in all reality, the first day Spyker had with Dave and me. You really can't count the morning's activities, either, as Mary was along and her sweet presence served as a silent tongue tamer. Barely 90 minutes into our guide/client relationship, the rules were understood by all. Anything goes. Spyker had keyed right in and, with both barrels of his big double .458 Lott, let Dave have it.

We got up to the springbok to watch something quite special, and something quite sobering. At the exact moment of death, the moment when all brain waves stop and all blood stops flowing, an amazing thing happens.

Stretching from mid-spine down to its base, springbok has a brilliant long white-haired ruff. You can't see it, ever. Except, that is, at that exact moment of death when the ruff rises up slowly through its tawny gold overcoat like a snow-white mohawk haircut on an otherwise deeply tanned bald pate. It comes up flared, you might say a bit defiant. It stays that way for maybe five seconds. And then, much quicker, it retreats back under the golden outer fur, not to be seen again. It's as if the ruff acts as a launching pad for the springbok's soul—sending it to the vast grassland plains to roam free and easy into eternity.

Some who have seen this happen up close say there is a scent associated with the ruff's unfurling. Nutmeg comes to some minds, vanilla to others. I did, we all could, smell a heady sweetness.

The springbok joined the two blesbok in the rear of the hunting car.

"Okay, Dan. You're up." This from Spyker. This not a question but an instruction. Seeing as the day was well past mid-afternoon, that the sun was nearly set to disappear behind the distant high hills, and that we were heading back to the com-

Dave Westphal and his springbok. Dave passed on one earlier in the day. This one was taken while it was rather preoccupied processing food. Dave didn't wait for it to finish.

pound in order to take care of Dave's critters, I wasn't too worried about not staying with my plan.

The blesbok had different ideas.

No more than three miles from camp, Awie stopped the car. We were on top of a long sloping hill. Hartebeest could be seen far off in the distance near a small lake, called a dam. Springbok were a bit closer, and so where a herd of blesbok. A herd of 200 or more.

"Spyker, see the bugger?" asked Awie.

"Yah, there's a good head on the left there."

"No—look on the right. It's the biggest one I've seen here."

"Foc! He is a monster!"

"Dan, that's your blesbok. That one's in the book."

I looked at Spyker, "Are you sure? They are awful far. It's early in the safari."

"Daniel! This is one big blesbok. This one is yours. I'll have you shoot no Mickey Mouse animals."

So much for my plans. My list. My wallet.

Spyker and I, along with Awie, worked up toward the herd. This was proving to be difficult as they were moving northeast and so were we. We were not gaining a thing on the steadily moving animals. I still did not set eyes on the one my two fellows were so impressed with. All I saw were butts and a lot of horns.

I'd guess we were a bit more than 275 yards when Spyker told me I had to take them from here. That we weren't going to gain any more ground.

A long shot to be sure, but I was confident that if given a broadside I could connect off a good and steady rest. The good and steady rest we had. The broadside we didn't.

"Okay, Dan, we're going to go for the Texas Heart Shot; you're going to put one right up its bum," Spyker told me.

Yeah, sure, I thought. Hell, if I wasn't comfortable, I'd turn the shot down. Dave did. No disgrace in that decision.

"He's the 37th from the right."

"You're joking. He's in the middle of the herd?"

"Yes, but he moved. Now he's 29th from the right."

I counted from the right and they, both Spyker and Awie, gave me the play-by-play.

"Now 30th . . . now 24th . . . Okay, he's moving more right . . . now 10th. Wait! Do you see him?"

"I do now. He's still 10, right?

"That's him." The blesbok continued to move a bit right while the herd moved a bit left. "Now he's the second from the right. Right?"

"Yes, Dan. That's him." The blesbok then did something I dreaded. The damn thing moved a good 10 feet or so to the right of the herd, virtually all by himself.

"Pop'em, Dan!"

I looked back at Spyker and Awie. "You guys sure you want me to try from this distance, facing away from us? It's awful far."

"Dan, give 'em one up the ass."

"How far?"

"325, maybe a bit more. Just hold right between the ears. The bullet will hit him at the base of the neck. Seven inches or so lower, just the way you've sighted it in."

"Yeah?"

"Take'em," Spyker pleaded. "Please!" I swear I heard them snicker at this no-chance shot. I remember thinking that I should shoot, even with no real chance, as there was no way I was going to do anything but kick up a piece of South African dirt.

Settling behind the gun, I turned the scope up to the highest setting. Seven-power. Yup, only seven. My trusty, old, beautiful 7mm Remington Magnum has a 2X7 variable, wide-field scope. Even on seven it looked damn far. The vertical reticle was nearly as wide as the straight away blesbok.

The crosshairs found the head, went right behind the ears. It still surprises me how steady that rest was. The firing pin fell. The blesbok's legs splayed out like a cartoon road kill, flat on the ground.

"Damn. You hammered him. Great shooting, Dan." Spyker and Awie started to giggle a bit. I believe to this day that they were as amazed as I was that the animal fell.

"I wonder just how far that is?" I asked Spyker.

Awie started to measure as we went up to the animal. From the exact spot where the shot was taken to where the blesbok lay was exactly 400. Meters, not yards. That's 440 yards. No, the bullet did not impact the critter at the base of the neck. Not even close. Move back the length of the animal and down just a tad. There, at the base of the tail, was a neat little hole, splitting the base perfectly in half.

I will never do that again, nor would I want to try. I was just plain lucky. Shots at such a distance like this are stupid, foolish, and the stuff that magazine writers want to write about. All of them but me.

"Dan, that is the second longest shot I've ever let a client make. Spot on, Dan, well done!"

"Yeah, just don't ask me to do it again. And no ass-man jokes."

Like Mary had this morning, I was shaking and enjoying every minute. We loaded him quickly in the fading light and headed back to camp.

We made it back to camp just as the sun released a blaze of red fire in the western sky. Doug and Margaret had already returned and were up at the other chalet. I could smell cooking. I was hungry. And thirsty. A quick shower was a requirement, first.

When I departed in the morning, I had just left a pile of clothes alongside the bed. I was going to ask about laundry at dinner that night, but there was no need. Freshly washed and ironed crisply, my clothes from the day before were found neatly folded on top of my just as crisply made bed. This was way too cool. It was also the way things would go with laundry and bedding for the entire trip. Spotless and clean and no waiting.

I was the last one up for dinner. But before dinner there are, of course, before-dinner drinks just there are after-dinner drinks after dinner. Wine is served with dinner.

And with these before-dinner drinks, scotch whiskey for me, were some of the biltong and sausage sticks from the night before. Just after I arrived, Moses brought out a plate of hot snacks. These were grayish pieces of meat neatly cut in the size and shape of casino dice and sautéed with a bit of garlic and white wine. They smelled great.

"Come, come. Have some snacks," called out Pierre.

We all gathered around and asked what we were diving into. "Try them," was all Pierre would say. Then he'd stab one with a toothpick, plop it in his mouth ceremoniously, and smile the smile of contentment. They were as good as advertised. After everyone ate a few pieces, Pierre told us what they were.

"What you are eating are the testicles of Mary's hartebeest. It's rather a tradition to do this with the first animal killed on safari. It's the strongest part of the animal; it is to give us all strength." No one gagged, or even turned green. Not even a little burp was heard.

I think it was Doug who simply said, "Long live tradition! Now pass the damn balls back this way."

Moses delivered kudu schnitzel to the table for dinner. Pap, a cornmeal-like starch that looked like bright white mashed potatoes, was served with it. Unlike mashed potatoes, this pap, which is pronounced "paup or pop," actually had a very good flavor. The kudu he served could be cut with a fork, it was so tender. Unlike most schnitzels, this one came with a gravy that complemented rather than covered the taste of the meat. I believe Doug and I each had thirds. On everything.

After dinner Pierre stood up and raised his glass. "I'd like to propose a toast. To Mary, for killing a huge trophy red hartebeest. And to Dave, for killing two blesbok with one shot." He giggled a bit. All of us chuckled.

"We have a tradition in safari camp. It is a naming ceremony. For Mary, you will now be known as Mama Mojo, which means Mama One Shot." Mary beamed. Dave gave her a big hug. "And Dave, because of your accomplishments this day, you'll be known as Bwana M'bili, Master Two." This brought a bit of laughter to everyone but Dave. He just looked at Pierre, raised his glass in a returning salute, and grinned broadly, a bit like a young child getting his hand caught in the cookie jar.

The day was getting too long. Even without the mule for encouragement, I cried uncle and made my apologies for pooping out. I wasn't alone. Doug did the same a few moments later.

I remembered having slipped the night before, and so I took my good time. I could hear Doug behind me and thought of waiting, but didn't. He'd be at the chalet just a minute or two after me.

A stumble, a thud, and an "ouch" came from behind me.

"Doug, you okay?"

"Yeah, I fell. I'm all right. I think." Guess the ground didn't come up to catch him as it did for me the night before.

I waited and heard him try to get up. "Yeow!"

"Doug?"

"This thing hurts. My ankle, I think. I can't put much weight on it."

Make that no weight. I went back up to him. I tried to help him up, but the slightest bit of weight on that leg caused him to wince. I remember him saying that "we should give it a minute." Doug's no wimp, not by a long shot. His pain tolerance is legendary. He was really hurting. I helped him back down to the ground.

EFFECTIVE SHOOTING

Bullets, and their exact placement, are everything. You can take that .470 Nitro, load it with premium bullets, screw the shot, and you're left with a wounded, angry critter. Load a rifle, even a .223, and make a brain or spine shot, and as long as the bullet doesn't fail, you'll kill just about anything. Yes, within reason, but you get the point.

A brain shot will kill animals stone cold. A spine shot will anchor an animal to the ground but will probably need a follow-up to stop the blood from flowing in its veins. A heart/lung shot will kill the animal, but there's an awful good chance you'll track a few of these for more than a few yards, and anxious minutes.

Before you go to Africa, it would behoove you to pick up a copy of Robertson's *The Perfect Shot: Africa.* You'll find real-life photos of the big five, as well as dozens of other representative game animals, in quartering, straight on, straight away, and broadside poses. The animal's anatomy is superimposed, showing you the exact placements of a perfect killing shot. You'll find that the anatomy is a bit different from North American animals. There are also in-depth chapters on guns and bullet types. The pocket-sized edition should travel with you to Africa and be the last thing you read at night, and the first you review in the morning.

It is also true that some calibers will kill better than others. They launch bigger bullets, at better speeds, and with premium bullets that will cause more damage. That's why, when hunting in many countries, there are minimum calibers that can be used. In other words, you *can* bring the smaller stuff, but you *will* have the big stuff, too. Generally these are .375s or better.

Having these minimums does make sense. What I found as somewhat of a surprise is that a fair number of fellows who hunt really don't know what is doing the killing. It's not the rifle. The rifle simply launches the bullet. In the words of my wise friend Doug Chester, "It's the bullet, stupid."

No bones showed through the skin—no bumps or bruises, either. I took his shoe off, and his sock. I could move his knee up and down, bend it a bit side to side. No pain. With his ankle I did the same. No pain here either. I had him wiggle each of his toes and extend them up and down. Again no pain. I had him press a bit with his foot on my hand. That, he said, he felt but just a little.

Then, using my hands, I went up and down his leg from his ankle to just above the knee feeling for anything strange. It all felt fine. I did hear a crinkling just above the ankle, a crinkling like cellophane. By that time the others heard us and came down.

Professional hunters must be able to handle a lot of medical issues, many of them life-threatening. I told Pierre what I did, and the results. He went through the same motions I did in pretty much the same order.

"I don't like that crinkling," I told Pierre and Doug. "I don't think anything is broken, but that sound is like a tendon curling up on itself. Not torn all the way, but partially, and it's curling up on itself."

For the plains game we were after, I chose Winchester Supreme Partition Gold in 165-grain for my 7mm Rem. Mag. That's a bit heavy in a bullet for the smaller antelope but quite acceptable and quite good for larger antelope. This bullet is known for its rapid expansion and ability to drive through, maintaining a good deal of its original heft. I didn't want to sight in every day, so I decided to use the same bullet for every day with this caliber. I only brought the 165-grain style on this hunt.

For the .375 H&H, I brought Winchester Supreme FailSafe bullets in 300-grain. That, my friends, is a lot of bullet. That will kill a buffalo and then some. I had no dreams of buffalo. I did have nightmares of a muffed and unrecovered kudu or zebra or gemsbok. I heeded the advice of Doug Chester.

Doug—and in fact everyone but me—was using handloads. Doug and Dave like playing with the intricacies of powder charges and such. I do not. As long as I can get premium bullets loaded for me by a premium manufacturer, which is much easier to do than it was even ten years ago, then I am perfectly happy and content to pay them for the service.

If you do load your own, the wise reader will pay heed to this advice from Doug: "Use Barne's X bullet. The end."

It doesn't matter a hoot if you can't hit what you are aiming at. Firing from the bench will get the rifle sighted in, but it won't get you sighted in. You have to practice the way you will or may have to shoot.

That means practicing from the prone, or lying down, position. From kneeling and sitting. Certainly from standing, both supported and unsupported. And, for heaven's sake, practice shooting off some sort of shooting stick. Chances are, on safari, you'll be put into most if not all of these positions. That miserable kneeling shot may be the only one you get when a trophy kudu is disappearing in the mopane. You need to be ready. You are now warned. ▪

"I don't think it's broken, either. That tendon could be it, though."

Spyker went up for a vehicle, and we loaded Doug on the back and drove him the short distance to our chalet. In the chalet Pierre wrapped the ankle in an ace bandage, and I dosed Doug with Celebrex, a prescription painkiller and anti-inflammatory. In fact I double-dosed him.

Pierre and I carried Doug to bed. "We'll check that leg again in the morning. If it's still hurting like that, we'll get you into a doctor to check things out. Don't be trying to get out of bed without help. Dan's here; call him if you need anything."

I handed Margaret two more capsules, telling her to give them to Doug if and when he woke up in the middle of the night.

This was Africa. This could be a bit of trouble.

The lions grunted.

CHAPTER 6

Springbok Prongs and Rhino Watutsi

leep came easy that night. Even keeping an ear open for a call for help from Doug didn't stop the sleep genies from doing their work. Everything was right in the world as I got up just before 5 A.M.

As the water was heating for coffee, a herd of wildebeest set up shop right off the front patio, using the rails as rubbing posts. This was all too good to be true. Their soft grunts were melodic.

The sunrise was a replay of the day before, with the sky lit up in all the shades of yellow, orange, and red that you can imagine. It was a feast for the eyes. Laughing doves shouted their appreciation. Lions growled and haa-rumphed in approval.

Doug and Margaret started to stir. Knowing Margaret would want coffee immediately, I had a cup ready for her. Doug's night was uneventful. Thankfully. The leg was still mucked up though.

We double-dosed him again, much to his disapproval. Doug is a tough bird with a high pain tolerance. The double wasn't so much for the pain; as long as he didn't put any weight on it, there was virtually none. It was to keep the swelling down.

In a broken bone you expect some internal bleeding that shows itself as a sizeable and brilliant purple bruise. There was no bruising except for just a few varicose veinlike bruise lines. It was swollen, but nothing beyond what a sprain would show itself as. This was looking almost okay. Pierre came down, had a look, and came away with the same impression.

The pain from weight bearing was an issue, though. Any weight at all on the leg sent daggers up the leg. Pierre told us that he'd have Anneli take Doug in to Vrede, a small town nearby, and get it checked by the doctor there. "Just to be safe, Uncle Doug. It's best to be sure."

Dave and Mary decided to sleep in. Spyker was to take them on a critter cruise when they woke up. A critter cruise is just what the name implies, a cruise looking for critters. In Africa they call them game drives, but I like critter cruise better. It simply sounds more fun. Margaret, Pierre, Tielman DeVillers, the other owner of Moreson, and I were going hunting.

Hunting demands a bit of concentration. Doug's questionable status had our levels wavering from the task at hand. Up on top of a butte, Margaret and Pierre spotted a good bull black wildebeest, something Margaret definitely wanted. Black or blue (there are black wildebeest and blue wildebeest, completely different species), variety didn't matter. She simply wanted a gnu.

Wait a minute, aren't we talking about wildebeest? What's all this gnu stuff about?

This is Africa. Africa is different than anyplace you've been. What Africa decides things should be called doesn't always meet our expectations. Africa forgives your confusion.

The blue wildebeest is more properly called a brindled gnu. You'll find dark vertical stripes (brindles) on the flanks and on the neck. The mane is black. Its body is generally gray in color. The tail is short and gray at its base with long black wisps on the last half to the tip.

The black wildebeest is more properly called a white-tailed gnu. This fellow has a chocolate coat. The mane, white to light yellow at its base ending in chocolate-colored tips, is quite striking. The tail is more cream to light yellow than white, and is horselike, with long wisps from base to tip.

Margaret is a bona fide, honest-to-God rocket scientist. It's her job to design rockets and satellites, manipulate their flight into and through the heavens, and then gather and interpret the data they send back. One of the jazzy computers she works with is called a Gnu. Margaret wanted a real one for her office.

The grasslands are a lesson in long stalks and long shots. Take these black wildebeest, for instance. We couldn't get within 500 meters before they would stampede off.

THE SAFARI WARDROBE

First of all, realize that excess baggage fees charged by the airlines are outrageous. Slightly overweight on two bags is much cheaper than an extra bag. And packing three separate bags means there are three bags that could get lost. I'll stick with two, thank you. And one of those is my gun case.

With this in mind, pack well and pack light. Your clothes in any good safari camp will be laundered, pressed, and folded daily. Just break the rules your mother taught you, and leave the dirty stuff at the base of the bed in the morning. When you return in the afternoon, you'll find them neat and clean, pressed and folded upon your perfectly made bed, as if done by laundry fairies.

On the plane trip to Africa, wear one set of hunting clothes, pants, and shirts. Pack two additional sets in one of your bags. You are going to want good canvas or cotton pants and shirts that will stand up to the thorns. I chose Cabelas's Trail Hiker pants and their Serengeti Plains shirt. Both performed wonderfully. Good medium-weight cotton construction, the pants have extra layers of fabric at the knees and butt. Same goes for the shirts, with roll-up sleeves. Pockets on each are plentiful and well designed.

As for underwear, remember you are going to be sweating. Wicking fabrics will be best. Bring five pairs. You never know if one is going to get soiled after an unexpected encounter. For undershirts, again the wicking variety will serve you very well indeed.

You must take two pair of good hunting boots. These must be well broken-in. Don't bring your insulated deer hunting boots; your feet will sweat too much. Anything with more than 200 grams of Thinsulate is simply foolhardy. Heavy lug soles make too much noise, so get something softer and less aggressive. Bird-hunting boots seem almost perfect. Hunt in one pair today. Hunt in the other pair tomorrow. This ensures they get dried out after a hard day of hunting.

Socks are nothing to take lightly. Bring five pairs plus the ones you are wearing. In actuality you'll be bringing ten pairs: Five pairs of good quality hiking socks and five pairs of sock liners. The sock liners draw sweat away from

They stalked the wildebeest, a creature that can never make up its mind as to which way to go, but never got within range. If they ever got close, the wildebeest would do a quick about-face and dash off, just a short ways, but enough to get outside the comfort zone. It would mill about a bit, dash back at the pair, only to peel off left, or right, and start all again. It reminds me of early flirting where the girl says, "Oh, come here." Only to dash off when you gather your courage and make the slightest effort to do just that. Then she pleads again, "Oh, come here." And dashes off once again.

A nickname for the wildebeest is "clown of the veldt." They just never seem to know which way to go so they go all ways. I would suggest "tease of the veldt" is more appropriate.

the foot and into the hiking socks. This is a very good thing. Wet feet bring blisters. Blisters mean misery.

You'll want five pairs for a number of reasons. It is awfully nice to change socks at midday when you come in for brunch. You will just feel better. And carry an extra pair with you on the hunt. Don't believe your boots are waterproof. If you find yourself in a stream crossing, you'll be glad you had that extra pair to change into on the other side.

I really like gaiters, those funny-looking things that cover your boots and the bottom section of your pants. I like the ones that come up to just below my knee the best. Gaiters do a number of things. They protect your laces and knots from coming untied and loosened with every grab of a stick or rock. They protect you with an extra layer of protection from thorns. And, they prevent irritating seed heads and burrs from falling into your boot. Most professional hunters wear shorter styles, called sock covers.

The nights and early mornings can be cool to cold. You'll want to pack a sweater or two. A fleece coat with a wind-stopping fabric is a very good idea. I have found Cabela's WindStopper line to be next to perfect. The one problem with sweaters and fleece is that they pick up thorns and seed heads and burrs. A lightweight canvas coat worn over the fleece prevents this from happening.

Take a pair of gloves or two. One pair of lightweight shooting gloves and one pair of lightly insulated gloves will do quite nicely. Those insulated ones come in very handy while riding in the back of the hunting car when you leave in the morning and return in the evening. The shooting gloves, even if you shoot without them, help get those pesky thorns out of your way.

A watch cap will help fend off the cold. A baseball-style cap will help deflect the sun as it gets warm.

After the day's hunt, after your shower, you will want to get into something comfortable. I like sweat pants and a super-soft sweatshirt, with the very comfortable sandals that I wore on the plane ride over and tomorrow's hunting socks underneath. ▦

After an hour or so, the hunt for wildebeest was abandoned. On the way back to the car, a wall-worthy springbok stood up in the grass. It was the last time it would stand, as Margaret's .270 bark was as bad as its bite.

While all this was going on, Tielman and I were playing cat-and-mouse with another springbok he described as "quite huge." I knew it was a ram, a good one, but that's as far as I'd go in estimating its worth. Like the blesbok of yesterday, they all looked alike to me. Three hours we chased that ram. He was alive when we saw him last.

Breakfast went the same way as the day before. The cubs were played with. Doug and Anneli were off to the doctor in Vrede. I figured we'd get going again around 2 P.M. I was wrong. And that made me a very happy camper.

Margaret and Pierre heading out after a springbok. Low grasses do not allow a close approach. Maybe below that little dip, they'll find them. Or the one after that. . . .

Cubs do grow up, fast. Just over a month or so old, this one's coming over to play. Go ahead and play, as long as mama is tucked safely away. Just don't turn your back or you will be pounced on. They have teeth. They have claws.

Just after 11:15 A.M. Spyker came by the chalet. I was sitting on the patio, glassing the herds that were milling about below. "Dan? No nap for you?"

"Nope, can't deal with them."

"When you want to go back out hunting, let me know."

"Spyker, I did not come on this safari to sit on my ass. I'll sleep when I'm dead. If the others want to nap, that's fine and I can wait. I'm easy. The river flows and I'm just floating along with it. But for me, you do not ever need to ask when. You know this country and the game, not me. You tell me it's time and it's time. All I ask is a five-minute heads-up to gather my gear. Deal?"

Spyker chuckled. "Dan, that is perfectly fine with me. You now have five minutes."

"Really?"

"Five minutes, now four and three quarters."

The five minutes turned to fifteen. Mary and Dave, Margaret, Tielman, and Awie, along with two trackers, all wanted to go and watch us hunt, too. It was quite a crew in that hunting car. Six people crammed themselves into the back of the car. Think of that old college prank of how many people can fit in a Volkswagen Beetle, each hanging in and out of the thing. Tielman and I had the honors up front.

While out looking, Tielman answered a lot of my questions. Seems Moreson translates from Afrikaans to English as Morning Sun. With the daily show to the east, it's no wonder the place is named as it is. Vrede translates to Peace. Can't say why it's called that, but it is.

The cosmos plants that are intermixed with the prairie grasses are not indigenous. The Boers brought them over and planted them as feed for their cattle. Now

Not all the grass is short at Moreson. In ravines where water pools, the grass grows above a man's head. Above the trucks, too.

they have naturalized. That grass, about five feet high and in some cases up to seven and eight feet high, is called blackjack. You know it when you come up on it. There's a heady, musty-sweet perfume from the seed heads. It's one of the smells that I would come to associate with the grasslands of South Africa.

Untold numbers of birds looking like small quail squirted out from the car as we made our way down the track. They were, in fact, quail. Other grouse-sized birds, various species of francolin, flushed in front of us. Guinea fowl ran ahead of us only to dash into the nearest cover. On one of the small dams, a pair of Egyptian geese had set up housekeeping. Cranes and herons stood sentinel on its edges.

Certainly I had seen all these yesterday and during the morning's hunt. I remember them. But I didn't really see them.

The first day in a new place, I'm still unsettled. I'm in sensory overload, synapses on overtime. There's only so much input my brain can take in with the new environment. It takes at least a day to settle, for my brain to efficiently engage and start soaking in the specifics. I was finally seeing, with the help of time and Tielman, the individual trees from the forest. It was a sublime moment. I remember taking a deep breath and holding it in, savoring it. I remember sighing in the wonder of it all. God, this really is Africa.

Tielman broke the moment with a sharp slap across my chest. "Dan, springbok. Good one."

Maybe from glassing so many others, maybe from finally being settled, I was able to pick the best ram out of the herd in front of us. "Third from the left. Right?" I asked.

"That's him."

Or was him. The group dashed off before we could even think about the stalk. It took a good hour to get back up on this one boss ram.

Finally we were on him. Settled behind the gun, I put the crosshairs on his shoulder as he stood broadside and facing to the left, about 200 yards away. Trouble was his lady friends were all around him. When a shot presented itself, a lady would stroll by mucking up the works. Fifteen minutes I waited.

The ram was finally clear of his harem. I squeezed the trigger and watched a puff of dust kick up just to the right of the ram. "Damn."

"Right on the height and all, Dan. But you forgot about the wind," said Tielman.

No kidding. I didn't even realize the wind was blowing until that precise moment. Not a breeze, either, a true wind that Spyker estimated at a good 30 knots. No wonder the bullet drifted a good 18 inches. What a dummy. It shouldn't have drifted that far, but that's my story and I'm sticking to it.

Africa forgave that bit of thoughtless shooting and allowed us to regroup and find, once again, the ram with all the ladies. This time we were perched upon a rather tall hill covered by grass and rock. The springbok were below in a wide ravine.

The ram was facing right this time and the wind was still an issue. I thought of the last shot, the miss, with all those spectators judging me, but worse still was how I was judging myself. I should have paid more attention back there.

"Dan, he's a bit farther this time. From the top of this hill where we are to the bottom of the ravine is 300 meters. He's just a touch on the other side of the bottom, say 325. Put the crosshairs just right underneath his head and 6 inches in front of his neck. You'll clock 'em right in the heart and lungs," coached Spyker.

I had other plans. No matter if the wind sent the bullet two feet to the side, this guy was mine. Rather than risk the bullet going too far back resulting in an agonizing and aggravating gut shot that would certainly turn into a miserable recovery, I settled the crosshairs at the top of his head and moved them directly in line with the neck. This shot, I thought, would take him in the spine, anchoring him. No matter if the wind blew or suddenly stopped, that beautiful spine shot would put him down.

It did, too. "Spot on!" yelled Spyker. The others gave me a few pats on the back.

Rather than retreat to the vehicle and drive to the springbok, I wanted to walk up to him. Driving up is impersonal, without feeling. Walking to the kill is personal. It honors the animal. It's the way, whenever possible, that it should be done.

The rocks were a bit interesting to negotiate. Particularly with the thick grass, often more than head-high. I did make it just fine, a good five minutes before the car came up.

The time difference was needed to collect myself. He was beautiful. I wept a few tears of the hunter, tears of joy, and a bit of remorse. I shook the tremors of the hunter, adrenaline coursing through my veins. I saw the ruff quickly flair and just as quickly disappear.

"Thank you," I said softly while stroking his golden back. The bullet had done its job well, hitting directly in the spine in the middle of his back.

The horns were bigger than I remembered them through the scope. They were taller and wider, his bases thicker, the inward curl was deeper. I ignore the record keepers who judge their animals by size. These types are compensating for something. This mature ram needed no compensating. Nor did I.

We returned to camp and found Doug and Anneli were also there. Doug was in a cast.

"The clinic doesn't have an X-ray machine, but the doctor thinks it's probably broken," Doug told us.

"I'll be taking Doug to Ladysmith tomorrow to a hospital. He has an appointment with a doctor there, and they will take X-rays," Pierre added.

Pierre then informed us that, as Ladysmith was a good ways away, it may be best to move the entire show to another concession, one closer to Ladysmith, a day earlier than planned, just in case. "Don't worry about this one. Lots of kudu, lots of gemsbok, you'll love this one, too."

Mary was a bit disappointed; I guess all of us were. Of course we were concerned for Doug's condition, but we were beginning to really see Moreson and we wished for more.

Mary and Dave, on their morning critter cruise, didn't find the rhinos that were setting up housekeeping, and the giraffes behaved badly, only showing themselves from too far a distance. These were critters Mary really wanted to see. With only a few hours of daylight remaining, a plan was developed.

Spyker was to go quickly into the bush and try to find the rhinos. It would not be a fun ride, fast and bumpy, something that Mary probably wouldn't enjoy. If he found them, he would beat feet back to camp, gather us up, and take us to the rhinos.

"Ah, Spyker?" I asked, "Mind if I come along?"

"No problem, Dan. Let's get going."

The hunting car found its second breath while Spyker took it past "normal" driving speed in the bush. It also found its leaf springs as we sped over rocks, in and

This is only a fair springbok as far as springbok go. They get much better in the Kalahari region. We're not in the Kalahari; we're in Free State Province where this one is referred to as a "big dude."

out of gullies, and scattered more than a few flocks of birds and herds of blesbok, springbok, and wildebeest.

Awie and Tielman told us before we left that the rhinos had been frequenting a certain valley on the concession. A valley that was filled with acacias and scrubby-looking pines that pushed up into the mountain that dominated the landscape.

No rhinos. Onward to the end of a long grass-covered butte overlooking the grassy plains below. Two oryx, my first sightings of these straight-horned majestic antelope with a masked face, galloped off in a rather dignified and upper-crust manner. It was almost snobbish. From the edge of the butte, ancient rocks sent up spires. They appeared as medieval battlements towering over a castle.

From these we could see until sight disappeared. The grasslands went on forever. Ever look out on the ocean, or one of the Great Lakes, where you start gazing at the water in front of you and then look outward? You see nothing on the horizon but a line. You know the water is still there. It doesn't disappear. But it does. Crisp skies allowed a long view, but eventually the curvature of the earth took over, swallowing the grass into nothingness. Even in the prairies of the United States or Canada, there's always something to define the horizon. There was nothing here.

We looked hard for the rhinos. We found the giraffes, but they were still uncooperative. We found a group of eland equally unimpressed with our invasion.

Back toward the valley we came on a small river. All but dry, it still had enough water to create a jungle-thick canopy of grasses and acacias and assorted other trees. Spyker drove the car through the tall grass and trees. An old homestead and barn sprang up from the grasses. Barely held together by 100-year-old hopes, it was mostly coming down. Piles of something were just outside the barn.

Spyker and I got out and looked closely. To me they looked like cow pies. Spyker smiled. "Rhino. Dan, I think they've been here very recently. This is fresh and warm." Yes, he used his finger to determine warmth and wiped the dung off on his pants.

Back in the truck, Spyker drove ever more slowly through the thickets and grass. Around a bend he stopped suddenly. He didn't need to explain. There, maybe

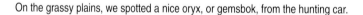

On the grassy plains, we spotted a nice oryx, or gemsbok, from the hunting car.

Giraffes were in the tall grass, the short grass, any grass. From a distance they look rather funny; up close, when they have an attitude, they do not look so funny.

75 yards away, were two white rhinos. The closest one standing in a patch of short grass. The other one maybe 10 yards farther and standing inside the tall grass, only his back showing above the seed heads.

They aren't called white rhinos because they're white. Their technical name is the southern square-lipped rhinoceros. "White" is a bastardization of a poor translation of the Afrikaan word for wide, "whyde." They get the name due to their wide or square mouth. The black rhino has a narrow mouth, like a stubby trunk. White rhinos are grazers. Blacks are browsers. The white fellow is also twice the size of the black, with an average male pushing more than 4,500 pounds. While the black is generally thought of as being more ill-tempered, both can possess the attitude of a drunk redneck.

I started snapping photos, prints specifically, just to get them on film. The lens was too short to capture anything except memories, but I wanted the photos. "Dan, let's get closer. Bring the slide camera and get some really good pictures."

"Uh, okay." I mean, what would you do? You're with a professional hunter who definitely knows his business. You both have guns. "Ya sure there, Spyker?"

"The wind is good for us. They have very poor eyesight. Mind where you put your feet. They do have good ears." Yeah, I thought. And I also thought of the John Wayne movie *Hatari*, where the rhino gored the feller, actually gored two. *Mutual of Omaha's Wild Kingdom* also came to mind, where Jim and a rhino do-si-doed a few squares together.

We got closer. I kept two steps back and two steps right per Spyker's instructions. In case we had to beat feet, Spyker didn't want to be tripping over me. I wondered who could run faster, Spyker or me.

This white rhino smells something he doesn't like and steps out of the tall grass to investigate.

Within 20 yards, I still felt the breeze on my face. I also felt my heart racing. I clicked the shutter fast, wanting to get it all. I did, too. Until the wind decided to play a practical joke and sent a swirl from us directly into a rhino's prominent nose.

That rhino immediately snorted, turned directly toward us, blew his nose, and five gallons of rhino snot sprayed out, snorted again, and started to come. God, are they quick! The world stood still as two tons of angry rhino stomped his way toward us. I swear the ground trembled.

The camera was hanging around my neck and the gun raised as quick as Spyker raised his. "Don't move!" he hissed. At no more than 5 yards, the damn thing stopped dead, growled softly, and then turned and walked back to where he was.

Spyker inched back, something I had already started to do when the rhino switched direction. "You didn't shoot; most would have," he said back at the truck.

"Yeah, but you were in front of me. I had my gun up to defend your sorry ass, though," I replied.

"You took the safety off, too. I heard it."

"Just like I heard yours. You know, just in case."

"When would you have shot?"

"Two more steps."

"I thought one, but then I was closer."

"Yup, and you are the professional."

"Christ, that was great fun."

"Fun? You shit! Here I am. Entrusted in the hands of the great white hunter. It's only the second day, and already you're out to get me killed. Christ! Fun? Well, yeah . . . I guess it was. Sort of."

"Think of the pictures you just got. They'll be great. Let's get Mary and Dave. Rhinos'll still be in the area." The drive to get Dave and Mary was again at high speed. I'm glad the trip was fast, since it prevented me from stumbling over my tongue in a post-excitement, adrenal gland-shutdown stutter. Good Lord, two days in Africa and already this PH has my pucker factor tightly shut and me thankful that I'm not a spot of oozing raspberry jam.

We found them again, too. Mary and Dave snapped away. This time from a good 100 yards or more. No one got out of the vehicle. No one asked to.

We watched ostrich high-step in the grass. Mixed herds of antelope marched across the plains. We were even graced by a small herd of zebra that came out of nowhere, buzzed in on us fast, and vanished into the same nowhere just as quickly. On the drive back to camp, the sun was washed out, surrendering itself into a smooth red haze by the dust of the animal's movement.

It was the magic or golden hour. The night sounds were just beginning, and the night-loving animals were just starting to make their presence known. We watched a group of clownlike meerkats come out from a termite mound. A jackal's yip sent them scurrying back to cover. Night was coming on and so was the cool wash it brings to the plains.

We stopped at the top of the hill before heading back down to camp. Whether we knew it or not, we needed time to taste the coming of night. We could have been on top of the Big Horns of Wyoming, on a mesa overlooking hundreds of mile of grasslands. Grasses etched in shimmering gold hillsides. Looking east, even through the purple dusk, we could see tomorrow coming. To the west, yesterday was still waving its goodbyes.

Dinner was roast hartebeest, compliments of Mary. I'm generally not one for roasts, but this one was exceptionally tender and moist. I have no idea what herbs or spices Moses used in preparing it. I'm just glad he did. I was glad three times. I was glad for the scotch the same number of times.

God bless Moses.

CHAPTER 7

Zulu

 reakfast in Moreson's dining room was just as full as the prior two days. It was earlier, around 7 A.M. We had miles to put on in order to get to the next concession by nightfall.

During breakfast, a lioness decided it was a perfect time to give birth. From no more than 30 yards away, we watched as the fruits of Awie and Tielman continued to ripen. Three cubs, born under the shade of a huge acacia, licked clean and now suckling on mama's belly. Soon they would be a part of the land.

Doug and Pierre headed for Ladysmith and the hospital. Getting around on crutches isn't exactly Doug's forte, but he did manage, with help, to get into the Land Cruiser. Margaret gave him a hug and whispered something in his ear. Other than that, no words were spoken. None dared.

The game plan for the rest of us was to head for a "day of culture." Specifically, Anneli had arranged a special tour of Basotho Cultural Village, a Zulu living history museum located inside Golden Gate National Park.

Driving down the washboard gravel road leading away from Moreson, a blesbok decided to pace us. No more than 15 feet from the road's edge, he trotted along in an almost Tennessee walking-horse style. The front legs jumped in front, one after the other, while the hinds seemed to barely move. At 50 kilometers an hour he hadn't broken a sweat.

The thing stayed with us a good mile. We decided to race and sped up to a solid 65 kilometers an hour and still the blesbok stayed with us. In fact, we watched as it glanced over, gave us one of those looks and sped up, leaving us in the dust as it turned away. Then he stopped, standing stock-still as we passed, and finally trotted off with that superior attitude of his, having proved who was faster.

We drove south over excellent roads into Harrismith. Like any other mid-size city in any other place, it has what you need and not a lot more. Not to disparage the fair residents of Harrismith, but at first glance it could be anywhere. Except that it serves as the gateway to Golden Gate National Park.

Golden Gate Park sits on the southern border of the province of Free State. One of the two countries located entirely within the boundaries of South Africa, Lesotho,

Moreson has a captive breeding program for lions. Here's mama licking a cub all of a minute old.

provided the boundary. The other country within a country in South Africa is Swaziland, to the northeast.

Upon turning out of the city, higher mountains, not unlike those of the desert southwest, started to pop up. The area gets more rainfall so there is a lot more plant life, but the mountains look surprisingly similar.

I thought I saw a sable, one of the "royal" antelope species. In fact, I was so sure I demanded we stop, turn around, and look for the thing. I knew seeing a sable here would be quite rare, actually quite rare anywhere except the northern reaches of the country, where they are still very uncommon.

Ah, but it wasn't a sable at all. It was standing just as I see them stand in the photos. Head held high, chest puffed out—yup, had to be one. But it wasn't. No, what I saw was a rather ordinary member of the blesboks. He was standing just like a sable, though, even Spyker said so. Spyker then made a whistling sound and shook his head just a touch. I guess it was a monster blesbok, or else he was making fun of me.

At Basutho Cultural Village, we were met by Adam, our tour guide. His English was better than mine, and he seemed thrilled that we were taking the time to learn more about the land and, more importantly, its people.

Zulus are a proud people. Handsome to a fault. Reserved at your first meeting, and then quick with a smile.

Along a path lined in thorny acacias along a rocky cliff, we made our way to the village. From high on the cliff, high-pitched squeals, like a third-grader learning the violin, could be heard. "That's the village sentinel," said Adam. "He's announc-

Basutho Cultural Village at the east side of Golden Gate National Park. The village traces Zulu history through time, and does it in the living history style.

ing our arrival to the village." Rounding the bend we could see him up on the cliff, perched like a raptor, and also like a raptor, watching our every move.

Through an archway of vegetation, we entered the village. Another Zulu greeted us and told us that the chief expected us to visit him. It was not a request. Something more like a firm insistence.

Now, I don't know Zulu from Portuguese, but from the tone of voice and hand gestures going on between Adam and the king's right-hand man, I could tell something was expected. It turned out that a "gift" was expected. Adam explained that upon entering a Zulu village and meeting the chief, visitors were expected to bring a gift. Nothing major and not money—just a simple gesture of thanks for being invited. Between us we came up with a handful of hard candies, which were accepted with genuine thanks.

A clap of the chief's hands brought out two Zulu women from the king's hut, both carrying a large covered calabash. They knelt in between the chief and us and took the covers off. With a nod of his head, the ladies took a smaller gourd, made for dipping liquid, and filled two small gourds serving as cups with an amber liquid.

This was Zulu beer. It did not come from a bottle, can, or keg. Fermented in the calabash and with some of the grain still in fair-sized pieces, it looked like some health food freak's protein concoction. To say it tasted much better would be a stretch, but drink it we did. At least enough of it to be polite. I had two small sips. Natural carbonation gave it some fizz, showing itself in a rather weak head. Thick and more than a little yeasty, the big brew houses have nothing to

The chief, the brightly dressed fellow in the middle, even "treated" us to his Zulu beer. Home brew, served from a calabash, it was, as Spyker is finding out, interesting.

fear if Zulu Brew comes to market. If you go, and if you are offered some, taste it. I'll pass, thank you. I already punched that ticket. But I will pretend to taste it, to be polite.

Anneli had told Adam of the troubles with Doug. She received a phone call from Pierre on her cell while we were with the king. He and Doug were in Lady-smith at LaVerna Hospital, waiting to see the doctor. Adam suggested a visit to the witch doctor.

The walls of his small hut were made of cow dung, hardened and smooth as concrete. Like most all other buildings, thick thatch covered the ceiling. Two porcupine quills were stuck into the thatch over the entrance. Adam explained that the striped quill was used as protection against lightning and the fires they bring to the bush. The solid-colored quill was used to ward off evil spirits and welcome the good spirits.

The witch doctor was a picture of fashion confusion. His polyester slacks and button-down shirt under a long cape made of skins, along with the unshined black oxfords on his feet, were enough to make you scratch your head with a "huh?" On his closely shorn head, he wore a hardened skin hat resembling something like a fez. His bright eyes were a stark contrast to his face and hands wizened with age. The doctor spoke softly to Adam, asking who we were.

After satisfying the pleasantries of greetings, he brought out a small skin bag and placed it on a larger reed mat in front of him. Adam told me that the doctor wished me to dump the contents of the bag onto the reed mat. A mish-mash of small

No, I am not praying. I just dropped all that stuff sitting on the straw mat. The witch doctor will now commence to read my fortune.

Adam, our guide in Basutho, explains to the witch doctor or shaman what we are doing there. Anyone want his or her fortune told?

bones, buttons, rocks, shells, and beads spilled out. The chief motioned for me to gather them up in my hands and then let them fall to the mat.

I did just that. The chief looked over the pieces, turning one or two over, and then looked at me and gave me a quick smile. Adam told me that the old man had just read my fortune. But, in order to get the meaning of it, a slight payment was expected. Ten dollars was suggested.

Adam laughed when I pulled out a $10 bill. "No. Not U.S. dollars. Rands." Ten rands is equal to about one dollar and fifty cents.

I told Adam that fortunes and I aren't getting along. That I would give the old man 20 rands if he could tell us about Doug. Adam translated my request to the old man who asked if any of us were related to Doug. Margaret, being Doug's wife, was pointed out.

He motioned for Margaret to take my place and gather up the bag of bones and such. Then motioned her to let them scatter on the mat. With more than necessary force, Margaret let them drop so hard some tumbled well off the mat. The witch doctor did not look amused.

Taking a close look at the scattered design, he spoke softly to Adam, never making eye contact with Margaret or the rest of us. Adam translated. "He says that your friend Doug is hurt very badly. It's his leg. That he will need much healing. That you will not see him for days."

None of us said anything. Heck, this was such so much mumbo-jumbo, a little show for the stupid tourists. Doug wasn't hurt that bad. We thanked the old man and continued into the village.

After leaving the Zulu witch doctor, we continued our tour of Basutho. The cultural village is set up as a timeline, beginning with the huts built as they were hundreds of years ago and continuing until the present. You could point out the oldest without any trouble.

The older buildings had no paint. The dung walls and floors, though hardened, were not all smooth. The cooking area, a single small fire pit in the center, was bordered by rough stick bed platforms covered with skins.

The newer buildings did have paint, some with quite gaudy pinks and blues. The floors and walls were still of dung but were carefully smoothed out. The fire pit was more formal, the beds now coming with a leather mesh instead of the sticks woven together. The most modern had store-bought shelves and an icebox along with a rudimentary stove. There were even glass windows and doors.

Just before leaving, Adam invited us to a large thatched building. He had arranged for a lunch to be prepared for us. Ginger beer, which I would gladly drink again, pap or mealie-meal, some stewed meat (I was afraid to ask of what), greens, and yams were placed in front of us. All of it was good. Some of it was better.

From Basutho we headed east into the province of KwaZulu-Natal, KZN for short. Passing the massive Sterkfontein Dam, a huge reservoir, we encountered the Drakensberg Mountains towering to our south and west. The road to Bergville, near our next concession, took us into the Drakensbergs and through Little Switzerland.

These are true mountains. It is as if a piece of Scandinavia was picked up and transported here. Emerald green grasses, rocky crags, high plateaus, and deep valleys with small towns popped up and stretched out in front of us with every bend in the very winding road. Guardrails were iffy at best, and an errant wheel could send you plunging down hundreds of feet. The drop would have been exciting. The stop wouldn't have been.

Into Bergville and soon after a jog back to the west, we came upon a gravel road. Or what passed for a road. One hour on this puppy and our kidneys were aching. The van was shaking. And rattling. A lot.

A huge gate stopped our progress. Kwaggashoek was emblazoned over the top of the gate. Kwaggashoek, or Zebra Corner, was where we would spend the next few days.

Driving through the gate, it was evident we were not in the expansive grasslands of Free State nor the Drakensbergs. Here the hills rolled with acacia of many varieties. Flat-topped acacias dominated, or at least appeared to with the way their upper branches reached horizontally across the reddening sky. The grasses underneath were like gold, and the contrast between the green and gold was what my mind had told me Africa would look like.

The road to the lodge twisted and turned over mainly a sand base. Impalas, the first I had seen, trotted through the trees as we drew closer to them. A small group of eland ambled across the road in front of us. My God, they are big. Think of an ox that's as large as an Alaskan moose. Tawny with faint white stripes and a pair of tightly spiraling horns spearing the sky. And, like the moose, huge dewlaps swung underneath their necks in rhythm with their ambling footsteps.

Cresting a rounded hill, the main house hung below us in a small glade. Beyond that a small dam, inky now in the fading light and with a cross-hatching of

MEDICAL CARE IN SOUTH AFRICA

South Africa is a modern country. Mostly. Their hospitals and clinics are good. Mostly. Getting to them is easy. Mostly.

Even though most of the facilities you may encounter may be of good quality, that doesn't mean you shouldn't take some precautions. They should be looked into well before you leave on safari.

Most of South Africa is not in a malarial zone. Ask your booking agent or professional hunter before you leave if you will be in a malarial zone. If so, do not pass go without getting your stateside doctor to prescribe some sort of malarial prophylaxis. There are more than a few out there. In my book, Malarone is the way to go. Yes, the time period for which you must take it is longer than the others, but it comes with many less side effects—like seeing things that aren't there or headaches or nausea. You may be different. Ask your doctor. While you are in your doctor's office, make sure your DPT shot is valid.

Still with your doctor, ask him or her for a few things that you can take along. Chances are you may twist an ankle. You may get a bout of diarrhea. You may pull a muscle. A small prescription for a painkiller, a muscle relaxant, and an antibacterial will cover most of these quite well. Motrin works, Vicodin and Flexeril work better. Pepto-Bismol and Immodium help relieve nausea and diarrhea; Cipro is an antibiotic that can knock out many bugs. Again, ask your doctor.

Next call your medical insurance company. This will be no fun at all. You may have better coverage than your senator as long as you stay in the states, but overseas it may be worth nothing. If you are one of the lucky ones whose coverage does extend overseas, ask for a letter stating so in writing. If you

V-shaped ripples from waterfowl swimming across its still surface. Beyond that, stretching north and south, was an imposing ridgeline. A prominent plateau towering a few hundred feet above the main ridge pierced into the quickening twilight.

The main house was a huge affair with a deck overlooking the dam just past a group of acacias. Marge, Dave, and Mary found their rooms there. I, along with Spyker and Anneli, found our rooms in, wouldn't you guess, a mobile home.

No, that is not standard, but in this case it would have to do. We learned that just a month before, the main lodge had burned to the ground. This mobile home was only temporary. So temporary that the plumbing had just been installed that day.

A quick shower had me refreshed. I left the trailer to join the others in the main house. Now at full dark, the land manager was out lighting the gravel pathway to the main house with the soft glow of hurricane lanterns.

Anneli had a scotch ready for me. That is what I call service. A new fellow, much younger than Spyker and Pierre, was standing on the porch. "Dan," said Anneli in that flute of a voice, "I'd like to present Clinton, Pierre's son. He'll be joining us for the rest of the safari."

aren't covered, then ask about purchasing a "rider" that will cover you overseas for the length of your safari.

Now, don't expect that the clinic or hospital will accept your insurance. Some simply don't want to deal with the complexities of filing for their payment. More often than not, cash and credit cards will be asked for.

Now, what happens if you don't want to be operated on, or convalesce in Africa? Then you are going to need a way to pay for evacuation back to your home country. These costs are into the stratosphere. Protect yourself.

Three companies that I am familiar with are Travel Guard, CSA Travel Protection, and Medjet Assist. Each has policies covering a wide range of possibilities. Some even include evacuation from the place where you were injured. Read the policy before you pony up the cash. Some require an initial hospitalization before the evacuation back to the States. Some only pay for evacuation to a "suitable" hospital—wherever that is.

All of these obviously cost a few dollars. Realistically, it is only a few compared to the price of your safari and well worth the peace of mind it offers. If you travel outside of the United States on a regular basis throughout the year, you can buy a policy that covers you year-round. If this trip is the only one of the year, there are policies covering a set number of days.

Outside of updating your DPT inoculation, you do not need any other shots. South Africa is not a yellow fever or cholera area. Not at this time. It is highly advised that you check with the Centers for Disease Control before you leave. The world is an ever-changing place. You never know when a beastie is going to show up.

Clinton is a handsome lad like his father. Maybe 21 years old.

Clinton and I shook hands. Margaret came in and was introduced, as was Dave. We went out onto the back deck and enjoyed the close of the day. That's when my evil twin came out.

"Say, Clinton," said I as I packed my lip with Skoal. "Would you like some?" I ask this of everyone. Not that I expect them to really try this disgusting habit of mine, rather to be funny. Okay, it's weird.

Clinton didn't miss a beat. "Sure," and reached his thumb and forefinger into the can to grab some. I pulled it away.

"Are you sure?"

"Sure, I always wondered what this stuff was like." He reached for the can again.

"Not so fast, cowboy. Take a small pinch. Place it between your lip and gum. Do not swallow the juice, spit it out."

Spyker nudged Dave, who nudged Mary. Margaret had been watching all along. She didn't need the nudge.

This is the main lodge at Kwaggashoek. Again, not so shabby. The wire you see is to keep the eland and giraffes and impala and so forth out of the pretty flower and shrub gardens. It doesn't work too well. They just come in via the walkway and are smart enough to go out the same way.

Clinton did just as he was told, taking a small pinch and then placing it in his mouth.

"Clinton, I already see that you're a smoker. This is different. You are going to get dizzy."

"Yeah, Clinton. When you get sick, use your tongue to spit it out," said Spyker.

Clinton was a bit woozy. Then, even in the darkness, I could see his face change color.

I quickly pulled him over to the rail. "Clinton, do not swallow it. Do not use your tongue to get rid of it. Use your finger to sweep it out."

Which he did. Then he yakked. Spyker howled in laughter.

Quickly Clinton jumped the rail of the deck and both ran and wove his way to the side of the house. Through the darkness, sounds I didn't associate with wildlife came from where Clinton disappeared.

A few minutes later he returned. His eyes were a bit glassy. His face a bit red, which was much better than the green of a short while ago.

"Shit! That stuff is wicked."

I just smiled and told him never to try it again. I don't think he will. I wish I hadn't so many years ago.

Dinner was just about to be served when Anneli's phone rang. It was Pierre. Anneli didn't have to say much to us; we could see the concern in her eyes.

Doug was going in for surgery any minute. His leg was badly broken. He would not be joining us this night, maybe any other on this trip. (How did that witch doctor know!?) Marge and Anneli quickly gathered together a small kit and off they raced for Ladysmith.

Maybe it was the nervousness. Maybe it was my scotch, Dave's rum, or Mary's wine. I don't know. What I do know was that one of us called LaVerna Hospital. One of us asked to talk to the surgical team before they began to work on Doug and was passed to one of the nuns who work there. The evil twin returned.

"Uh, excuse me, Sister, but our friend Doug Chester is to have surgery this evening. We were wondering, Sister, if it would be possible, when Mr. Chester is under anesthesia, could you be so kind as to instruct the surgical staff to shave off the poor man's beard? It will be a present for his wife. Trust me, Mr. Chester was considering doing it anyway for his dear wife. Besides, won't the surgical room be more hygienic if he doesn't have that big beard?"

"No. I will do no such a thing."

"Please, Sister, think about how much happier his wife will be. That, and there's $50 U.S. in it for you."

She hung up. Mary was rolling in laughter. Dave was looking in disbelief. "You really didn't . . ." Spyker had Coke coming out of his nose trying to keep from cracking up.

Okay then, someone thought, why not try this: "Hello. Mother Superior, please." Going right to the top helps many times.

"How may I be of help? This is Mother Superior."

"Ma'am, our friend Doug Chester is having surgery tonight. It's on his leg, which is badly broken. My friends and I, but especially his devoted wife, we were wondering if you could do her a favor. Could you please arrange for Mr. Chester to have a circumcision while he is under? He's always wanted one. He has one planned anyway when he gets back to America, and this will save him another hospital visit."

"My dear sir, I will not do such a thing."

"There's $300 U.S. in it for you if it happens."

She hung up the phone before whoever made that call could up the bribe to $500.

Oh well, at least we tried. What are friends for, anyway?

Later that night, just before the generators turned off, cutting the power, we got a call from the hospital. The surgery went well. Dr. Voitek Pieczkowski did his orthopedic magic. Doug still had his beard, and his, well, you know. He also had a dozen or more pins in his leg, along with a shiny new metal plate connecting all the parts of his broken leg together.

CHAPTER 8

An Oryx in the Salt

We woke up in a gray shroud. Sometime during the evening, Pierre had returned from the hospital. As did Anneli and Marge.

"I heard that Clinton tried some of that tobacco of yours. You're a shit, you know that. You should have waited for me to enjoy the show. That would have been great fun," said Pierre.

Anneli and Marge were busy gathering up some things for Doug and some clothes for Margaret. Margaret was going to Ladysmith to be with Doug. Anneli's sister offered her a spare room for sleeping and more hospitality than a friend normally receives, much less a stranger. Doug's surgery, we were again assured, went quite well, and he was resting comfortably.

The three previous days of high blue skies had given way to a cloak of gray that hung heavy all around us. It had rained the night before. It was misting now. Puddles marked the path to the main house like inkwells. There was no breeze to crinkle the water's surface. No leaf moved. Heavy gray clouds hung motionless, blanketing the mountains and valleys. Even the mist off the river hung still in the air. Only the dripping of water off the leaves proved it was not a painting.

Eland had visited during the rain. Heavy hoof prints pockmarked the groomed grass with large heart-shaped pools. Scat lay all around.

Dave headed off with Pierre in search of impala and whatever else might trigger his fancy. Spyker and I, along with Clinton and Isak, joined with Robert, one of Kwaggashoek's trackers. Kudu, that magnificent antelope with corkscrew spiral horns, was the quarry for us. Only kudu.

Hemingway hunted these in old Tanganyika, now Tanzania. So did Ruark. I remember their stories well. Their days-long searches. Their exhilaration. Their crushing defeats. Their long days searching the scrub and forested hills and valleys for a glimpse and a chance at a trophy. It is not a stretch that theirs was a quest for what is known as the "gray ghost."

If no other animal fell to my bullet on this safari, if I bagged a trophy kudu, the safari would be a success. If unsuccessful on the kudu, as long as I hunted them

68

See those clouds? That's where we're going to look for kudu.

A pair of eland strolled over to say hello one day at brunch. Not bad dining companions if you can ignore the rifle, crying to be used.

hard and well, as long as I could look myself in the mirror and be proud of the effort, well, then it would still be a success.

The first order of business was to sight in my .375 H&H. Yes, this is a big gun. No, you most certainly do not need a gun this big to shoot kudu. A .30-06 is more than adequate.

Pierre and Spyker had both told me that if you are only going to buy one gun for Africa, then the .375 should be that gun. Loaded with the proper bullets it will handle anything, in their words, "from rats to rhinos." It is also the minimum caliber allowed in most countries for the dangerous and big-game species like Cape buffalo.

The first shot off the bench showed that something had happened to the scope since I left home. It was not shooting where it was supposed to. Four rounds later it was back in sync. A fifth round proofed the fourth. Two inches high at 100 meters put the bullet I was using—a 270-grain Winchester Fail Safe—dead on at two hundred meters. At three hundred there was an 8-inch drop. Out to 350 and with a steady rest, I was fully confident that the animal was going down.

Spyker drove the hunting car up a memory of a trail toward the mountains. As we crested a hill, a pair of giraffes slowly glided through the tall grass. Down off the hill we found ourselves in a broad valley. Grasses dominated the flat with small shrubbery scattered throughout. On the edges, thick acacia forests reached up into the gray clouds still hanging overhead.

A stream blocked our way. Not the stream per se, but the very steep grass-covered hill on the other side allowed us to drive no further.

Under normal conditions, those of crisp nights followed by sunny days, kudu are often caught leaving the thick bush in early morning and going into small clearings. Kudu get cold. They like to be warm, and the sun on their backs makes them very happy. And it makes them vulnerable to hunters, too.

Giraffes were a regular part of the scenery at Kwaggashoek.

On days like today, the kudu do not want to go to the grassy openings where the grass will soak their fur. Instead they like to stay in the thick stuff.

This was no normal day. Spyker sent Clinton and the trackers into the valley with instructions to make the woodline and go no farther for 30 minutes. This would give Spyker and me time to climb the hill and get in a vantage point overlooking a few small openings. The goal was to have the trackers bust through the brush. Not haphazardly, but in a deliberate fashion. Kudu, and whatever else might be in the bush, would be pushed out, hopefully into a position where Spyker and I could get a shot off.

I knew the hill was steep. I knew that what I thought was the top was most likely only a sucker's top, that there was another and probably another after that before the true top was reached. This would not be a fun part of the hunt.

The grass covering the hills soaked us through and through as we pulled ourselves up the slope. Where there was brush, we used the branches to steady us. With each grab of branch, rain fell from the leaves. Baboons roared and barked at us from the valley and the ridgetop. As expected, the top wasn't the top at all, but three more climbs to small flats finally did put us on the ridgeline's grassy, shrub-covered top.

Spyker kept up a brisk pace along the spine of the ridge. It appeared to be easier. It wasn't. Sharp and unsteady rocks were littered on the ground. Most were covered by grass, and only the largest were visible. I caught them on my shins and thighs, on my hands, arms, and back as I stumbled along to keep up. I saw Spyker stumble. Once. I quit counting my own missteps at 34. But I did keep up.

A good half mile up we halted and Spyker set up the shooting sticks. Three small grassy openings in the flat-topped acacias and other assorted trees and shrubs were below us. The farthest was just under 200 yards away, the nearest a mere 75.

The land at Kwaggashoek is vastly different than at Moreson in the Free State. The hills are higher and covered in acacia trees.

"Dan, the kudu and other game will be in the heavy stuff. They don't want to come out into the grass and get all wet. Clinton and the boys are trying to get them nervous enough to move. We're hoping they move into these openings so we can get a shot. Be ready; if it happens, it will happen quick."

Branches breaking below us brought us to full alert shortly after. I laid the gun on the sticks and settled in. The treetops showed where the animals were better than the snap of branches. A treetop would shiver, a branch would sway, each marking the animals' approach. A flash of movement caught my eye near the first opening. Getting behind the scope, I followed its progress.

A huge bull eland came into the clearing, followed by three cows and a younger bull. I relaxed behind the gun.

"Dan, stay ready. Eland are the first things to move. Kudu often follow. Stay ready."

As if on cue, a kudu bull slid into the clearing. I settled the crosshairs behind his shoulder.

"Don't shoot. He's a puppy."

I couldn't believe it. Those spiral horns looked magnificent. That mane, the striping on his flanks. It was a good animal, for God's sake.

"Spyker, c'mon," I whispered.

"Trust me, Dan. He is a very young bull. This one is not for you. Not today, not the last day. He might go 44, he is certainly not over that. We're looking for a 50-plus. Let's go, we have to get ahead of those eland, or they'll spook everything in front and we won't have a chance in this valley. They are making a lot of racket."

We were off to the races again. Spyker in the lead, me stumbling along behind. I was getting the hang of it, though. In the next half mile I only stumbled twenty or so times. We stopped where the ridge again took a severe upward slope. The slope was covered in thick brush. Two openings were below us, each no more than 150 yards away.

We were soaked with sweat and rain. A slight breeze helped to cool us down a bit. The shooting sticks were set up again. I settled into the gun again. I waited again.

Just beyond the openings we saw branches move and heard their snap. One eland cow skirted the opening to our right. The others stayed in the bush. We never saw the kudu again. We didn't see anything else.

After fifteen minutes, Spyker let out a loud whistle. From deeper into the valley I heard a faint whistle in reply. "I just called the boys back. We'll need to look somewhere else."

After all that work, it was time to rest. Digging through my pack, I grabbed two water bottles. The first one was gone in a single swallow. The second one took two.

Spyker was glassing behind us when the boys met us on top. I passed a couple bottles of water around. Looking over to the ridge across the valley I spotted movement coming out of a group of trees. Kudu! Kudu bulls! Just over 250 yards away in the clear!

"Spyker, come here," I whispered loudly. Clinton got excited. The trackers got excited. I was excited.

These were bigger in body and horn. The rifle hit the sticks again, my heart pounding.

"Dan, these are not for you."

I couldn't believe it.

"Dan, these are bigger. The largest, the one in front, may reach 48, nothing more. If this was the last day maybe, but we can do better."

My trusted hunting team of Spyker, Clinton, and Richard.

Damn. Everything I had read before this trip said to trust your PH and listen to his advice. He's the professional. He's the expert. But damn, three kudu bulls. Each would grace any wall in proud fashion. I didn't need that magical 50-incher. I needed a kudu!

I really think the only thing that kept me from shooting that lead kudu bull was the fact that we had a lot of days to look for a better one. If we only had two left, that would have been one dead kudu.

After a slight rest we headed "elsewhere," which turned out to be the next valley over. This time done in reverse, heading down.

You would think that hunting down would have been easier. It wasn't. Any hill climber will tell you that going down is much harder on your calves and thighs. It is also much harder on your knees, feet, and especially your toes. Your feet and knees come down harder. Your toes jam into rocks. Balance, too, is harder. Falling up isn't nearly so painful as falling down.

On the way down, the skies lifted some. Still gray as ash, they had lost their mist. The breeze, too, had started to cut the blanket of clouds a little. A hint of sun could be seen between the cracks.

Besides the trees, grass and rocks were all we saw on the way down. Hunting fast, we made it to the car in about an hour's time. All of us were a bit winded. The last half-mile was almost a trot.

Clinton shot Spyker a questioning look. I noticed a slight nod from Spyker.

"What was that all about?"

"What?"

"Guys, c'mon, I may be an American, but if you ask me, I think this morning was some sort of test. I'm not pissed about it or anything; it was hard but fun. It was a test. Right?"

Spyker chuckled. "Mr. Donarski, a test of sorts? Yes. I walked you hard. If you couldn't keep up, I would have slowed down. But you did keep up. Your breathing was good enough to make a shot if one came along. In fact, you almost walked me into the ground. I couldn't go any faster. It's important for us to know our hunter's physical limits. There are places where we just can't take some." He broke out into a broad smile, stuck his hand out for me to shake, and said, "You, Mr. Donarski, you I'll take anywhere."

Just after lunch the skies cleared off completely. Except for a mass of clouds that clung to the very top of the mountain, blue skies were all around. A slight steady breeze bent the grasses in the valley and brushed the leaves of the trees in slow rhythm. Plans to head to a distant valley in search of kudu were halted when a small herd of oryx, or gemsbok, was spotted about a mile off.

The blondish-brown body with a striking facemask of black and white and straight, rapierlike horns make an impressive trophy. I did want one. I had more days for kudu. Spyker thought he saw a very good one from that distance, so what was there to do but have a go at them?

It was early in the afternoon, not a hair past 1 P.M. We'll take care of the gemsbok, then head back to the valley for the golden hour when the kudu would come out to feed and water. Plenty of time.

GETTING IN SHAPE FOR SAFARI

Do you have to possess super-human strength to go on safari? Nope. Do you have to be able to run a half marathon? Nope. But . . .

A simple fact of safari life is this: You will have more fun, you will hunt better, you will hunt farther, if you are in better shape on the day you leave than you are right now. Start your conditioning routine at least three months before the beginning of your safari. Six months is even better.

When it comes to physical strength, being able to lift a Volkswagen is not necessary. You will, however, be using your arm, shoulder, chest, and back muscles in ways you are not used to. Dumbbells are all you'll need for this. Simple arm curls, military presses, and bench presses will get you where you want to be. The more weight you can lift, the better off you are. If you don't have dumbbells, the basic push-up is a good all-around exercise.

If you're just doing push-ups, then be sure to vary the style. Three sets of standard push-ups, followed by three sets of decline push-ups, followed by three sets of incline push-ups will work wonders.

Leg strength is an altogether different animal. You will need a lot of it to truly go the distance. Leg presses, leg curls, and leg extensions, along with squats are the preferred routine. Your legs are going to take a real beating; make sure they are ready.

If a gym isn't in your future, then go out and buy some of those long fitness rubber bands, or tubing. You can do extensions, curls, even squats with these. The bands are not nearly as effective as the machines, but they will help.

Do the upper and lower body exercises on the same day. Do them every odd-numbered day. And, before you start lifting those weights or using those bands, do a quick 15-minute warm-up of light jogging or running/walking.

Foolish boy.

Kwaggashoek is a concession in two parts. Part one is a beautiful grassy plain: a mix of short and tall grasses with intermittent groves of trees. The herd animals are quite content here. Zebra and blesbok, springbok, and black wildebeest all run and trot and prong along doing their daily rituals.

The other part is where the plains give way to the mountains. A small river separates the two parts. Not deep enough to prevent the hunting car from negotiating its bedrock bottom, the river divides the grasses from the ever-increasing elevation and the ever-increasing shrubs and trees. Sharply defined valleys and ridges spill down the mountains like gnarled fingers.

The oryx were in the first part, in the short grass. It would have been better if they were standing in the tall grass. Thousands of years of genetics and instinct have taught them that tall grass means danger. Lions live there. Lions eat oryx. Oryx don't like to be eaten by lions. It's in the short grass that they are safe from most predators.

On the even-numbered days, you will not be resting. You will be having cardio fun. Cardiovascular fitness is absolutely vital. Walking, jogging, or using one of those strange-looking cardio machines on a regular and ever-lengthening basis *will* improve your chances of success.

At this point, I don't care how far or fast you can walk, bike, or jog. The only thing that matters is being able to go longer and somewhat faster when your safari starts. Your goal is to be able to walk at a 15- to 20-minute-per-mile pace for two hours.

That is not walking on a city street. That is walking through the woods, up hills, on sand and grass, and through slop. That goal is not going to be an easy one to reach. Then again, if you set low goals for yourself, then low goals are all you will ever achieve.

If you do have access to a gym, then I highly recommend using that confounded Marquis de Sade thing called a StairMaster. This will initially hurt you. But, I know of no other cardio machine or exercise that will speed up the conditioning process quicker than this baby. It also significantly strengthens the leg muscles like no other.

I'm no doctor. I don't know what sort of shape you are in. Do see a doctor before beginning or significantly increasing a workout routine.

Start slowly. Work up to speed. Each week try to go heavier. Try to go longer. Increase your speed a touch. Just get better. The more you work at this beforehand, the more fun you will have on safari. ▪

Relying on keen eyesight, a solid nose, and ears that are better than my mother's, oryx are very much at home in the short grasses and the desert environments. All those defenses are formidable enough. Now add a burst of speed, and any stalk can be a lesson in humility.

Between us and the oryx lay a mile-wide stretch of short grass, most not taller than a few inches, that stretched to the north. There was no way to make an easy stalk.

There was a donga, or ravine, formed by a small river that cut a deep gash in the plain. Along the donga-sides, grasses grew taller, maybe chest-high in places. This cover was sparse; we couldn't use it to hide our approach.

We drove along the two-track, getting farther and farther from the oyrx. We were slowly making our way closer to the donga's southern reach. There we jumped from the car. Spyker had me take off my hat, as he feared it might be too bright for a careful stalk.

Spyker led me to the edge of the donga. Slowly he worked down to its bottom. A small creek flowed slowly to the north, toward the oryx. Spyker thought that we could get a shot at them if we used the donga for cover on our approach.

Within just a few minutes, we were both sweating heavily. The temperature had climbed into the low 80s. Then we really started to work.

That small stream had formed wide marshy areas where water pooled. The water was thick and green. You wouldn't want to drink it. You wouldn't even want to walk through it. But we did walk through it, our feet sinking deep into the ooze of mud and slime. At times we tried to use the roots coming from the sides as hand-holds in an attempt to stay out of the water.

That was a good plan. But good plans often don't survive. The mud on the edges was as sticky as Georgia gumbo. The green slime water was easier. For a good three-quarters of a mile we slipped and slopped and groped our way. Normally, three-quarters of a mile isn't all that long. But these were not normal conditions. Just over 50 minutes later, Spyker stopped and pulled himself on his belly up to the top.

Through whispers it was evident that he thought we should continue. Sliding down, he told me another few hundred yards in the slop was needed. Sweat stung our eyes. Seed pods and grasses stuck to our necks and clothing.

The last 100 yards were relatively easy. The mud became stiffer. The water was shallower and less slimy. Spyker again belly-crawled to the top. A nod and a wink was all I needed to see to know we were finally there.

I handed my rifle up to him, then did my own version of the belly crawl, scrambling first through wet mud, then dry sand, and then over the top and into the grasses.

The strip of grass here was a mix of waist- to shoulder-high. It was also a lot wider than it looked, stretching a good 100 yards out into the plain before breaking into grasses no taller than a few inches. It was also not as thick as it looked from so far away. There was no way to make a careful stalk in anything close to an upright walk or crouch.

One hundred yards is a long way to crawl on your hands and knees and on your belly. It gets even longer when long thorns stick into your knees and legs and hands at every creep forward. These thorns break off easily, right at the skin, sending all their woody length into you. You feel the first few, and you always feel them when they find a particularly tender spot. But you continue.

Crawling behind Spyker, I hadn't dared to raise my head to see how far we had gone, nor how far we still needed to go. I simply followed, trying to stay in his path, knowing he was picking up the majority of the thorns.

Slowly he brought his knees up underneath him and raised his chest off the dirt. His head still in the grass, he used his binoculars to judge the oryx about 150 yards in front of us in the short grass. "Dan, we can't get any closer. They are looking right at us," he whispered. "The one we want is second from the left. It's a bull, a good one. The cow behind him has horns that are longer, but we want that bull."

Oryx cows normally carry longer horns than the bulls. The cow's horns are often more slender. Spyker and I had discussed what I was looking for earlier. He knew that a good bull was better than a great cow in my mind.

After wiping the sweat from my eyes and making sure the scope was clear, I slowly got into a sitting position. I hate the sitting position. Six pairs of eyes were locked on us. Their black and white striped mask beautifully framed in the blue sky. Their horns pierced the air in black, rapier pairs.

I found the bull in the scope, settled my breathing, and promptly missed him from less than 150 yards. I hate the sitting position. A termite mound just underneath his chest and behind his front leg showed a puff of sand. I aimed low. "Shit!"

Within no more than a second or two, the group was at full speed, heading toward a small scrub-covered hill. Spyker was just as disappointed as I was. Maybe more. We made our way back to the hunting car, licking our wounds and me feeling lower than low.

"Dan, it is too late in the day to have a go up the valley and try to find some kudu. Shake off that miss, everyone misses. Let's see if we can find those oryx before we lose the light."

We did, twice. Not once was a shot even considered. It would seem that every time we found them, they had found us just moments before and were heading away from us. They were always running away, and running beautifully. Their gait is like that of a thoroughbred. By simply trotting, they cover a lot of ground in a gorgeous pattern of glides and steps. When they run, they run with the wind, their feet barely scratching the ground.

The third time was a charm. We found them on top of a large acacia-covered knoll. We watched them as they disappeared down the other side. In a low crouch, Spyker and I, along with Clinton and Isak, hoofed it onto the hilltop. There, 285

Clinton and me with the oryx, a nice bull. Not a great bull, mind you; but one well-earned and I'm damn proud of him. A "Texas heart shot" brought him down. That hole you see is where the job was finished. That smile comes from a lot of things, including it being the first critter on my list.

yards away, the oryx were walking down a small valley, heading for a bit of thicker cover. They were heading straight away. Quickly.

"Dan, I don't know if we'll find a bigger bull than that one on this safari. He's a good one. Get steady and take him."

"From the back?"

"Just put the crosshairs on his neck and squeeze. You'll break his spine. Take him."

I settled behind the sticks and squeezed. The oryx fell as if hit by lightning.

"Spot on!"

Isak gave me a thumbs-up and a wide grin.

The bullet had hit the oryx just off center at the base of the tail. It did what Spyker said it would, it broke its back. His horns were heavy and the tops unbroomed. No, he wasn't the biggest oryx in the world, but he was a dandy. And he was mine. We toasted the oryx as the day softly faded away.

During the skinning process, we found that the bullet had gone all the way up into the right lung.

CHAPTER 9

Askari

he morning was clear and cold. A better-than-crisp wind whipped at our clothes. The same crew as the day before headed south, toward another ridge, another valley, another area that should be holding kudu. It was kudu again, and would be until we either ran out of time, or a kudu was down.

Passing the burnt main lodge, I could only imagine what it once was. Most of the walls were down already. Only the heavy pillars that had held up the two-story structure were left. These were fire-scarred, black and ugly as fire itself.

The sandy road took us into a thick forest of acacia. Giraffes cantered ahead of us, their heads bobbing above the trees. Zebra darted in and out of view. A brown rush of color streaked across the road as a group of impala scattered. One had magnificent horns. But it was kudu today. Kudu until we were done with kudu.

From where we parked, it was a good long walk to the top of the grass-covered ridge. Not as steep as the morning before, but much longer. There were no hidden steps that would give one a false sense of the top. Here the path, an old game trail, just continued up seemingly forever through a thick growth of trees and shrubs.

As was the case yesterday, Clinton and the boys stayed below. Same as yesterday, they were to push the animals into an opening where I would get my shot. Good plan.

Along the trail Spyker picked up a porcupine quill. "I don't know anything about lightening and evil spirits," he said. "But I do know these things bring luck when you find them while hunting."

After a good hour, we reached the ridgetop's finger. Spyker called on the radio for the boys to start pushing. Still on a forced march, Spyker and I sped through the grasses and scattered shrubs climbing higher up the ridgeline. A broad opening about a half-mile ahead on our side of the valley was where we were headed.

Just above the opening, Spyker and I halted. We got cold. The wind continued to blow cool air from off the mountaintop. And this cold air snuck through every bit of clothing we had. We had sweated heavily on the climb. Now we were paying for it.

A large rock served as a minor windbreak. At this point, any break would do. Both of us hunkered down as close to the ground as we could get. We just wanted out of the wind.

A pair of oryx, both females with long slender horns, appeared on the ridgetop from where we first broke out of the trees. It appeared that they were following us, as they came directly toward us on the same game trail we had taken to our rock perch.

Ah, the wind. When the two were but 100 yards away, they lifted their heads and stared holes into us. Then, without a single good-bye, they ran lickety-split through the grasses, to the south, disappearing into the next valley.

While we were watching them dash off, we heard roars from the valley and from the scattered trees higher up the ridgeline. It was baboons, and it sounded like a lot of baboons. They were none too pleased by our intrusion. One in particular sounded very pissed off.

After an especially long and ferocious roar, we heard what seemed to be shorter roars, or growls, and they were getting closer. Much closer.

Something was coming and coming quickly. A stone tumbled down toward us. Spyker and I both turned around and there, up on another rock, was a big dog of a baboon. With his next roar, we could see his teeth—a set of canines that were easily 4 inches long. These are nothing to play with. He was only 20 yards away.

Spyker stood up and made himself look big. The baboon, now on the defensive, ran away with a barking call. It would seem he didn't think he was the baddest baboon in the valley any longer. Spyker was.

After the baboon departed, we could hear the boys making their way through the thick stuff. Just before they got to the opening, eland came out and scampered through. Zebra followed them, as did a couple of impala. But no kudu.

We then raced ahead again. Again the boys pushed on to the next opening, the last one before sheer walls of rock would stop our progress.

Just before the rock wall, we heard something. Our eyes peeled and scanned. Seeing through the trees, trying to detect a flash of horn or hide. None came. So much for the quills bringing luck.

The climb down was interesting. Rather than take the long way down, reversing the way we came, Spyker suggested we pick our way through the jumble of huge boulders and trees, which was not all that fun. The rocks were sharp. The trees had thorns. There were lots of rocks and trees.

No one said much when we got back to the truck. We were tired, hot, thirsty. And we were beginning to doubt that there was an animal called a kudu on this earth. Or at least one Spyker deemed big enough for me.

On the drive back to camp for brunch, just as we were driving by the burned-out lodge, a herd of impala skipped ahead of us on the trail. There at the front was a fine ram with tall horns, a wide saddle, and thick bases. Better still, he was black, a rarity that made him much too expensive in the trophy-fee category to even think about doing anything except admiring his grace.

When we got back, we found Dave at the skinning shed. He and Pierre connected on a nice impala while we were playing baboon boogie. Anneli had called back, too. Doug was doing fine and wanted to send his best wishes on the hunting.

The first full day at Kwaggshoek and Dave takes a nice impala. Moses, our cook, knows I don't eat liver, so what does he cook that night? The liver. I had thirds. Liver á la Moses is the only liver I will ever eat.

After eating, I went out on the deck in the back of the main house. As an avid birder, I wanted to see if I could identify the bee-eaters that had been flitting around. Anneli had lent me a superb bird book, and in an hour I had added an easy two dozen birds to my life list. A pair of young eland came up within five yards or so of the deck and ambled down toward the dam and back north. My eyes followed them through the acacias and yellow grasses.

They continued north a good while, following the small river leading out of the dam. About a half mile away, they went into a loose grove of trees with leaves like pine needles. Once there, smaller antelope rose from the grass. A group of impala had sought relief from the bright sun and heat. The eland had disturbed them.

Inside that group of impala was one big ram. Knowing Spyker and I were going to leave in an hour or so for a return trip to the "first valley of the kudu," I asked him if he thought we had time to take care of my impala itch. It wouldn't take too long, I figured. It should be easy.

Spyker called for the boys, and we were off. The impala had moved a bit farther away when we came up on them. The grasses concealed everything except their head and neck. Their coats matched the dying grasses perfectly.

After a short stalk, Spyker had me positioned for a perfect straight-on shot at the ram. One through the brisket and the job would be over. Except for that tree.

An acacia had the ram framed with two branches growing up on either side of the impala's neck. I once had a shot like that on a deer hunt in Michigan. I screwed the pooch then.

Here's the view from the back deck. Eland and impala often greeted us here around noon. Giraffes would come by for coffee in the early morning.

I screwed the pooch here, too, letting the trees spook me into a poor shot. The bullet whipped into the left branch, snipping it off as sure as a set of pruning shears.

Picking up the spoor was relatively easy. The tall grasses bent in nice neat rows from the scattering of the herd. Into the wide grassland they ran, and ran some more, finally settling down about a mile away.

Using an old road for our path, and the tall grasses for cover, we made our way at a 45-degree angle toward the group. The road made walking easy. With the tall grass, we couldn't see them, but somehow we knew they would still be there.

The road turned slightly left and began to head downhill. The grasses were getting shorter. A roadside tree would be the last bit of cover before we came into the big wide open. Spyker and I got next to the tree. The range was estimated at nearly 300 yards.

The tree was too thickly branched to use the shooting sticks. Spyker had me put my shooting elbow on his shoulder for better support. I couldn't get comfortable and told him so.

I couldn't stand and shoot. The impala, already showing signs of being very nervous, would have scattered. Kneeling was no better. The only position I could use was my least favorite—sitting.

After controlling my breath and getting as comfortable as I could in that gawd-awful position, I found the impala in the scope. As the animal quartered away slightly, the crosshairs met the neck just at ear level. I squeezed.

Through the scope I watched the bullet strike in a puff of fur just where the neck meets the back. I watched the impala crumple. The other impala disappeared into the tall grass.

Another car was called for from camp. We didn't want to waste any time going back to camp with the impala. Nope, it was up the mountain again, up that same mountain we had climbed the previous gray misty morning. This time it was hot. Knowing what to expect made the climb easier, at least on the mind. It wasn't bad. Not bad at all.

Monty Pienaar, Kwaggashoek's land manager, joined us. A sturdy fellow, it seemed he'd be more at home on the football field, or in his case rugby field, than trekking up hills. Early on, however, his fitness level proved him to be more than just muscular. His legs carried him very well indeed.

This time the boys stayed with us. In the afternoon, the kudu started moving through the thick brush to water. Gaining heat isn't the issue for them now as it was in the morning. Now they want water and something to eat.

We sat on the top of the ridge, using thorny scrub brush to break our outline. Below us a small river, with its banks well marked by hoof prints, eased through the valley. Directly opposite, on the other ridge, was a well-worn game trail. Monty had it pinned at 285 meters with his rangefinder. There we waited. And waited.

A duiker came down to the river to drink. A cow eland sauntered along the game trail. Baboons roared in the distance. The wind was blowing straight down the ridgeline, and we didn't have to worry about wind giving our position away to any critter except those directly on top.

Spyker and me with my impala, a true dandy. This was taken after, of course, a miss, and then another stalk.

THE RIGHT AMMO FOR THE JOB

Ruark said that you must use enough gun. That is certainly true. Yet now with all the premium bullets on the market, it is just as true for the bullet as the gun.

Any proper rifleman knows his gun. He knows how it shoots. Or does he?

I do not reload my own ammunition. If you do, great. I don't. I rely on high-quality factory ammo to do my work for me. I could care less about an extra 100 feet per second or 50 more foot pounds of striking power. I know the bullets I buy from Winchester, from the Winchester Supreme line, will get the job done. The same can be said for the premium lines from Remington and Federal.

With each caliber of gun I take to Africa, I generally carry two different bullet weights. When I'm done sighting in one of the rifles with bullet weight number one, I fire another three-round group with bullet number two. Nine times out of ten, the bullets strike in a different place. Not much different, but different enough that you need to know where that bullet is going.

I tape a small piece of paper on the scope of the rifle as a quick reference. The bullet strike at 100 yards and 200 yards is written on that paper. As I zero the guns for dead-on at 200, this is easy to do. I also write down where the bullet should strike at 300 yards based on the ballistic charts for that caliber, bullet weight, and bullet maker. As a general rule of thumb for guns in the 30-caliber class, a bullet that strikes 2 inches high at 100 yards will strike close to dead-on at 200.

Then comes practice. Shooting off the bench is easy. You have a solid rest. You take your time to get your breathing correct. You squeeze the trigger just so. You won't be doing this while hunting.

During the hunt, most of your shooting will be off shooting sticks. That means you'll have to practice with shooting sticks. You won't be shooting off of

A few minutes later a group of kudu cows came down to the water. Where they came from is a mystery. Where nothing had been, there they were.

"Dan, get on the sticks. There will be a bull with them," whispered Spyker. Ever so slowly I came to my feet behind the sticks and settled in behind the scope. The cows were still drinking. Every now and again they'd look up and back to the bottom of the valley. "He's coming, they hear him."

For nearly fifteen minutes the kudu cows lingered. For nearly fifteen minutes they drank, looked up, looked back. For nearly fifteen minutes I stayed glued to the scope. Then they walked away.

Minutes later a group of gray-coated animals could be seen making their way down that game trail on the opposite side. Kudu! We could see their horns, those huge beautiful corkscrew antlers bobbing in the branches. Kudu with horns!

Back on the sticks, settled in behind the scope, I waited for them to get into the open. They'd be broadside. They'd be 285 yards away. One was going to die.

sticks from the standing position all the time, either. You need to practice sitting with sticks and kneeling with sticks.

Practice using a tree trunk as a brace in all the positions. And be sure to practice shooting from the prone. Lying down and shooting isn't a sure thing. But with practice, it may be almost as good in the accuracy department as from the bench.

And, for heaven's sake, spend some time practicing shooting offhand—with no support but your own arms. Practice as you'll hunt, too. Have a buddy say "now" unexpectedly while at the range. That's your clue to acquire the target and fire. Quick and sure is the rule to follow.

Pay special attention to the clothes you wear to the range for practice sessions. Do not shoot with clothes you won't be hunting with. Besides practicing for accuracy, you are going to be practicing gun mount whether you realize it or not. Boots, a heavy coat or a simple T-shirt, gloves or no gloves—this all matters. Use the Army mantra about going to battle: Train as you will fight. The better you get with your rifle and bullets before the hunt, the more confidence you will have when the moment of truth comes.

Some of the antelope you'll be hunting—like springbok, impala, and duiker—are small. Others—the kudu, oryx, and eland—are quite large. You are going to need to look at some anatomy pictures to determine just where to put that bullet from any number of angles.

Some animals have an exceptionally thick neck. Some have a hump on their back. Some have long throat manes and dewlaps. All have a heart and lungs. All have a spine. Make sure you really know where these are, and you will make a good shot. These animals aren't whitetails or mulies. Don't for a minute get them confused.

"Wait. Let me get a good look. There's four of them, all bulls. We want the biggest," said Spyker.

When the fourth one broke into the open, it was evident that the first one was by far the largest. I swung the rifle to the front, centered the crosshairs just behind the front leg. "Nope, not these," said Spyker.

"What?" I whispered in desperation. "That front one is huge."

"No, Dan, he's not. Maybe 48, nothing more. On your last day maybe, but we have a bigger one in mind for you."

I couldn't believe it. I was a bit miffed. I took a cigarette from Clinton and smoked it. Then another from Spyker. And I don't smoke.

We continued to wait on that ridgeline. Then, just to break the tension, mainly from me, I played that old children's game on Spyker. When he wasn't looking, when he was least aware, I grabbed him quickly by the shirt and whispered excitedly, "Spyker! Kudu! Over there, much bigger than the others."

This doesn't look too thick, does it? Well, it is. Quite thick. That shadowed valley is where kudu and other critters like to hide. That's where the trackers and Clinton, the appy (apprentice), pushed through trying to get a kudu to come and play.

Spyker leapt to his feet and searched. Clinton broke out in laughter. Monty just smiled broadly. Isak covered his mouth and turned away so his boss wouldn't see him laugh. "Okay, Mr. Donarski. We'll see who laughs next."

When the sun went down behind the mountain, we headed back walking down the ridgeline. A group of waterbuck sprang out of the grass ahead of us. One of the bulls was huge. I pulled the gun up and found him in the scope. "He's very big, Dan. Take him if you want."

I brought the gun back down without using the trigger. "He was a big one, very big," said Spyker.

I just watched the waterbuck disappear over the hill and into the trees. "Yeah, but I want a kudu. I can't afford both."

That waterbuck still walks, all noble and proud, in my dreams. In those dreams, he taunts me with those curving horns reaching high into the sky above a head the color of a cinnamon stick. That white ring across his withers formed a perfect Texas bull's-eye.

Ruark took a record-book waterbuck on his first safari. He did not take a good kudu. I wanted the kudu.

CHAPTER 10

Bushbuck!
A Mental Shift

he previous evening we learned that Doug would be released from the hospital today. That was certainly a reason for celebration. This was much quicker than we had hoped with the bad break. That night my malaise left. Doug was coming back.

Upon waking, the malaise was back. Kudu fever. A definite sickness. I had it bad. No amount of Dr. van Tonder's or Dr. Joubert's Magical African Elixir would remedy it. Like a kid wanting the latest and greatest toy, I just had to get that kudu. You know the one—that one. Nothing would interfere. (Thank you, I think I will have some cheese with that whine.)

Up well before dawn for medicinal coffee and rusks, we would be off before the sun was thinking of peeking over the hills. Walking into those hills, busting a lung to get even higher, was becoming a daily ritual.

"Daniel," said Pierre, "you must get high in the hills and look for the kudu in the early morning when they come into the clearings to get the first rays of sun. They get cold overnight in the winter, and they want the sun. It's our best chance."

So, after passing up a half dozen perfectly spiraled kudu in the high 40s and maybe low 50s during the last three days, Spyker and I were sweating in the chilled air as we climbed higher into the mountains of Kwaggashoek. Joining us were Monty Pienaar, the land manager, Spyker's main tracker, Isak, and Robert, another tracker. And, let's not forget Clinton, on his first hunt as an apprentice professional hunter.

It should be noted again that I came to South Africa with preconceived notions. My "want list" included serious examples of impala, zebra, gemsbok, and kudu. All but the kudu and zebra were in the salt, along with a major blesbok and a good springbok. With plentiful zebra in the grass plains below the green and gold hills, kudu, *the* kudu, was the game plan.

I can remember Pierre telling me to come to Africa without a plan. "Dan, let Africa show you what is right to shoot. You never know what might show up and what might not. Do not squander opportunities."

Yeah, right. I wanted a kudu.

Diversity in habitat means a diversity of game. Zebra, giraffe, blesbok, and black wildebeest all out in the open. Meaning an easy shot, right? Take a look at how flat that terrain is. Count the eyes looking for danger, same number of ears, and half as many noses—it's not at all easy.

Up we climbed to the high ridgetop overlooking a deep valley. Acacias and aloes of every size and shape, along with viburnums and thick scraggly trees, generated a myriad of green below us as we made our way, stumbling over jagged rocks hidden by the glistening frost-covered golden grass. Giraffes had the same idea we did, it seemed. A group of eight watched us pass from no more than 20 yards. The mountain above us wore a heavy cloak of white against the crisp, brightening blue sky.

At the valley floor a small river flowed black as ink in the early light. As we crossed a 20-foot, thickly vegetated ravine, we heard an animal bark and watched as a flash of black ripped through the trees no more than 10 yards away, heading down into the valley. "Bushbuck!" said Spyker in that shout of a whisper you use when startled. Grabbing me by the shirt collar, he pulled me up to him. Not letting go, he scampered like a mountain goat to another vantage point. I don't think my feet ever hit the ground. Kudu brain was cured.

"Dan, the man," said Spyker in the excited whisper of the afflicted. "That was a monster bushbuck. Mama Mojo bushbuck—we can get him."

"Beeeg N'konka," chimed Richard, using the Zulu name for bushbuck, his face beaming like a kid on Christmas morning. "Beeg N'konka." Isak, too, had a huge smile on his face.

I had only seen the flash of black, indistinguishable from the early dawn shadows except for the movement. A quick lesson in bushbuck was given. I learned from Spyker that they are very territorial. That especially during the winter they generally will stay in the same area. The thickest of thick he told me. "It's an animal of a lifetime. He's huge, this one is."

He also told me that they weren't hard to put down. But, and heavy on the "but," you wanted them down hard or risk being attacked if you had to wrestle him out of the thickets.

Now, unless you are lucky enough to jump one and get a quick shot, or ambush one coming to water, the hunting is a matter of flushing him out of that dark and tangled piece of forest he calls home. Then you pray to the gods that the bushbuck makes a dash across an opening between two thickets where you might, just might, get a shot.

I had seen a picture of a bushbuck just once. I never thought I'd have a chance to see one, and now one was just ahead of us. I wanted him.

Spyker sent Clinton, Richard, and Isak down into the steep valley through a finger of thorns and vines and trees. They would try to push the animal into a clearing for a shot. From our perch above we could hear them struggling through the thick, tangled mess and stumbling over rocks along the steep face.

They spent a good hour and a half working through the valley floor and up into the fingers of thorn and vines that crawled up the ridge through ravines and dongas. My eyes were red with straining through the scope and the glasses. The boys below were soaked in sweat when we met them at the bottom of the valley where the sharp ridge petered out into a gently rolling hill.

"Damn!" said Spyker. "He has to be here." The boys looked dejected. Blood oozed from thorn punctures and cuts along their arms.

"Well," said Monty, "do you think he could have gone farther up the valley? He might have, I think." Farther up meant thicker, it meant more thorns, more sweat, a lot more sweat.

Spyker pulled Clinton over and in a mix of Afrikaans, English, and Swahili, started discussing a game plan. When they were done, it was decided that Clinton would once again join Isak and Richard and push up into the valley, coming out on top only when they knew a bushbuck could go no farther.

Clinton knew this particular ravine very well indeed. Seems just three months ago he went on a personal head quest to figure out what his 21 years had meant and where he was going. The search lasted a full 30 days, all of it in this place. He knew that a waterfall at its upper reaches, and the associated cliffs on either side, would stop virtually any animal's progress.

Clinton relayed the game plan to Isak and Richard. With an audible sigh of resignation, the trio set off. They made quick work on the terrain they had already worked. Getting to the original starting place, their pace slowed, and thankfully, so did ours. Sweat was burning my eyes, blurring my vision. Heaving lungs were more in tune with shooting a kangaroo than laying steady crosshairs.

Quick whoops and sticks banging together marked the group's progress. Every now and then, when a forested ravine cut toward the top of the ridge, we could hear one of them below us, breathing heavy, stumbling, falling, and uttering muffled curses.

Another hour, and Clinton called up to us, telling us there was no way a bushbuck, or anything for that matter, could make it up the now near-vertical sides. Spyker called back to him, telling them to make their way on top and join us.

Getting the entire group back together was an admission of defeat. After silently passing water back and forth, we decided to follow the ridge up until it topped out on a wide grassy plateau just before the mountain's final 600 feet pushed absolutely vertical into the crystalline blue skies. The clouds had burned off its summit. The sun was burning us. It was only 10 A.M.

Not far along the route we came upon one of those finger ravines cutting to the valley floor. This one was steeper and ran the entire length of the ridgetop. It would take a bit of work to get through. We took a break and started glassing, lazily, the other side of the valley, up the opposite ridge. We were tired and wondered if we really needed to go through all the trouble to reach the plateau.

Nope, not worth it. Spyker called for a five-minute break before starting back down to the Land Rover and regrouping.

I looked down the ridge, not relishing the walk back to the Rover. We were getting ready to leave when Spyker hollered, " Dan! There he is! Grab your pack!"

Spinning around, grabbing my pack, I searched to where Spyker's eyes led— across the valley, onto the opposite ridge. I couldn't find him.

"Dan, he's right across! Moving down. He's in the open above the trees, in the grass."

"I see him," said Monty. "The rangefinder says 290 yards. Do you see him?"

Lying amongst the rocks and thorns, I pushed the pack into a rest and settled behind the scope. I searched but didn't see him.

Finally, leaving the scope, I saw him. Still in the shadows of the mountain, appearing as a dark gray animal moving in a sea of lighter gray shadows, he was making his way into the cover, walking straight at us and angling down the slope. Back on the scope I found him. Five meters and he'd be in the trees.

"How far?"

"278."

Crosshairs settled on his spine, halfway back. He was alongside a rock shelf that tumbled down into the valley in the last two meters of open country. I don't remember the trigger pull, or the recoil of the .375 H&H. I do remember the puff of dust and fur as the 300-grain Winchester Fail Safe found its home just above where the shoulder blades meet the neck. I watched him crumple with the scope still squarely on him. He didn't move.

Spyker hollered, "Spot on!"

The next thing I know Spyker is slapping me hard on the back. Monty and Clinton were hollering. Spyker, I think, pulled me to my feet and gave me one helluva bear hug. Clinton shook my hand so hard I thought he'd break it. Monty followed suit, and Isaac just smiled and gave me a serious thumbs-up and a quick nod of his head.

More hugs followed. I sat down and tried to collect myself but found that I was weeping.

"Dan, the man!" shouted Spyker. "That is one animal that few will be able to beat. Well done. You don't know it yet, but this is the animal of your safari, or your many safaris. Screw the kudu! You got a trophy bushbuck!"

I turned away from the group and wiped my eyes. Then, without warning, Spyker grabbed my shoulder and said, "He's up, Dan. He's moving!"

My heart jumped as I looked toward the bushbuck.

He wasn't up. Spyker was just paying me back for startling him the day before. I think I called him a fatherless child, or something like it.

Now the fun was to really start. The only way to get to the bushbuck quickly in the rising heat was to go down into the valley and then climb up the other side. The Rover could only get within a mile or so on that opposite ridge. And to there only after a long and circuitous route.

There was no way I was not going to where the bushbuck fell. Even with a questioning look from Monty regarding the steep terrain, there was no way I would be denied. The animal deserved that much. I needed to go.

A quick gear switch was handled. Spyker and Monty carried my pack and my cameras back to the Rover. "See you guys in about two and a half hours," Spyker called out as he and Monty hiked off.

If it wasn't for the vines, I don't think we could have made it down. Sharp boulders, 15-foot sheer drops, and a tangle of forest blocked us at every footfall. The vines acted as ropes, as footholds, and as emergency braking devices. Still, we skidded on our butts and our faces down the knife-sharp rocks all 400 feet to the bottom. Clinton and I led, Isak and Richard followed. Tentatively at best.

We bottomed out just below the waterfall. The air was heavy with mist and mosquitoes. Lots of mosquitoes. The rocks in this eternally wet grotto were covered in a fine moss as slippery as moose snot. We took a break here, for only a moment, as the mosquitoes found fresh blood.

Then it was back up the other side. It was just as steep, but after the first 100 feet, the ground changed from rock to a thin layer of soft dirt. Two steps up, one step back. To gain elevation I pushed Clinton up to a perch where he would grab my rifle and the shooting sticks. From his perch he used the sticks to pull me up, and the process started all over again. Near the top, and no more

After shooting the bushbuck, we rappelled, climbed, and fell down a cliff, ending at this neat waterfall. Now we had to climb up the other side to recover him.

This is where the bushbuck fell. The shot was taken in that open patch just off my left elbow. The ravine is between the shot and the critter.

than 10 yards above us, a gorgeous golden-coated, white-striped female bushbuck bounded off.

Finally, after a good 90 minutes, Clinton and I topped out onto the ridge. Sweat soaked, as if we had taken a shower, we were there. Just off to the left we saw the large rock shelf the bushbuck had fallen next to.

Walking up to it, my heart sank. I could only see the horns and the base of the hindquarters. It was too dark for a bushbuck, the horns were too large, the points had too much ivory. I had shot a young nyala. Damn, I thought silently. I was wrong.

Getting closer the "damn" turned into "Damn! He's huge. Clinton, look at this animal!" Using his hands he quickly measured the horns at between $16\frac{1}{2}$ and $17\frac{1}{4}$.

More handshakes. When the trackers met up with us, giggling like madmen, they broke out in smiles and whistled in approval.

Quickly Isak took out the stomach and intestines. When Clinton told him to take the heart and lungs, too, Isak grunted a word that must have meant no. The heart and lungs were to be his and Richard's reward for the work they had just done, and the work they were to do.

"The boys want a Coke each to haul him out. They are negotiating with me now," Clinton told me.

"Hell, give them both two, on my tab. Now let's get going; we need to get this one in the salt."

Clinton started the task of carrying the bushbuck out. Using front legs hooked to hinds, he formed a backpack, and with a grunt of "La Fontaine!" started carrying.

Up, always up, for the first half hour it was all uphill to get to the ridgetop where the carrying would be easier. I was thinking how nice it was that I wasn't the appie hunter. On top he turned the job over to Richard and Isak.

There were more gorges to negotiate, with more thorns to tear arms and faces. Three hours from when we left Spyker and Monty, we met them again, with the Rover. Spyker slapped my back again. Sweat sprayed through the air. "Tough walk, eh?" he laughed, then added, "Dan, I've never seen one shot any bigger."

Driving back to camp Richard and Isak were talking away in Zulu. Clinton started smiling. "Dan, the boys think this is very special. Richard says his people are afraid of bushbucks, as they have killed many dogs and even people. He and Isak have given you a name—N'kosana N'konka—Boss of Bushbucks. My smile couldn't have been broader. I shook their hands; we slapped each other on the back. We had done something magnificent.

A mile from camp the trackers started to sing and dance. Bob Seger's song "Like a Rock" boomed out of the stereo. The horn started to blare, and rounding the last curve into camp we saw the entire camp lined up waiting for us.

Spyker had radioed ahead and told them of the kill. He hadn't told them how big. Pierre gave me a hearty handshake and said, "Well done!" I left to take a much-needed shower and change clothes before he had even seen the animal.

Walking back to the main lodge, I was greeted by Pierre, Spyker, and Anneli, standing just inside the entrance in a formal line. Each held two shot glasses filled with scotch. One by one they toasted me, and I toasted each in return. "Dan," said Pierre, "that is the largest, or second largest, anyone has taken on safari with me. I score it on the tape at $16^7/_8$. It is simply huge, beautiful, with perfect horns. Now, how about we try for kudu tomorrow?"

I just smiled and nodded my head.

While we were eating, Anneli's phone rang. It was Margaret telling us that Doug was ready to be discharged. In a flash she was out the door and on her way to Ladysmith to pick up our friend and his wife. We'd be a whole group again tonight.

Just over two hours later, as Spyker, Pierre, and I were heading out to collect a zebra for me, Anneli's little car came up the drive kicking up a dust cloud and spitting small stones.

Doug is not a small man. Getting him out of the car was no easy matter. Seeing Doug try to use his crutches would have been comical if it didn't look so damn painful. Margaret was smiling one of those forced smiles. You know the one. The one that says something like "I'm not so sure this is a good idea, but I'll keep my mouth shut." Yup, it was one of those.

Doug was feeling a little woozy. He was unsteady on these new crutches. Slowly we maneuvered him into the main house and put him on the bed. After a few hugs he fell fast asleep.

Zebra time.

Zebras get no respect except from those who have hunted them. They are not horses. They seem to have a sense when they are being hunted. When that mojo kicks in, they like to join other animal herds like impala or blesbok, using them for shields and extra eyes. Their own eyes and ears are extra fine as well.

Spyker and me with my zebra stallion. It ain't like shooting horses or circus ponies. Not one bit. These are tough critters and can be a devil to sneak up on in the short grass.

We found a herd out in the short grass not far from camp. They were on the move toward a section of tall grass as we started after them. Using a small knoll as cover, we paralleled them, hoping to catch them before they made the tall grass.

We didn't. Rounding the knoll the zebra, seven of them, were in waist-high grass. The last one, according to Spyker and Pierre, was the stallion, the one we wanted. His head was blockier, as was his body. Through the binoculars I could see his hide had a few nicks and scratches on it.

Zebra stallions do a lot of fighting with each other. They kick, head butt, and bite. Their teeth are formidable weapons. Unlike horses, these things have huge canines, and they know how to use them.

These zebra were of the Burchell's variety. Here in South Africa, they are known to come in a variety of colors, not just the standard white and black. In fact, this one, this stallion, had a golden hue across the top of his back. And, like most Burchell's, he had the shadow stripes. These are light gray in color and are found between the solid black stripes upon the white base.

We entered the small grass, still paralleling the herd. The zebra headed up a small knob and stopped to look back at us. The stallion was still in waist-high grass as I placed the rifle on the sticks. Picking an exact spot, where the black meets the white, and right at grass-top level, the bullet should hit the lungs. I squeezed and heard the bullet hit home with a thunk.

Except for kicking in the after-burners, the zebra didn't even flinch. He just shot off with the herd and disappeared over the hill. Moments later we saw them running back across the grasslands to the west, the stallion still with them, bringing up the rear.

This baboon wasn't very happy to meet me, as it first was required to meet a 300-grain bullet. We still shook hands.

Then, without a stumble, without the slightest bit of a stagger, he fell over. Dead.

From where he was shot, he ran a good 500 meters. He took all of 300 grains of Fail Safe from a .375 H&H, and yet he ran hell-bent-for-leather. He ran all that way after being double-lunged and spouting blood from both flanks. These are seriously tough critters. He was a beauty.

Pierre called for another hunting car. When it arrived, the zebra was loaded and Pierre headed it back to camp.

Spyker and Clinton had another plan for me. They wanted to celebrate the morning's bushbuck by having a sundowner in a very special place. They took me to a grotto hidden by a tangle of trees and vines. Inside the grotto was a high rock face marked with bushman paintings from hundreds of years ago.

On the way to the hidden grotto, a troop of baboons headed up a ridge spine. A big female baboon was in the rear. Clinton yelled to Spyker for the hunting car to stop. He did, saw the baboons running quickly away, and set up the sticks. "Take him, Mr. Donarski. He's our gift to you."

Easier said than done. They were running uphill, at a good 200 meters. The bullet launched, the baboon crumpled. "Well done!" Spyker yelled. "Damn fine shooting!" I don't know what came over us, but we giggled like schoolgirls. I also thanked the gods for sending the bullet true.

We parked the car at the top of a hill looking over the grasslands below. Spyker grabbed a small cooler, and the three of them headed off to what looked like a small rocky hill. Rounding that hill we headed down an incline, maybe 100 feet and

The grotto with the San art was hidden behind a thick grove of trees. You wouldn't know it was there at all. I'm glad we knew.

turned into the tangle of trees and vines. A small path brought us into an opening where the 100-foot-tall solid rock face looked exactly to the east, to the sunrise.

The rock held numerous paintings. Most were of animals. Some of rudimentary humans in suggestive positions. Looking from right to left, you could see the progress of evolution in their painting skill. On the far right they were very crude and highly faded. Moving to the left they got more intricate, more lifelike. According to Clinton, the oldest were 1,000 years old. The most recent from 150 years or so.

As the sun set, we stayed next to the rock. It was a very spiritual place. We didn't say much. When we did speak, we spoke in hushed whispers. If there truly are such places as power points on this earth, this was certainly one of them. We toasted the day with Tusker beer as the sun disappeared in a blaze of orange and red.

CHAPTER 11

Doug's Return

t dinner that night it was evident that Doug was feeling no pain. Seems that the good doctors at La Verna Hospital had him well supplied with painkillers. No scotch for him tonight; he didn't need any. I couldn't have any either— Spyker had me ready for a night hunt for small cats and jackals.

Doug, through his medicinal haze, spoke of something he called "velvet sledgehammers." Seems these are actually some sort of opiate drug and come in a blue and white capsule. According to Doug, they beat anything he had ever had before. In fact, they were so good that he actually requested a smaller dose than the one he was given at the hospital. Doug is not exactly small. It takes a fair amount of meds to put him into la-la land. If this was the smaller dose, those velvet sledge-hammers must have really been something.

When the meal was finished, we floated Doug back to bed. Spyker and I mounted up and took off to the grasslands for some predator hunting.

Duiker scattered in front of us like jackrabbits. This little antelope is a night lover, and if the drive to the grasslands was any indication, the place was loaded with them. Night jars, a small variety of night hawk, were in the road ahead of us. We couldn't see them except for their eyes. The eyes are a bit spooky as they appear as just two glowing red spots seemingly coming out of the sand and piercing the dark.

The moon was near full and the sky crystal clear. Stars like you wouldn't believe glittered like snowflakes falling through a streetlight. Jupiter was easily seen just to the west. Through our binoculars we could see two of her moons.

We didn't hunt long. We were tired. Our day had been a tremendous success. We decided to slowly drive the roads rather than set up and call. We crept through a large group of eland. Impala moved away slowly when we approached. A bushbuck was surprised when caught in the headlights. Jackals yipped and howled.

The night was magic. A gunshot would have disturbed it. There was no reason to do that.

I got to the main lodge the next morning just as Moses had the coffee ready. I could hear Doug and Margaret "discussing" things from their bedroom. Not loud, just pointed.

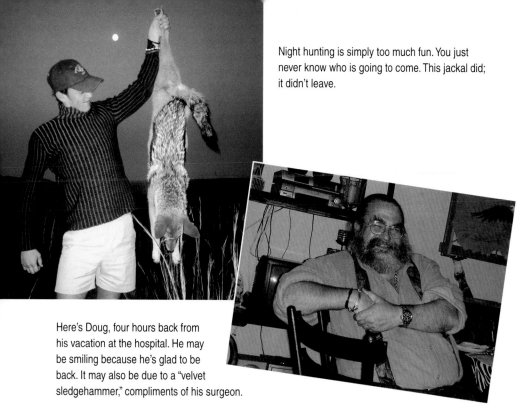

Night hunting is simply too much fun. You just never know who is going to come. This jackal did; it didn't leave.

Here's Doug, four hours back from his vacation at the hospital. He may be smiling because he's glad to be back. It may also be due to a "velvet sledgehammer," compliments of his surgeon.

Doug was in some degree of pain. Margaret wanted him to dose himself with one of those magic pills from the good doctor at La Verna Hospital. Doug wanted to hunt. The prescribed pills wouldn't allow him to hunt. Motrin would do, I heard him say.

Doug won. Hobbling on his crutches to the table, you could see the pain was more than a tickle. Four Motrin, 800 milligrams in total, were consumed. And right after that, as is his habit each and every morning, a plop-plop-fizz-fizz.

No, not common AlkaSeltzer. These were Morning Relief AlkaSeltzer, chock-full of a mix of caffeine and aspirin and whatever else they put into those things. Doug swears by a dose every morning to get him going. I swear by my gallon of coffee and Skoal chewing tobacco. Doug gets his nicotine from his pipe, which he lit now.

Getting him into the hunting car was not easy. Doug did not complain. "A little broken leg isn't going to stop me. Hell, boys, let's go hunting." There wasn't much of a grimace on his face while he said it, either.

Doug was certainly ready to launch lead. He claims his Griffin and Howe .375 H&H was crying when he took it out of the case this morning. Before the accident at Moreson, he was quite content to let Margaret do the shooting. He hadn't even shouldered the thing yet except for the range that very first afternoon. He was due. It was time.

Pierre and Doug discussed a game plan.

"Doug, there's very good zebra here, as well as blesbok, springbok, and black wildebeest. We'll try to sort some of those out."

"What about oryx and kudu?"

That's Doug Chester with his blesbok. We haven't seen much of him yet—he broke his foot on the second night, had surgery, and now five days later he's back. You can see the cast just to the right of the blesbok's head.

"Oryx here are quite good, Doug. Kudu, too, but Dan and Spyker have hunted them hard and saw nothing worth shooting. Tomorrow we leave here for another camp. Much better kudu there. If we come on a good oryx here, we'll see what we can do. Dan and Marge took fine ones here a few days ago."

"Christ, Pierre, I just got here. And we're leaving tomorrow?"

"Doug, don't worry; you'll love the next place too. There's a lot of game. It is quite pretty. Kwende-tu! [Let's go!]" With Margaret riding on the back, they were off.

Spyker and I, along with Clinton and Monty, followed behind in the other hunting car. Clinton was driving; Monty rode shotgun. Spyker and I were up on top, looking for critters.

Just before we came to the knoll where we took my zebra, we spotted another herd. Pierre pointed out the stallion as Doug ever so slowly slid out of the seat and onto the trail. Using the window as a shooting rest, he found the animal in the scope and squeezed. The zebra ran maybe 50 meters before falling over stone-dead.

Now, it should be noted that during this safari some provinces in South Africa allowed hunting directly from the car. Doug, like me and I hope most, don't think this is very sporting. Beginning on June 1, 2007, the entire country has banned that practice. However, with special permission, exceptions are allowed to this new law when the hunter has a debilitating condition that prevents mobility—in Doug's case, a broken leg.

Whoops and hollers went up in congratulation of Doug. Blood had been drawn. Doug got his first critter. When it came time for photos, Doug did his best to hide the cast and abandon the crutches. In the end it didn't matter a hoot. It also didn't

CHOOSING YOUR PROFESSIONAL HUNTER

When it comes to professional hunters, be aware that it is illegal to hunt without one here in South Africa. These fellows, and ladies, are licensed not by the country of South Africa but by each individual province. As we were hunting in two provinces, ours needed to be licensed in both. Ask for the license number. Ask for references. Do your homework. And, oh yes, ask for a picture.

Why do you need a picture? You do not want to hunt with a fat PH. You want to hunt with one who looks like he can go the distance. Otherwise you'll be doing an awful lot of diesel stalking. Now, if you are fine with this, if you want to do a lot of riding followed by short stalks, that's fine with me. I, on the other hand, like the stalk. Sure, let's spot them if we can from the car. Then let's get out and work the wind, work the terrain, work the animals. The word "hunt" is a verb. A verb is active. Active is good. It is worthy.

You need to know what to expect from the land. Virtually all of South Africa is fenced one way or the other. On the concessions, or game farms, or ranches—whatever you call them, you will find fences. In South Africa the landowner owns the animals on that land. Years ago the fences were meant to keep game in. Now, while they are still certainly used that way, they are also used to keep the poachers out. Some concessions are free range, as I was to find out on our next move. Fenced, but not the high game fences. Fenced like a U.S. cattle ranch.

You will want to know how big the hunting area is. This will normally be described in hectares. A hectare is 2.5 acres. The smallest concession we

matter that this eyes welled up. Nor did it matter that mine did, too. Doug was back in the game. He had his zebra, the one animal that, as Doug puts it, "has Africa written all over it. When you see one of these live or as a rug, you know it didn't come from Hong Kong."

We loaded the zebra up and continued to cruise the grassland areas of Kwaggashoek. There was more hunting to do.

As if cued by a benevolent director, a herd of blesbok appeared. A small herd, maybe thirty or so strong, but with a heck of a ram leading through the grasses. Again the hunting car with Doug and Pierre maneuvered on them, getting ever so closer—if close means 200 meters or so. Spyker, Clinton, and I hung a good 75 meters behind in the other car. Margaret was with us. We didn't want our hunting car to spook them.

We watched as Doug again started to slide out of the seat. We watched as Pierre and Doug got into a discussion. It turns out the discussion was about shooting directly from the car, and not just using the window as a rest. We watched as Doug, with a look of resignation, took the advice and swung his legs back into the cab.

hunted was just shy of 3,000 hectares. The largest was four times that size. If you want to hunt without seeing the fences all day long, look for one at least 2,500 hectares. This means the game is wide open. You won't see animals along a fence line. And, if there are more than two professional hunters working with your group, you won't be running into each other at every bend in the trail.

Ask if you'll be hunting a single area or if there are other concessions you can travel to. On any safari lasting more than seven days, moving areas is a damn good idea. You'll be able to hunt different terrain, different habitats, and different animals. God didn't put kudu with springbok. He gave them specific areas in which to prosper. Hunt them where He put them, and you will generally get a much better trophy. In our case we hunted the blesbok and springbok in Free State. We could have taken black wildebeest there, too. The rest of the animals I was after were scrub and forest animals. Hence the move to that habitat at Kwaggashoek.

Another very good reason to find a PH that has multiple areas to hunt is that you will have a better opportunity to score on a real trophy. Imagine a professional hunter who books in thirty clients a year and hunts a single concession. Of those thirty, say twenty of them want a trophy kudu. You do not want to be the 19th person looking for that kudu, do you? Multiple areas help ensure that the quality heads are not all shot off when you arrive.

When hunting with a professional hunter on a single concession, you also may find yourself in a drop-and-shop situation. I've heard of this more from

Next to the window Pierre was pointing out the ram, now the third one from the right. Doug got behind the gun and fired. All of us saw a puff of dust behind the ram and just above his shoulder. And we all saw Doug open the door and swing his legs out and slide out onto the sand trail. He didn't look happy.

The blesbok were still there, and obviously a bit nervous. Doug got behind the gun and used the window as a rest. Another shot and the blesbok dropped like a stone.

While we were taking pictures, Doug swore us all to silence. Silence over missing that blesbok from inside the car. "Guys, I swear, you can't tell anyone. If the folks back in Penn's Valley find out I missed one from the truck, they'll send me to Jersey. Broadside no less. Now, c'mon, promise."

Some of us did. But not all of us.

After all the pictures were taken, Doug told us he needed to take a break for a while. All the climbing in and out, all the excitement and photos had taken their toll on him. He just wanted to sit in the cab and enjoy the rest of the morning. It was Margaret's turn.

CHOOSING YOUR PROFESSIONAL HUNTER

packaged hunts than from á la carte hunts. This is a dirty little secret that some operators use to ensure the game is always there. Here's what happens: While you are eating dinner, or asleep, a truck loaded with game comes into the concession. The game is unloaded onto the ranch. You get up the next morning, and all of a sudden your luck changes. There, no more than 20 minutes into the hunt, stands the kudu of your dreams. After seeing neither bulls nor even spoor for a few days, there he is! Generally right next to the fence.

Yes, a good number of concessions buy animals at game auctions every year. It is also true that most landowners don't like to continue to purchase critters for us. They would much rather have their animals be self-sustaining. The very good ones tell the professional hunter who has permission to hunt the land how many of each species he or she is allowed to take to make sure that happens. That's called smart.

There's another reason to hunt two or more concessions while on your safari. You simply get to see more of the country. You'll see the grasslands and river valleys. You'll see the mountains and high hills and the forests and the scrublands. You'll experience more.

You need to find out, well before you go, what the rules of camp are. In other words, who you'll be in camp with. Some, if not most, professional hunters and outfitters work as a team. That's a good thing. That means if you'll be bringing along more than a single friend, that your PH will be able to handle

---

As mentioned earlier, Margaret Chester is a rocket scientist. She is responsible for satellites going up into space, courtesy of Swift Laboratories, and responsible for something called gamma ray bursts. I don't know much more than that. She has tried, on numerous occasions, to explain these things to me, but my brain just won't wrap around the concepts.

One of the equipment companies she deals with goes by the name of Gnu. As there were some very good black wildebeest on Kwaggashoek, she decided she wanted one for her office. The correlation comes in the name. The black wildebeest is, more properly, the white-tailed gnu. Margaret wanted a gnu to sit on her Gnu.

Also called "the clown of the veldt," the black wildebeest is rather ungainly looking. It seems that God must have taken a bunch of spare parts and threw them together to create this animal. It has a head like a bison and a big tuft of yellowish-white hair sprouting off the top of his nose. Then there's a scraggly beard. The head is "graced" with horns that first curve down and then sharply turn upward.

The clown nickname comes from their behavior. These things will start bucking and jumping for no reason at all. They will hit the afterburners going lickety-split south only to turn, again for no apparent reason, and head due north. They will scatter if a fly farts or if a penguin at Cape Town burps. Then they'll rest for a moment or two, only to resume this spastic dance.

the group. A PH is only allowed by law to guide two hunters. If there are three of you, there must be two professional hunters. If there are five of you, then there must be three PHs.

What is not so good about this is that you may find yourself in a camp with folks you don't know from Adam. They will want to fill all the beds. Some of the people will be obnoxious. Count on it. Or at least count on them not fitting in with your group. They will probably think you are bit off, too.

This is not good at all. A safari will prove to be a very personal experience for you. Your friends and/or family should enjoy it. The camp should be full of hail-fellows-well-met; people who accept each other as they are because they know each other. It should not be shared with every Tom, Dick, or Harry who has the same vacation time as you and wants to go on one of these things. Sure, there is always the chance that you'll meet some great folks. There's the same chance that you'll meet some people who just seem, well, odd. Don't take the chance.

You and your party should be the only people in camp. You know each other's strengths and weaknesses. You know when to kid around and when to lay off. You know which buttons not to push. You know when a word of encouragement may be needed to go the extra distance. Don't screw it up by ending up with Sally Pop-Tart and Johnny Toast and their friends in camp with you.

My, how we chased them. Every time we came up on this herd and started the stalk, they were off. We'd climb back into the car and then watch as they returned to where they started. It was more than a little frustrating. A new plan was needed.

Spyker, Monty, and I convinced Margaret to follow us on foot about a half mile. There, in the middle of the grass, was a low-rising dirt berm along a now dry waterhole. Pierre and Spyker figured that the damn things would come near there on one of their moves. As we walked away, Pierre gave another bit of advice, "Stay very low, shoot from the prone. If they see you, it will have been just a walk and a long wait."

It happened as if preordained. The four of us got to the berm. We could see the wildbeest a good mile off. We could see Pierre take the other truck and move slightly toward the animals. After going no more than 200 yards, and still a good half a mile from them, the wildebeest broke and ran.

Spyker pegged the biggest bull for Margaret, making sure she knew which one was the good one. The four of us screwed ourselves deeper into the soft sand on the berm. When the herd got within 150 meters or so, they stopped. The bull was in the rear. Exposed. "Take him," Spyker whispered.

Margaret's .270 sent a big whoomp into the air. The barrel, being within an inch or two of the sandy berm, sent a cloud of sand and dust up, completely obscuring our vision.

Can you see the wildebeests, just beyond the ridge? Nope. More walking and hoping . . .

That's Margaret again. She still wants a black wildebeest. The waterhole, also called a dam, has been used regularly by the beasts. That's why she is there. Hoping . . .

"Did I get him?"

"You hit him. I don't know where because of all the dust in my eyes. But, I did hear the bullet hit," answered Spyker.

We stood and watched as the herd ran off. One of the herd on the right side started to peel off. He wasn't keeping up with the others. "Shoot that one, he's the one!" instructed Monty. Just as Margaret lifted the rifle, the animal fell. Sometimes a plan does come together.

Doug and Margaret shared a hug and kiss over the wildebeest. More than a few photos were taken.

It was still before noon and time to eat. After we filled our bellies, Doug took a nap. The plan was for us all to get out by about 3 P.M. for the final few hours of daylight. This plan didn't come together.

Doug couldn't sleep. At 1:30 I swore I heard a roar coming from his bedroom. I did hear a roar. It was Doug, and he was not happy. The Motrin he took with lunch dulled some of the pain. The excitement from the morning still had him wired. If he couldn't sleep, he wanted to hunt. He wanted to hunt now.

"No problem at all," said Pierre. "Let's go."

After a quick episode of Boots and Saddles, the two hunting cars left the main house. The one issue was the animals. It was hot this afternoon with the temperatures easily breaking into the mid-80s. The animals would be hunkered down in the shade, hiding from the heat. They were also hiding, or so it seemed, from us.

We crisscrossed the grasslands. We drove through the acacias and trees. We drove down toward the river and over to the dam. Everywhere we went, except for the birds flitting through the trees, nothing moved but our cars.

This what a happy rocket scientist looks like who uses Gnu equipment at work and now has a white-tailed gnu for a trophy.

The animals remained hidden until 4 P.M. or so. Then, from out of nowhere, they appeared. Zebra galloped in the distance. Giraffes came out of the thick forests and nibbled on the tops of acacias butting up to the grasslands. Blesbok walked stiff-legged across the plains. Where fifteen minutes ago there was nothing, now we were in a park full of animals.

Pierre angled his hunting car to the east where he knew a springbok herd had set up housekeeping. He had seen a nice ram a few days ago, a very nice ram. That was what he and Doug would be after.

Doug's luck was appearing to hold as we found the ram herding a group of ten to twelve ewes around. It was more than obvious that this ram was boss. We watched from afar as a much smaller ram came close to the herd. The old male, the one with the perfect lire-shaped horns towering over his small head, chased him away quickly. The younger one didn't even put up the smallest fight. He just skedaddled when he saw the big ram.

It was getting close to 5 P.M. The sun was beginning to fall fast. The light shining on the ram's golden coat glowed in the softening light. His black Nike-esque stripe was dark as coal. And he was staring at us. Not moving a muscle, just staring at us like a statue. In an instant, and a burst of speed, he topped a hill and was gone.

Slowly we took the cars to the hilltop. The ewes had followed him but were a good 10 meters or so to his left. Clinton maneuvered the car so Doug could get out and shoot.

The ram moved into the ewes during the repositioning. He was still free of the ewes for the time being. Another few steps left or right and he'd be in line with one ewe or another, taking away the shooting opportunity.

Nothing special about this sunset. Except it is in Africa, at Kwaggashoek, and signals the end of a very eventful day.

The ram started to twitch a bit. Through the binoculars we could see his eyes darting left and right. We watched as he loaded his back legs, ready to spring away. He was preparing to bolt.

That's when Doug's gun roared and the springbok tipped over. He was as beautiful up close as he was from afar. Deep black horns were perfectly shaped. He sported a coat of the most beautiful amber. All of our eyes welled up. What a day for Doug! What a day for all of us.

After loading the springbok into the car, we just stood there. Not a word was spoken. We stood there in silence, in the grasslands of Kwaggashoek, and watched as the sun disappeared behind the mountains. We watched as the stars started to capture the sky across a purple backdrop. The moon was already well into its nightly journey.

When the last vestige of the day had given way to the west, the jackals started their nightly chorus. That must have been our cue; without a word we just loaded up into the trucks and headed for camp.

CHAPTER 12

On to Kameelkop

oug became much more comfortable at dinner last night. One of the velvet sledgehammers had him grinning from ear to ear. As did his ability to put that bum leg of his up on a padded cushion. The tremendous day of hunting didn't hurt, either. I, on the other hand, was jolly with scotch. Wine was the drug of choice for the others. Our feet stayed on the floor.

It was an early night. As much as we didn't wish it to end, it had to end early. The game plan for tomorrow was to get up at the regular early call, have a good breakfast, and then head out for the next hunting concession. This meant that we had to get packed up tonight.

Dave and Mary were up well before the crack of dawn. Anneli was driving them to Durban to catch a plane for Cape Town and a couple days of touring. They were already loading the car when I arrived for breakfast.

Once our gear was loaded and our bellies full, it was off to another concession, a place called Kameelkop, or Camel Head. Pierre had us excited. "Big kudu there. Lots of game. Very pretty."

We did need to make a small detour on the way. As it is with any hospital, the paperwork never ends. Same goes with the financial aspects.

Ladysmith is built up and around a big hill. During the Boer War, it was a very strategic location. The Boers had it under siege for months until it was finally broken and the British prevailed. It was your typical city. If you needed it, they had it. If you wanted it, they had it. Chain restaurants and chain department stores. Banks and suburbs, poorer sections and more well-to-do.

La Verna Hospital sits on top of the hill overlooking an expansive valley. In the distance the city disappears into grass and scrub lands. Well-kept grounds surrounded the hospital, and like hospitals everywhere, parking is an issue. We finally found a place right on the edge of the hill with a fabulous view.

That was a good thing. Taking care of the final payments for Doug's surgery and stay took a bit of time. It was a pleasant day. High clouds, somewhat cool, a good day to simply watch the world pass by below us.

After Doug was firmly entrenched in the bowels of the hospital bookkeeping section, Pierre came out of the hospital and pulled me aside.

"Dan, I have a big favor to ask. Doug has just been told that he can't fly home on his scheduled flight. Margaret is already changing their flight so that they can leave on June 2. Is it possible for you to stay an extra few days and help us, help Doug and Margaret?"

My schedule had me flying home on May 31. I'd been away from home since May 13.

"Pierre, can I think about it a bit?"

"Sure you can. Just know it would be a big help."

My initial impression was to say yes right from the start. Hell, I'm in Africa—it is probably a once-in-a-lifetime deal for me. Of course I wanted to stay. Then came thoughts of family, my wife, Kris, and my children, Karen and Eric. I'm away a lot. A few extra days could well be a lifetime in their eyes.

Margaret spent an awful lot of time with Doug at the hospital. But not all of her time, as this gemsbok is testament to. Heck, Doug was sleeping most of the time anyway.

An hour or so later Doug and Margaret came out of the hospital, all the bills paid. In cash. It surprised me to no end that they could take care of the bills with cash. If Doug had the same surgery and stay in the United States, I'm afraid of what the bill would have been. The curious fellow that I am, I had to ask how much.

"When I first met the doctor, I asked him how much his fee was. He told me, and I peeled off just over $1,500. Dan, he just put the bills in his shirt pocket. I couldn't believe it. The rest of the bill, including what I paid the surgeon, the gas-passer, the surgical team, the hospital stay—everything came to around $8,000. I figure that if I was going to break my leg anywhere, that South Africa was a bargain. Just imagine what it would have cost in the States."

The sky had clouded over by the time we left Ladysmith and headed for Kameelkop near the very small town of Wasbank. Just outside Ladysmith a situation developed with one of the hunting cars. The alternator wouldn't alternate, or whatever it is an alternator does. Not good. It was mid-afternoon, most shops close mid-afternoon, and we needed that car to be at the next camp.

The chalets at Kameelkop were tucked into an acacia forest. Very private, very secluded, very romantic. I was by myself. The romance part was wasted on me.

Then there's Clinton. One of the apprentice PH's jobs is to do anything the professional hunter doesn't want to do. Even if that PH is your father. It may be more correct to say especially if that PH is your father. Clinton became the auto mechanic.

Now, Pierre did stay behind, too. After we cross-loaded as much as we could into the combe and other hunting car, he thumbed his way to town, found an auto supply store, and thumbed his way back to Clinton and the sick car. We found out about this later as we took the moving vehicles and headed for the next camp.

We arrived in Kameelkop around 3:30 in the afternoon. The clouds had thickened. There was a light mist in the air. Kameelkop's staff unloaded our gear and brought it to our individual chalets. Though the trailer I stayed in at Kwaggashoek was fine, this was a dream. I had the chalet to myself. A huge picture window overlooked a small dam. Even lying down on the bed, which is to this day one of the most comfortable I've been in, I could look out over the water. Acacias surrounded it on three sides. The walls were built of wood and beautifully stained. The roof was made of classic thatch. This was going to be great.

I had no intention of hunting that day. The clouds had the light flat. The mist was more like extreme humidity, and heck, it was late. I figured this was to be a nonhunting day. That was fine with me. A day of rest wouldn't be such a bad thing at all. I was wrong.

I heard footsteps coming down the path to my chalet. Spyker didn't knock; he just came in. Handing me a Coke Light, he said, "You aren't ready yet? Let's go. Kwende tu!"

A view of the unfenced section to the south of Kameelkop proper. The aloes come in all shapes and sizes. This one is nearly six feet around and just as tall.

In ten minutes I was at the car. Spyker started to explain the land. "Kameelkop comes in two parts. Where we are now is high fence, about 5,000 hectares. Across the road we drove in on is another area, maybe 7,500 hectares, and there are no game fences. This side has some high hills or small mountains, which you've seen, as well as some grasslands to the west and north, which you haven't. Where there is no fence, the hills are more rolling, but there are some very deep dongas, dry stream beds. Mr. Donarski, this is a great place. We'll have high fun here."

Spyker is always optimistic. That's a good thing, as attitude is everything. The way he said it, the way his hands sliced through air to punctuate a point, the way his eyes danced—this place must be someplace very special.

"Let's get going . . . " and I stopped in mid-sentence. From the hills behind us, I heard what sounded like the bark of a kudu. The only problem with claiming it was a kudu was that a kudu's bark is a short one. They generally only bark once, maybe twice before they disappear. These barks were longer, and they came in a set of three.

"What was that?" I asked. Spyker gave me the hush sign. Then the barks continued, another series of three. Deep and guttural, they sounded more like a throat clearing this time than a bark.

"Dan, it has to be a kudu. It has to be. If we were anywhere else, I'd swear it was the cough of a leopard. It's exactly what a leopard sounds like. There just aren't many, if any, leopards around here."

At that instant a crashing was heard coming down the hill. Flashes of gray screamed through the trees and horns danced in the limbs. The kudu bull came tearing down the hill, stopped at the side of the road not 50 feet from us, gave us the once over, and leapt over the road and dashed for the cover at the other side of the dam. He disappeared into the thick brush.

"Damn." It's all I could say.

"Damn straight," replied Spyker. "That was ever so close to the 50-incher we're looking for. Load up."

Just as we were pulling out, Pierre and Clinton were pulling in. The alternator job took them no more than an hour. Clinton jumped into the back of the hunting car with me.

Driving back down the entrance road, a tall black man in olive green coveralls and wearing a watch cap was waiting alongside the road.

"Cyril, you are on time. I like that," said Spyker. "Climb in with me." Cyril was one of the camp's trackers. He led us into the unfenced area. He led us into kudu country.

Cyril saw them first, followed by Clinton a split second later. Clinton's hand pounding on the roof of the Land Rover and Cyril's excited pointing brought the car to a halt.

"Kudu. They are over there, behind those trees. Eight, maybe ten of them," Cyril whispered. This man's English was very good. Very proper, with a bit of a British lilt to it. Cyril spoke better English than a lot of people I know. "If these are the herd I know best, there is a huge bull with them. This is where they like to be."

Very quietly we left the truck. Spyker looked at me, pointed to my watch, and had me turn it around so that the face was under my wrist, not above it. "The glare," he whispered. Never before had he taken the time to give our clothing or guns or equipment the military once-over. This must be a serious deal.

Cyril picked up the spoor quickly. Maneuvering so that the wind wouldn't give us away, we cut a long U in an effort to get ahead of the herd. The going wasn't all that easy. The trees and shrubs, as always, were thorn-filled. We crossed more than a few narrow dry streambeds bordered by high sand and gravel banks that gave way underfoot. One step forward, two steps back seemed to be the rule.

After about 30 minutes we came to a junction of two streambeds. Cyril said that this would be a good place to try for a shot. They would come by here. Setting up in the V we had both avenues covered.

Soon we began to notice the flick of a tail here, a flash of gray there. The kudu were coming. As they drew closer, we could hear them scuffing the gravel and sand. We could see movement. We could see one set of horns.

A huge cow, her ears and eyes constantly checking the area for danger, led the kudu. The ears are incredible to look at. From a distance the inside of the ear looks like a red stop sign bordered by dark gray. From close up the entire animals looks as huge as it is. Going up to 700 pounds, sometimes more, they are elk-sized and sport a gray coat with thin white strips that start at the spine and drop to the belly. Kudu have a fine black, gray, and white mane and eyes that can see tomorrow coming.

These were close. The lead cow, followed by two smaller cows, came within 50 feet of us. We were up on the bank, more or less hidden in the shrubs. The kudu were in the streambed. The lead cow veered up the right fork with the other two. Behind her were the others. One had tall spiraling horns.

A minute later they came out into the streambed. I had the gun leveled on them, steady on the sticks. "Dan, he's a pretty one. But he's not the one we want. High 40s, that's all he is." I couldn't believe it. I was, again, a little miffed.

After all the kudu had disappeared I pulled Spyker over to the side. He could see I was miffed. "Spyker, you're the pro from Dover. But c'mon, that was a dandy kudu. I don't need, hell, I don't even want to think about a record kudu. That one would have been just fine. He was gorgeous."

"Mr. Donarski, Dan, we could have taken that one, certainly. We can do better. You deserve better. I want to be as proud of your kudu when we take him as you are. That was a nice one, but it was not a *nice* one. I don't want you to shoot a Mickey Mouse. I want to be able to say that I'd be proud to put it on my wall. Trust me, please. We'll get our chance."

"Okay, it's just that, well . . . "

"I know, trust me."

We made it back to the car with a little less than an hour of light left. The skies were still cloaked in clouds. "Boss," said Cyril, "drive please to the east. We'll find a clearing there and one where kudu often come out just before dark."

Fifteen minutes later we were there. Spyker tucked the car underneath an acacia and instructed Clinton to stay on top and glass the clearing. Cyril, Spyker, and I walked over to another donga, a steep ravine with a dry river as its bottom. Kudu tracks filled the soft sand and mud.

After a few minutes we heard Clinton pounding softly on the roof of the Rover. It sounded like the beat of far-off drums. Spyker didn't like it at all, fearing Clinton would spook anything that would come our way.

A quick glance to Clinton proved otherwise. He was pointing low to the ground, into the grass in front of the truck. Looking at us he lifted his arms into a big "U." Even I knew he was indicating a warthog, a big warthog. Then he started gyrating his hips.

Seems this big warthog was, right in front of him, in the process of making more warthogs. I guess that warthogs aren't very modest animals. Being as ugly as they are, they must figure why bother with modesty. We could see Clinton doing his best not to laugh. It was no use; he finally gave in to the urge and started up. That scattered the hogs. It also signaled our time to head back to camp. It was getting quite dark.

Spyker had me climb up top, into the back with him. Clinton drove, Cyril rode shotgun. Through the headlights on the slow drive, Spyker pointed out different tracks to me. He had the car stop when he spotted the tracks of a brown hyena and again when a caracol's tracks traced the path. Nearing the edge of the property, a gray, lightly spotted cat tore down the road.

Spyker got very excited. "That was an African wildcat. It is one very cool cat. We'll have to set some baits, maybe do some calling here."

I spent the rest of the ride back to camp thinking of Pierre's request: that I stay until Doug could fly.

After a quick shower I headed for the main lodge and poured myself a tall scotch. Doug called for me to come over; he had a question for me. I asked for a moment, as I had to make a phone call right away. Doug looked puzzled.

AFRICAN TRAVEL ARRANGEMENTS

Flying to South Africa is easy. As mentioned earlier, South African Airlines and Delta both have direct flights from the States. Any number of carriers can take you through Europe and into Johannesburg. Getting there and back isn't the issue. How you book the ticket is.

Yes, Orbitz, Travelocity, Expedia, and any number of companies can sell you a ticket over the Internet. I use these companies all the time to book flights in the United States. Sometimes I save money, sometimes the fares are the same as from one of the airlines. As travel agents have to charge you now for their services because the airlines don't give them a penny, a travel agent will cost you around $50, sometimes a bit more. A good travel agent is worth every penny. Pay them. Bring them back a small gift. They deserve it. Here's why.

Say you need to change your reservation after you are already overseas. If you book with one of the online companies, just whom are you going to call? Even if you can find a number to call, do you really expect to talk to a person who genuinely gives a damn about you, if in fact you actually talk to a live human being?

You need someone who knows you, or at least has done business with you. You need an advocate to state your case for you to the zombies reciting chapter and verse of company policies. You need someone to be in your corner and come out fighting when the chips are down. You need an agent.

We're not talking "Jan's Discount Travel Emporium," either. This is Africa. This can be complicated. The agent you use must know the ins and outs and the schedules. The agent must know people at the airlines so that they can get through and talk to someone when they have to. You are going to be in the bush. You are probably hours from an airport that has international connections and anyone who *may* be able to help you.

I don't generally think naming names is a good thing, but there are three agencies that I personally know of and have dealt with. Gracy Travel in Bourne, Texas; Custom Travel in Hales Corners, Wisconsin; and Superior Travel in my hometown of Sault Ste. Marie, Michigan. These folks are experts. They get things done.

On this trip, I booked my air and first night hotel through Superior Travel. I'm damn glad I didn't book with some discount service or over the Internet. ▪

"Pierre, can I use your cell phone to make a call to the States? There's something I have to do."

"Use the satellite phone; we don't have a cell connection here."

Even with the satellite phone, I had to climb up a tall hill in the dark to get a good signal.

"Hello, Bev?" I asked. (Bev is the "Big Boss Lady" at Superior Travel.)

"Dan, is that you? Where are you?"

I explained quickly what had happened to Doug and my desire to change my departure so that I could help out. I told her that I could fly out on the second of June or a day or two later. That I just couldn't fly home before that.

"Dan, that is going to take me some time. Can I call you or you call back later today?"

"Uh, Bev, it's 8 P.M. here, and I'm on a satellite phone. How about I call you tomorrow at this same time?"

"Okay, call tomorrow. I'll be waiting for you to call tomorrow."

When I got back to the camp, I handed the phone back to Pierre. "Done. I'm staying with Doug and Margaret," I whispered to him so the others wouldn't hear.

Pierre smiled and shook my hand. "Thank you."

I walked across the room to Doug. He was sitting next to a blazing fire. Maragret was in a chair alongside. "Dan, is everything all right? You grabbed the phone and left pretty quickly. Kris and the kids okay?"

"I don't know, I guess they are. I wasn't calling them."

Doug gave me a sideways, questioning glance. "Dan, I need to ask you something. It's a big favor."

I cut him off. "Doug, if you're going to ask me to stay until you can fly home, don't. You don't have to ask, it's already done."

"What?"

"Yeah, I'm staying until you can leave. Hell, I'm in Africa, you think I want to leave?"

Doug sat up, reached his arms out and gave me one helluva hug. Margaret had heard the conversation. When Doug finally let me go, she came over and planted a soft kiss on my cheek and murmured, "Thank you."

Now I just had to somehow let my family know. I needed another scotch. That call could wait.

CHAPTER 13

A Kudu Encounter

 don't know why this morning is so important to me. Maybe it's the new location and the sense of discovery. Maybe it's because I had a good night's sleep. Or maybe it is because I'm staying an extra few precious days. This morning simply feels special; there is electricity in the air.

Clinton padded down the path to my chalet and knocked softly at the door, announcing that it was time to get up. The lad had a steaming cup of coffee for me, too.

We had more coffee at the main lodge, and before the sun was above the hills on the horizon Spyker and I were off. Cyril was where we dropped him off yesterday, waiting for us.

Somewhere along the course of this safari, I picked up a rather bad habit. Each morning with my coffee I smoked a cigarette, sometimes two. In the evening, when we were having cocktails, I'd have another, and another after dinner. That was in addition to my Skoal habit.

Cyril was a smoker, as was Spyker. Spyker bought his from the store. Cyril may have bought his tobacco from the store, but he got his "rolling" papers anywhere he found them. Newspapers, magazines, it didn't matter. If he could roll it, he smoked his tobacco rolled up in it.

Figuring that store-bought cigarettes are a luxury for Cyril, I slid him a pack on the sly. His eyes glowed and he shook my hand with more than a bit of enthusiasm. He then shook two out of the pack and offered me one. I accepted, and we smoked the things in the back of the Rover as Spyker turned the Rover to the left and up the start of a very high and steep hill.

Land Rovers and Land Cruisers are the most popular models for a hunting car. They have been since they made their debut decades ago. These things can go almost anywhere. They hold up incredibly well. They do what they are meant to do; they just get the job done.

But they do bounce. They bounce particularly well off the bowling ball-size rocks on the trail. As they bounce you also bounce, especially if you are riding in the back. If you suffer from hemorrhoids, you will either bounce so hard you'll cut the itchy suckers off or you'll bounce them back where they belong. Cyril and I

115

This is on the upper knob on the first day at Kameelkop, high above the camp. It's cold, it's very cold. Spyker took his hat off, reluctantly, just for the photo.

held on as best we could. We wanted to stand in order to get a better vantage point but found sitting was definitely safer.

As we climbed, the already cool morning got colder. The metal handrails turned icy, forcing us into our gloves. Cyril pulled his balaclava down into the face-mask style. He was cold. Hell, so was I, but I was accustomed to it. For him it must have seemed like Antarctica.

We got to the top of the hill and entered into an extremely wide and flat grass-covered plateau. The grasses were a mix of green and gold. A very heavy frost covered nearly everything. In the early dawn light, the landscape glittered like gemstones of pastel oranges and yellows. A few scattered dams appeared as ink blots in the grass. Higher hills were both to the east and west.

We headed west. But not far. Still coursing along an old trail, a whitetail deer-size animal broke from the 4-foot grass just to the right of the car. His tail was up and flagging its white underside just like a whitetail. Its coat was tawny just like a whitetail. Except for the horns, it could have been a whitetail.

Spyker stopped the car with a squeal and hopped up into the back. "Dan, that's a monster reedbuck. He's a gold medal for sure. Dan, you have to take him! He's huge!"

He was, too. The horns curved well beyond the ears and rose high into the sky. A good one goes 12 inches. Spyker said this was an easy 16-incher. And he was standing broadside, stone still, at no more than 75 yards.

I wanted to lift the gun, I truly did. If I were flush with cash, I would have. But my finances were drained, with only cash for the kudu left. And it was kudu I wanted.

This is the high plateau, just underneath the lightning-struck knob. It's also the very same place I passed on a huge reedbuck.

"Spyker, sorry, I can't afford the thing."

"Dan, forget the kudu. You won't ever see a bigger reedbuck than this one."

"I just can't. I'm sorry, I truly am." I put down the binoculars. I turned away after taking one last glance. I knew Spyker was not that happy and figured he probably couldn't understand. Ever so slowly Spyker got down from the truck, climbed back into the cab, and started to take us to those higher hills in the west. Looking back I saw the reedbuck walk a few paces and bed back down in the grass. Damn.

We made it to the top of the hill just as the sun broke over the horizon. The road ended here; from here we'd be on foot. We'd be looking for kudu.

The top of the hill was bare rock. Thick groves of trees spread out below us on the slopes. And in those trees were crooked fingers of deep ravines formed by eons of erosion. Very small openings in the trees meant that any shot would be a quick one. Kudu are known to disappear. Here it would be easy to prove just that.

Just off the crest of the hill, as we made our way down the rocky knob, we came upon what appeared like a mirror broken in the center. A solid black hole, shards of rocks with scorched edges, reached out from the center like a broken mirror pane. These shards stretched down the solid granite face for a good 30 to 40 feet. The geometry was impressive, the scorching of the rock dangerously so.

The vegetation near the top was short, at first. Just a bit farther down the slope, where there was obviously more dirt for purchase, it grew tall. The trees grew taller and thicker the lower we went. Not that we went too low.

Down the hill we walked, about half the distance to the plateau, and then back up a neighboring hill. Slowly working the ravines and the trees, trying to glimpse a

The vegetation here is different. Acacias and thornbush are joined by prickly pear, something that looks like skinny organ pipe, another like cholla, along with yucca and this big thing called sisal. Back in the bad times, folks used to dip nasty stuff onto the ends of these barbed leaves to poison people they didn't want around.

kudu. On the third hill, as with the first two, we stopped to glass the surrounding area. Spyker saw them first. Them being kudu.

This group of six or seven had just passed through an opening on the upslope of the next hill. He said he saw horns that were worth investigating and we had to move quickly but quietly in order to catch them.

We did just that. The problem was that once we caught them, and happily they were caught moving through another opening, the bull decided to stay in the trees. There was no shooting.

There was more hustling on our part. The group of kudu was moving through this dragon's back of hills, always staying on the eastern slope and never venturing far from the elevation they were at. They didn't know we were there. They were just walking away. We hustled to catch them.

We may have gone a bit too far before stopping and glassing carefully. Then again, they were just on the other side of the hill. And we wouldn't have been able to see them until we stopped where we did.

What we saw were six kudu cows, no more than 40 yards away, working down and across the neighboring rise. The bull was there, too, but only for a second. And he was the biggest bull that I had seen. I couldn't get him in the scope before he did his disappearing act. One of the cows saw us, too. A quick bark and the group disappeared in a crashing of trees.

"That's your kudu, Dan. That's the one for you. Don't worry, we'll get him."

It wasn't much past 9 A.M. My kudu was walking these lands. I had seen him with my own two eyes, if only for a split second.

After spooking the kudu, Spyker suggested we go look after that reedbuck. "Dan, I know that the reedbuck is not what you want. Margaret does want one, and this is the biggest I have seen anywhere. Would you be okay with calling them and having them meet us down on that grass. We know where the kudu is, we can get him later."

"Why not? Let's do it."

After a few radio calls back and forth, we motored back onto the plateau where we jumped the reedbuck. "Dan, these things are very territorial. They know their home and they like to stay there. That reedbuck is in this grass. When Pierre and the others get here, we'll get him jumped up so Marge can have a shot."

Now, I grew up hunting deer in the deep north woods of Wisconsin. After opening weekend, everyone knew that the only way to get those big, smart bucks was to drive them out of the thick stuff to shooting lanes where the standers waited for them. I, being a youngster, was always a driver. And, I can honestly report that of the dozens of deer drives I have been on, only twice was a deer taken. I do not have a lot of faith in that method.

Yet that is exactly what we did. Except for the fact that there were no standers and that we pushed through grasses rather than forest. If you would have seen us you would have sworn we were somewhere in eastern Montana or the Dakotas doing a pheasant drive.

Besides being territorial, reedbuck are also very wary. Like a pheasant, or white-tailed deer for that matter, they will remain hiding in the grass up until you almost step on them. Or so I was told.

There were eight of us walking through the grass. Doug stayed in the hunting car. A new member to the hunting party, Petra, the land manager's wife, was along

Here's our group glassing the plain to see if we can find a reedbuck.

for the fun. Eight of us hoped that we'd jump that reedbuck and Margaret could collect it. We swung north, then west, then south, and finally east in a square of easily two square miles. The walking was slow; rocks were hidden in the waist-high to shoulder-high grass.

We regrouped at the cars and decided to try one more time. This time we would walk to the south, down a slope covered by rocks the size of pickup trucks with the grasses in between. I hadn't walked more than 50 feet when a sudden and quite loud "Whoa!" sprang from my lips. Everyone turned to look at me, and at the reedbuck doe that sprang up only a foot or so in front of me.

I was more than a little startled. I watched as she bounded away down the hill. Laughter came from up and down the line. Only the two people on either side of me saw the doe. The others, when they heard the reason for my startled cry, only saw the hilarity of me being startled by something. I was more than a little startled. Heck, you would have been, too.

We didn't find the male before we decided to head in for lunch. The sun was high in the sky, the frost was gone, and we were hungry.

These brunches or lunches, whatever you wish to call them, are something special. Sure, one of the reasons they are special is because you've been up since before dawn and out hunting hard. Of course you are going to be hungry when you began the day with some cereal and fruit plus caffeine and nicotine, followed by an extra heavy portion of adrenaline. (It's pronounced a-drena-leen out there.) The -een diet.

Consider the brunch: It starts with eggs to order, as many as you want. (Choose three.) Then there are three or four types of breads. Different jams and marmalades. Oh, and something called Boveril. (I'll give you my share of that.) Three to four types of meat in the form of sausages and steaks. Fresh tomatoes and other veggies.

Doug resting his broken leg after brunch. He's smiling because he has just eaten and he is in Africa. You would smile, too.

Potatoes or pap. Fresh fruit juice. Coffee, tea, and cold drinks. Heck, it's all here, each and every day. Always with a different twist and always served up by Moses with a smile that stretches all the way from here to there. And if by chance you would like something else, it magically appears on the plate as if it were planned for all along. God bless Moses.

A change in plans was in order for the afternoon's hunt. Margaret really wanted a mountain reedbuck as well as the common reedbuck. Mountain reedbuck are cute little antelope, a big one goes to all of 65 pounds. Horns barely reach the tops of their ears. Dry rocky slopes are where they make their home. Plateaus and open peaks are not to their favor; they prefer instead those hideously treacherous slopes, covered in rocks with slick grasses in between.

This was no place for Doug, not unless Doug wanted to spend the afternoon by himself in the cab while Marge and Pierre got out and hunted. Doug was coming with Spyker and me, along with Cyril. After his nap.

Spyker and I walked down to the dam in front of my chalet. A group of kudu cows and calves ran into the acacias on the far side as we approached. This was the start of the dry season, the dam was slowly losing water, its edges now a foot or so below the normal water line. A ring of black mud surrounded the water like a necklace.

Spyker again started to point out the tracks of various animals. Kudu here, waterbuck there, more than a few impala. On the northern edge he pointed out the tracks of a nyala, arguably the prettiest of African antelope and a member of the spiral-horned family. Someday, maybe, I'll hunt this one. On this trip I'd be happy to just see one of these beauties.

On the western edge of the dam, a thick stand of what the locals call "cane" grew. You call it tulies, or reeds, but these were African-sized, easily 8 feet tall. Bordering the thick black ring of muck, animals had pounded the cane into the soft mud, making a path along the edge.

"Whoa!" Spyker yelled and high stepped it away from the edge.

I heard a rustle under the cane mat and followed quickly behind him. "What the hell was that?"

"Focin' cane rat! Bastard scared me a bit."

"A rat? You?"

"Not the rat, but what you often find with the rat. Cobra feed on them, and where there are rats there are snakes. I don't like those so much."

Ostriches strutted all over the lower elevations right at the edge of the grasses and trees. If you go to Africa, please shoot one. Then eat one. My bet is you'll shoot another just for the table.

DANGEROUS ANIMALS AND PESTS

Before we start, let's get one thing straight. Yes, there are critters in South Africa that can make you quite miserable, or even dead. The same can be said for most of the southern United States, with the region's snakes, scorpions, and assorted beasties.

Timing, no matter where you are, is a controlling factor. May starts the winter season in South Africa. It extends through at least mid-September. In winter a lot of these beasties are simply not flying, slithering, or crawling around. It's too cold, particularly at night, for these things not to be hunkered down in some sort of hidey-hole waiting for warmer weather.

Just about everyone who has read anything about Africa has read about cobras. They're here to be sure. Seeing one in the winter is very rare. The most common member of the family is what South African's call the Mozambique spitting snake. You know it as the spitting cobra. None of our group saw one on this safari.

Another common snake is the puff adder. Short and very fat, this puppy has very long fangs and an incredibly beautiful skin. I know because I've seen a lot of pictures of these. None of our group saw one on this safari either.

There are other poisonous snakes to be sure. Think mamba, green tree snake, a few other adders, another cobra or two. None of our group saw any of these on this safari. In fact, our group didn't see a snake of any kind. Not even tracks in the soft sand. I'm not complaining, either.

Then there are the scorpions. This place has them. It has a lot of them. Big ones, little ones, they are here. Ones that can make you wish you were dead and ones that just hurt like hell. They like to hang out until night, when they start to crawl around. Under cabinets, under logs, in between rocks, and, oh yes, in your boots or your pack, your suitcase, anywhere they can get into a dark hidey-hole as the day grows bright.

We left camp around 3 P.M., the sun already starting its slide down the sky. Driving out of camp, we came upon a group of ostriches. I tried to convince Doug to take one. In fact I told him I'd split the fee because they are so good to eat. He declined, and we watched them strut off into the bush.

A herd of impala stood in an opening at the base of the big hill. These animals, maybe all animals, know when they are safe and when they are in danger. We all had our impala in the salt. They just stood there and looked at us.

Then I saw him: a huge-horned fellow, easily a third again as big as the one I had taken at Kwaggashoek, and that one was a dandy. I had Spyker stop, and I glassed him with the binoculars. That he didn't like. Or he didn't like the way my brain waves were playing the "should I, or shouldn't I" game. Jerking his head straight up, he tossed his horns and with that the herd scattered deep into the trees.

What can you do to prevent a surprise encounter? Keep your pack and your suitcase zipped shut. In the morning, before you put your boots on, shake them out. Don't go reaching under cabinets or between rocks or under logs. Now, if you live in a scorpion zone in the United States, you already know this. This last part was for those who live where we don't worry about those long curving tails of dread.

Then there are the spiders. You will see some of these. In all shapes and sizes. Some very intricately patterned, some vividly colored, some as drab as a dead leaf. There isn't much you can do about these. Heck, in the dead of winter I have them in my garage in Michigan's Upper Peninsula. I hate spiders more than any other beastie. In fact, it would be a true statement that they give me the heebie-jeebies. You are just going to need to deal with them. Complaining wouldn't help anyway.

Other little fellows you are going to deal with are ticks. Not just wood ticks, deer ticks, and chiggers, either. No sir. This is Africa. Africa knows ticks. They are carried by animals. Any time you handle an animal, you are in tick central. You'll find ticks in animals' ears, on their necks, on their legs, and all over their bodies. They feast on blood, warm blood—maybe your blood.

Let's start with the pepper tick. These are seriously small bugs. They get their name from their size, not much bigger than coarse-ground black pepper and about the same color. Pepper ticks like to party; they like to hang out with their friends. If you have one, you have dozens. The good thing about them is that they don't eat too much. Another good thing is they don't travel too far. Clinton, while backpacking out my bushbuck, found that the pepper ticks on my bushbuck took a liking to him. They eased on down his shirt, found an opening where his shirt had pulled out of his pants at his sides, and took up housekeeping then and there.

Once we reached the plateau, we headed straight across it, toward the west where a long rocky ridge cut a swatch at the end of the dragon's back hills of this morning. Marge was with Pierre far to the north looking for her mountain reedbuck. We were looking for an oryx for Doug.

With Doug we were pretty much relegated to the trails. That was fine with me. The walk this morning had my feet screaming from rock bruises. Besides, having Doug along allowed me to play wannabe apprentice professional hunter and watch the hunt unfold. Not since Dave and I hunted together at Moreson had I been able to enjoy the show as a spectator.

We drove slowly on the trails. When we cut a track from an oryx on the road, we stopped to glass the area carefully. Spyker pointed out the bird life. Hornbills flitted through the trees and screamed at us. Laughing doves did just that. Francolin

DANGEROUS ANIMALS AND PESTS

They itch like hell and cause what looks like a rash, or a bad case of hives, to form in the affected area. One really good thing about these pepper ticks is that they do not really get a good bite into you. A shower and gentle scrubbing gets rid of the itch and the ticks. At least that's how Clinton got rid of his.

Then there are the blue tick and the red tick, both about the size of our wood tick. Their names come from their body color. You don't need to imagine the color; these things are definitely blue or red. Like our wood tick, they grab a solid purchase on your skin. Standard tick removal methods are effective on them. Unlike our wood ticks, they don't stay on as long, nor do they get as big as a grape before falling off. Normally they grow to the size of a fat pencil eraser in two to three days.

Finally, we come to the striped tick. They get their name from distinctive yellow and black striping on their body and legs. These fellows have a damn big needle nose. They hurt like the dickens. And, wouldn't you know, they are stalkers. They track you down. Unlike the others that survive on off-chance encounters with warm-blooded creatures, these guys sense your presence and walk on over and jump on board. On our safari we saw pepper, blue, and red ticks. We never saw a striped tick. I'm not complaining here, either.

With ticks, there are proactive measures you can take to keep them at bay. Tuck your pants into your boots. Keep your shirt tucked in. Check yourself out completely at the end of every day of hunting before you shower. Run a comb along your scalp just to make sure your forest of hair hasn't been made into a home.

and buttonquail busted from the roadside grass so frequently we should have had our shotguns with us. Good Lord, it was a pretty afternoon.

It's amazing to me that a diesel-powered car like a Land Rover can move so quietly. Starting them up creates a lot of coughing and sputtering and that clank-clank of a typical diesel. But once they catch their breath, and the blood is running smooth through their lines, they are almost catlike. They purr. This one was purring quite well.

And then, there up on the slope, was a pair of oryx. They were not close. Standing underneath a huge fat-topped acacia in the middle of golden grasses and rock, they were in the shadows. Gray bodies in gray shadows are hard to separate. White and black striped faces, in dappled sunlight, are hard to separate from the low branches. Only their rapier-straight horns on a field of arching branches gave them away.

Spyker tried to maneuver the car closer, only to be stopped by a huge rock, a warthog hole, or a deep ravine. He tried left, right, straight. Then went twenty yards forward and stopped. Seventy-five yards that way and we got optimistic, until the rock. Fifty this way, and the ravine. We were as close as we were going to get.

Then there's permithrin. This is a wonderful tick killer. There are three rules when using this stuff. Rule 1: DO NOT spray your skin with this stuff. Rule 2: DO NOT spray your clothes, boots, gloves, or hat while you are wearing them. Rule 3: Read numbers one and two again and DO NOT screw up.

This stuff comes in both aerosol and pump sprays. One bottle or can will treat two sets of clothes. Before you leave on safari, hang your hunting clothes outside and spray them down, according to the directions. Let them air dry. Now, pack them into big zip-lock bags. And, bring along a couple of bottles of the pump spray variety to treat your clothes while on safari.

The treatment lasts up to two weeks and will go through a wash cycle or two without losing its effect on ticks. I swear by this stuff in the turkey woods of Michigan and Wisconsin, which is where all ticks go when they die. In ten years of using this stuff, I have had one tick on me. I watched the thing crawl up my gloved finger, making it to the second knuckle, and then die. It may not be as exciting as watching them pop like a popcorn kernel under a flame, but this stuff is very cool.

And it even works to fend off other pests such as mosquitoes, black flies, deer flies, stable flies, and horseflies. I know it worked fairly well in the mosquito-infested grotto the morning of my bushbuck. I imagine it would work on tse-tse, mopane, and the other biting flies of Africa, too, though we did not encounter any of these flies on the safari. They don't live where we were, even in summer. I'm not complaining, either.

The oryx certainly saw us. If I were them, I would have been laughing at us. The oryx, relying on their superb camouflage, simply did not move. A tail may have twitched, an ear flickered, but I never saw such.

Spyker thought we might as well wait them out. The sun was quickly starting to head toward tomorrow. A purplish tinge was already showing in the east. They were nearly 300 yards away.

Doug takes his shooting seriously. He doesn't rely on shooting tables to tell him bullet drop. He makes sure he knows it by testing out to 300 yards at range near his home. He also doesn't believe in some factory worker to recalibrate the powder measure or the seating mechanism in the reloading process. He reloads his own, and to exacting standards.

Doug and Spyker got out of the car and walked/hobbled maybe 40 meters. Now the oryx were twitching and flicking; they were nervous.

Through the binoculars I watched as the oryx repositioned. They turned their bodies so that they would be heading up the hill if the flight response kicked in. They looked back over their right shoulders, trying to determine just what was out there and if it presented a threat. Their ears worked like a radar arch, front, back, left, right.

Both of these oryx were bulls, their horns thick. The front one took a step, and through the binoculars I saw a flash of white right behind the front leg, lung high. At the same time I saw the flash, I heard Doug's gun. The sucker should have fallen. Instead, both oryx beat feet over the hill.

Doug thought he shot well. I saw the flash of white. Spyker thought the shot was a good one, too. None of us could understand why an oryx, shot perfectly, acted as if nothing happened.

Spyker and I went up to the acacia. There was no blood. There was no hair. The flash of white was from a thick grey dead branch that matched the color of the hide exactly. None of us saw it. The branch had a small hole where the bullet struck and a mass of splinters of pure white behind it and angled down where the bullet exited. The bullet had hit the branch, angled down, and exited into the ground below. The oryx may have received a shower of sawdust, maybe an errant splinter. Nothing more.

On the drive back to camp, we came upon Pierre and Margaret. We told them our sad tale. They showed us their happy one. Margaret got her mountain reedbuck in the rocks, in between the grasses. The horns curved delicately up just beyond the tops of the ears.

The sunset, up on that plateau, was a happy one.

Margaret (joined by Isak) hunted hard for this mountain reedbuck. Up high in the rocks and the grass, these things are tough to see. They do have a pretty whistle, which gave this one away.

CHAPTER 14

Askari, Again

inner that night was full of Margaret's tale of her mountain reedbuck. How they heard the whistlelike call. How the small antelope almost flew in bounding leaps among the rocks and grasses. How there was only a small window of opportunity to shoot, and an even smaller target to shoot at.

Doug surprised all of us with a quick one-sentence tale of a long-horned impala he took in the morning and neglected to mention. Like the well-trained husband that he is, he made sure that this day was all about Margaret.

After dinner, Spyker and I announced that we were going back out; we had a date with a cat, or maybe a jackal.

Night hunting is a strange sport. Predator hunting is a strange sport. Here, in Africa, it takes on new meanings. Sure, where we are there are no large predators except for the hyena, whose tracks we see in the sand on an all too frequent basis. That cough we heard on the first day would have been a leopard anywhere else, but only small cats and jackals here—nothing to worry about.

That's an easy statement to make; it is much tougher to live by. When the light goes dark all sorts of critters, real and imagined, start to prowl and howl. It's when you become the hunted. As insane as that sounds, it is even more insane to relish the sport. Question my sanity, I love it, like a horror movie fan searches out his squeamishness, I search out the hunter.

I feel very comfortable in the north woods of the United States. I know the night. In Africa it's another story. Call it a comfort zone issue. Call it anything you want. Trepidatious may not be a real word, but, I like it better than 'fraidy-cat.

This was not the first night Spyker and I headed out after supper or stayed after the sun went down. However, it was the first time we actually had an area set up to work.

Setting up an area for predator hunting is an involved process. While Spyker is a virtuoso on the whistle, what we call a predator call, you need to set the table as well. Setting the table entails gathering the entrails from an animal you already have in the salt. You place these guts in a bucket, or simply in a pile in the back of the Rover, and drive to an open area where there is at least one good hiding place to sit

127

Doug with his impala. He's back in the game in a big way, broken leg and all.

along the edges. If you are very lucky, you find an area that has a small open knoll or knob.

After a few hours of the guts sitting in the sun, they do get a bit aromatic. This is a good thing. Once you have the area chosen, you gather up the guts in your hands. Using a strong wire or length of rope, you tie the guts into a loop on one end. You tie the other to the Rover and start driving, dragging the guts behind you. You do circles around the knob, you drive the trails leading into the opening, all the while trailing this wad of stink.

Then, once you think the area is well dragged with the stink, you drive back to the knob and place the pile on top. Now you chop down anything obstructing the view from wherever you'll be hiding. Grasses, shrubs, all of it comes down. After the chopping is done you rake the ground clean of any footprints or tire prints.

The goal, when all is finished, is to have the guts placed on the knoll, have the area raked clean, and have plenty of stink or scent trails leading to the pile. The scent is meant to attract the predators. The knoll is needed to give you a good line of sight when the time comes to shoot. Raking the area around the gut pile is used to see if anything comes by to visit while you are away.

Spyker and I, along with Cyril, had done all that using the guts of Doug's springbok from two days previous. Two days in the sun and they were well on their way from odoriferous to awful. Think gag reflex when the wind was right, or wrong, depending on your point of view.

We lasted just over two hours before calling it a night. The ground was cold beneath us. The wind was raw in our faces. Nothing Spyker could play on the whis-

tle brought in a night dancer. The perfume we set brought in nothing. Only
the Southern Cross and its neighbor
stars moved in our view.

Jackals did taunt us. We could hear
them yipping away behind us in the
high ground. Most likely from the
plateau. We could hear them in front of
us, over the gravel road in the unfenced
area. Once, when the world went still, a
hyena erupted from across the road, too.
That was a bit unnerving.

The morning brought new hope. It
always does. Doug and Margaret went
off with Pierre looking for kudu and
whatever else might come their way.
Doug did have a special mission. He
wanted to make like a bush.

Doug likes gadgets. He likes all
sorts of gadgets as long as they are
meant to make the hunting or fishing
experience more enjoyable. Actually I
think Doug just likes toys. He had
brought along a Ghillie suit, one of
those burlap monstrosities with flaps of
fabric hanging all over them that is supposed to make you disappear into the
woods and brush. These things are

That's me in the morning. It's chilly again, with
more than a little frost.

heavy. They get caught on every twig, every thorn. But they do work.

His plan was to have Pierre drop him off near some waterhole or off a well-
used game trail and see what comes by. The theory being that as he could not stalk
the way he wanted to with that broken leg of his, the animals should come to him.

After dropping Doug off, Margaret and Pierre would drive away and then begin
to hunt. Spyker, Cyril, and I wished them well, without laughing all that much, and
headed for the backside of Kameelkop. It was still quite dark as we made our way
up what was now named Ball Breaker Hill, leveled off in the plateau, and headed
across the frosted grass to the far south side of the property. Two oryx were sky-
lighted moving across a knob to the east in the early light of dawn. We watched
them walk off the knob, disappearing into the bush on the bottom.

The sun was now just hitting horizon. The grasses glowed on the plateau. Frost
on the rocks glimmered like skim ice in the soft light. By the time we hit the south
side of the plateau, it was awash in sunlight.

Spyker thought that the kudu we had seen the morning before might have come
from this far corner of the concession. Leaving the vehicle we walked down a game
trail covered in kudu prints into the bush.

Then there are these. Palm tree-looking, don't you think? Well over 12 feet tall, very bushy bark, these have a tendency to fall over when you really don't want them to. Best not to lean up against them. Besides, I'm told scorpions like to hang out under those shaggy bark "leaves."

The bush here wasn't all that thick. If you were patient, any kudu using this trail, or using the bush on either side, would offer a shot. It appeared as a tree-filled park with acacias and aloes every 10 yards or so and very short grass. Cyril kicked at the print-softened trail. The dust he kicked up went to the west. We left the trail, silently following the dust.

Seventy-five yards or so off the trail, Spyker motioned for a halt. A small rocky berm, no more than four feet tall, stretched 20 yards or so down the slope. We quietly maneuvered around the rocks and set up on the other side. From here we could see a good deal of the game trail both up and down the slope. We could see beyond the trail, through the loosely forested bush. We would wait for the kudu here.

And they came.

Just as the sun started to slowly trickle down the hill, and no more than ten minutes after we set up behind the berm, a group of kudu cows and calves walked down the slope, down the trail. Spyker got excited, looking behind the group. He saw horns, which got me excited and up on the sticks, ready to shoot. Just off the trail, on the other side, I saw a head and the base of the horns moving slowly down. They looked thick. They were thick.

Once in an opening, once in full view, I don't know who was more dis-appointed. The horns were short, and only a curl and a quarter. It was a puppy bull, still hanging out with his mom.

A kudu cow sauntered down the trail next, all alone. For nearly an hour, kudu of all shapes and sizes came down that trail. It was like dairy cattle going to the milking parlor. Actually they weren't *all* shapes and sizes, as there were no mature bulls among them, the largest stretching the tape to maybe the high 30s. In total, well over thirty of them came down that single trail in just over 90 minutes.

It's a funny thing, really. The kudu kept us on our toes. You just don't know when a good bull will come by. Every flash of gray, every sweep of any horn could be that one kudu of your dreams. They could be, but they weren't. Your adrenaline levels skyrocket. Your heart races. Your breathing quickens. Then it drops.

Over and over again your body goes through the pump-up and the letdown. I felt like I was drained. When, after 30 minutes of watching birds flit through the trees, Spyker said, "Enough," I felt as limp as a dish rag. A walk would do me good.

Although Spyker maintained a positive outlook, it was evident that he and I felt much the same. I thought about the big kudu the day before and how I might have gotten off a shot on him. A snap shot, needing more than luck. Kudu fever.

The walk back up to the Rover did both of us good. Sweat does that. Feeling troubled, or overwhelmed? Do some physical work. Work it out.

"Okay," said Spyker, "There's lots of kudu here. There must be a good bull. Maybe the one from yesterday. Let's find him. Get in."

Cyril drove with Spyker and I in back, scanning the trail leading down the mountain and farther south. This road was steeper than on the other side and full of switchbacks. With the addition of a sandy base, it was more enjoyable than Ball-Breaker. We could actually look for animals rather than hanging on for dear life.

We found them, too. A herd of a dozen or so zebra just off the road to the east. If it wasn't for an errant tail switch, we would have missed them. A cow eland plodded in a shallow ravine off to the right.

No more than fifteen minutes later, and near the bottom of the hill, more kudu. I refused to get excited. I had seen too many already. They were walking down the trail, the same trail we had been looking at from the rock berm. They had to be cows.

Spyker rapped on the cab with his fist, a signal for Cyril to stop. Spyker grabbed his binoculars and started scanning. "Dan. Kudu," he whispered.

"Yup, saw them. All cows."

"Oh, so now you're the professional hunter? Dan, you always have to be ready."

Christ, I never felt so crappy while hunting. Of course, he was right. Binoculars let you see more besides seeing farther. And it's true that you always, always need to be ready. Here I was, in Africa, hunting kudu. And, while I hadn't given up, I had lost the edge.

Spyker was kind. If I were him, I think I would have grabbed myself by the shirt collar and given myself a rough shake. I did give myself a solid kick in the ass and got back in the game.

The group did turn out to be all cows. The next group was a different story. Turning west near the bottom of the hill, we skirted the hill. The road didn't separate anything. It only served as a path through the much thicker bush. Kudu below us would be safe. There was no way to see through it downhill. Uphill was the only way to look.

A half mile or maybe more down the trail, I softly slapped the roof of the cab. "Kudu," I whispered. I had seen a flash of gray maybe 100 yards uphill. At least I thought I did. I hoped they were kudu. I wanted Spyker to know I was back.

"Up the hill, maybe 2 o'clock, 100 yards."

"Okay. I got them. Dan, there's a bunch of bulls in there."

I hadn't seen the bulls. I did see the cows.

"Where? I see the cows."

"Above them, maybe 25 meters, and to the left."

I saw legs, I saw patches of bodies. And then, walking in between two aloes in a sea of acacias, a kudu bull was walking east. Followed by another.

"Dan, there are four of them at least. One behind the other."

I don't remember leaving the Rover. I just remember finding myself 200 yards or so behind the truck and trying to walk as silently as I could behind Spyker as we climbed the hill. Spyker laid out the sticks and I got on them. And we waited.

We heard them before we saw them. A rock tumbled. A twig snapped. I swear I heard the click of hooves. If the kudu continued the way they seemed to be coming, they would pass above us at no more than 50 yards.

And they did. All five of them, each a cookie cutter of the others, passed by. None sported headgear greater than the mid-40s. It would have been easy to be disappointed. I was elated. We got close. We got close enough to smell them, the breeze kicking their scent down the hill to us. They didn't know we were there. Any of them could have ended their life at that spot.

After they passed, and after we waited a good 30 minutes to see if these "Askaris," or lieutenants, were marching in front of the granddaddy, Spyker and I looked at each other and smiled. We were elated. While it may seem a hollow victory, it was anything but.

"Mr. Donarski, those were all nice kudu. Now you've seen a nice one up close. It's time to get close to a great one. We will. Don't worry."

I did think, briefly, of Ruark and Hemingway, of how they struggled for kudu. We are struggling, too, but we're close. Ruark and Hemingway were close, but I doubt this close. If at no other time, I felt like the hunt was now joined.

Back at the truck we continued on the trail skirting the hillside. Going around a tight turn, ducking from the thorn-filled branches that now covered the trail in a hideous arch, I thought I heard something. I tapped the roof.

"What?" asked Spyker.

"I swear I heard something. A voice, I think."

Poaching is still a problem. Not a major problem, but a problem, and I thought I heard a voice. Spyker, Cyril ,and I scanned the area. Nothing. Not a sound even.

We started to drive off. I heard it again. I tapped the roof again. Again we got out and scanned. Nothing.

"Dan, you're hearing things. It might have been a baboon, but I really think the sun has cooked your brains."

As we climbed into the Rover, a voice boomed from the hillside above us. "I'm no baboon." And a hearty laugh rang down. "Jesus, I've been called a lot of things but never a baboon!"

It was Doug. His voice and his hearty laugh are unmistakable. "Where the hell are you?" I asked.

"Over here."

Cyril desperately wanted his picture taken with him holding my gun. He was quite an actor and camped for the camera at every opportunity.

We looked. He sounded very close. We couldn't find him.

"Okay, move your arm, Doug," I asked. "We'll come up and help you."

"I don't need any help. This Ghillie suit is pretty effective, don't you think?" With that he waved an arm. No more than 25 yards in front of us, tucked in next to an aloe with waist-high grass surrounding it, Doug stood up. Effective doesn't begin to describe the camouflage job this suit did for him. I want one now.

Doug hobbled down on his crutches, looking like a moving bush. When he got down to us, he quickly got out of the suit. It looked like he went swimming. Sweat drenched him head to toe. It ran in rivers down his face. "These things are really good, but they are really warm, too," he said.

I don't want one anymore.

Over the morning Doug had a group of impala within 10 yards feeding in front of him. A group of kudu cows came by no more than 20 yards away. A flock of Guinea fowl had a few of their members walk on the edges of the suit.

"It's time to feed the bear!" announced Doug. When Doug is hungry, we eat. A quick radio call to Pierre told him we had Doug with us, and back to the camp we drove.

When we arrived, Anneli had just returned from Durban with Dave and Mary in tow, back from their trip to Cape Town. We were all together again.

After the usual hearty brunch, and after catching up with Dave and Mary, Spyker and I gathered them both up and drove to a dam in the northwest section of the property. Dave and Mary wanted to sit on a waterhole and see what developed.

The dam was located at the base of the mountain. High rolling hills rose up immediately behind the waterhole. Acacias and aloes grew in a thick mass surrounding the sand-colored water. Tracks from warthogs, impala, kudu, and a host of

TOURING SOUTH AFRICA

Telling someone you are going to South Africa is like telling someone you are going to Europe. South Africa is a big place. Of all the habitats found in the world, all but one is found here. (In case you are wondering, the one not found here is the arctic habitat.)

When you choose to go on safari, you might as well do as Dave and Mary did, and see more of the country. A few extra days isn't going to break the bank.

Cape Town, and its namesake, Cape Point, is just one area. Besides being at the bottom of the country, the farthest point south, it also serves as the location where the Atlantic and Indian oceans meet. Table Rock, one of the most common photos you see of South Africa, is found here. From Cape Town you are only a short distance away from one of the finest grape-growing and winemaking areas on the entire planet. It is well worth the stay.

Then there is the Garden Drive, a driving tour through immense forests and lands filled with wildflowers, and the previously mentioned Drakensberg Mountains with unbelievable natural beauty and more than a handful of serious art galleries and even artists' colonies.

Farther up the Indian Ocean coast, the area surrounding Richards Bay offers a wealth of choices. From touring Imfolozi National Park to the spectacular beaches, there's plenty to do—like cruising the Greater St. Lucia Wetland Park or visiting Shakaland, where the Zulus still live as they did 200 years ago.

Kruger Park in the northeast is very well known. Nearby, a rare piece of land called Vendaland traces the natives back even farther than Shakaland. Kimberly, with her diamond mines, is yet another option.

---

other game were cast in the soft mud along the edges and hardened to rock where the sun had baked the earth.

Cyril and Spyker found a spot of high ground just 10 meters or so from the water's edge. There they cleared and leveled an area about 8 by 4 feet. An acacia stood on either end of the area. Now the cutting and building began.

The work is not done haphazardly. Only a branch from here, another from there, and maybe another one. Then it's the same from a spot no closer than 10 meters away. The goal is to keep the thickness, only taking a limb or two from any one area. By the time Cyril and Spyker were finished cutting, they were a good fifty meters away.

Spyker took two camp chairs from the Rover and placed them between the acacias. He had Dave and Mary sit in the chairs. Then he and Cyril began building the blind around them. When they were finished a good hour and a half later, we left them with a healthy supply of water and the promise to be back in an hour or so. Back at the Rover, I looked for the blind. I couldn't find it.

Over the next hour we drove from waterhole to waterhole, looking for tracks of a big kudu. While both Spyker and I wished to take the kudu on a walk and stalk,

You'll notice that, except for Cape Town, I didn't mention any large cities. I don't like large cities. If you do, I'm told that Durban is quite nice. Parts of Johannesburg, too. I fly in there and out of there. That's all I want to do with big cities.

Dave and Mary took their tour in the middle of their safari. No offense to Dave and Mary, but I don't think that was a wise choice. For my money, I'd do the touring before the hunt. Touring prior to the hunt allows you to recover from jet lag before you are asked to pull the trigger. Doing the tour before the hunt also starts your time in Africa at a relaxed pace. And, because you are doing it before, you won't be tempted to skip the tour and extend the hunt instead. If you are traveling with someone who is only going along to appease you, do the touring first.

The other good option is to do it last. It's something to look forward to. You are going to be tempted to skip it and continue hunting. Again, if that appeasing someone is along with you, do the tour. In the end, you'll be glad you did.

The problem with doing the tour in the middle of the safari is you are changing speed twice, rather than once. That's a hard thing to do.

A good outfitter or professional hunter will have contacts all over the country. Some even lead touring safaris when they aren't hunting. Before you set up a tour with a travel agent, someone who likely hasn't been there and done that, ask your outfitter or PH. They have been there and done that. Take their recommendations. Have them make suggestions on your itinerary. These people stake their reputation on the recommendations. They won't blow it on a chump's tour.

we also wanted a fallback plan: that if we couldn't go to the kudu, maybe the kudu would come to us.

We found tracks, big tracks. We found big tracks at nearly all of the waterholes. There seemed to be no pattern, the kudu were being kudu, going where they wanted when they wanted.

Back at the waterhole blind, we gathered up Mary and dropped off Cyril. Dave decided that he wanted to stay and see what developed. After dropping Mary off back at camp, we returned to the blind with more water and food for Dave.

Driving up we saw a warthog, a huge warthog. Still a good 100 yards from the blind, the pig ran hell-bent-for-leather up onto the berm and stood still. We expected a shot, as Dave really wanted a Poombah. None came.

We yelled for Dave to shoot. Dave yelled back, "Nope. Got one."

Dave had taken a warthog in the short time we were gone. It wasn't a big pig, but it's the one that Dave saw in his dreams and the one that would have a place on the mantle back home. Size doesn't matter, at times. What does is the take, the setting. In this case, a group of pigs had come down to drink. After watching them for

Dave checks to make sure he has a shooting lane before the upper section is put on the blind. It takes a fair amount of time to get things right. It takes a fair amount of blood, too. Those thorns reach out and bite you.

five or so minutes, Dave took one, the largest of the bunch, and, in his words, the ugliest. Four big and hairy warts, scruffy coat, and caked in mud. So ugly it was almost cute.

It was only just after 1 P.M. Dave wanted to stay at the waterhole for the rest of the afternoon with Cyril, again to see what might develop. Spyker and I loaded the pig into the Rover and hustled back to the skinning shed. Just as quickly, we drove off for the far eastern end of the property looking for kudu.

To be honest, we probably wasted the afternoon. That is my fault. I began doubting the land, the hunt, the kudu. I was, in a word, discombobulated.

Don't let anyone tell you that kudu don't get into your head like a bad dream. Sure, maybe you get lucky and one prances out all nice and pretty-like. You make the shot easily and the kudu dies easily. No fuss, no muss. Maybe that's the way it was with yours, or will be with yours. It wasn't for me.

Askari bulls barked and laughed at us. Cows giggled. Hell, even the warthogs showed us no respect. It was not a good showing for me. I needed a break. I told Spyker so.

"Hey, let's get to a high spot and watch the sun go down. I don't give a damn about the kudu this afternoon. We have an hour before sunset. Get me where I can see it disappear."

"You sure?"

"Damn sure. I need to relax and calm down."

We drove up onto the high plain and to where it plunges down. The sky to the east was already turning a dark blue. Spyker climbed up into the back with me and shook a cigarette out of his pack.

"Want one?"

We worked late into the day, never losing hope that we'd see a trophy kudu.

"Yup, maybe two."

Then he reached into the cooler box. "How 'bout one of these?"

He was holding a couple cans of beer. "Hell, yeah."

"I was saving this for when you shot your kudu today. Guess that's not going to happen. Only one, though. We're going back out tonight."

The beer wasn't cold, but it was cool. It cut the dust. The cigarette was harsh but soothing. It buzzed my head.

Far off in the distance we heard a shot. Doug and Margaret were out there somewhere. We toasted in hopes of their success.

Once the sun had disappeared, we drove the 30 minutes to gather up Dave and Cyril. Back at camp we found it was Margaret who had shot. They had just returned, and something was really stinking up the joint.

Seems a kudu bull, a very nice one, had fallen for Margaret. Clinton was the first to come upon it in the fading light. As he was reaching around the neck to pull it up for a good look, his hand had found something soft and slimy. He pulled away quickly.

At the base of the neck, on the opposite side, was a gaping open sore, a sore festering with maggots and rotten flesh and pus. Clinton's hand was now covered in the ooze. Without thinking, he tried to shake it off. That only spread the mess all over his clothes in thick droplets. Then, again without thinking about anything except getting the stuff off his hands, he wiped it on his pants. Big mistake.

I'm told that just about then, Clinton yakked, more than once. From what I was smelling now, I wouldn't doubt it for a moment that he yakked a third time. A cesspool could take lessons from what Clinton smelled like.

This was the first kudu we took. Margaret was the shooter. Her expression and Clinton's are due to a rather pungent smell coming from the side of the kudu you don't see. This one had a helluva infection. You can see where it starts just on the upper back.

This cute little guy is called a genet. Spotted on the body and with rings on the tail, he's a nocturnal critter. Or was until a few hours ago. Now he's a small rug.

The skinners weren't all that happy. Clinton certainly was not happy either. Margaret, on the other hand, couldn't have been smiling brighter. She had her kudu. I admired it from a good 10 yards away.

As it turns out, there was a good probability that a poacher's bullet had wounded the kudu many days earlier. A small caliber bullet was found under that mess during the skinning process.

After dinner all of us went night hunting. Sort of. Night hunting is always tough. With a group it is almost foolhardy. We did learn about the Big Magellanic Cloud and the Little Magellanic Cloud from Dave and Marge. Both are galaxies and both very visible in the crisp and clear night sky here.

We found nightjars, their eyes glowing red in the sandy road. Duikers sprang from the grass as we drove past. An owl swept through the lights silently. Impala scampered slowly alongside the car as we made our way back to camp. Clinton even reached out and slapped one on the ass.

Then, just before we got to camp, we saw green eyes glowing from the trees. "Genet!" hissed Spyker.

I grabbed the shotgun and ran after Spyker. A genet cat is almost weasel-like. A spotted coat with a ringed tail, it is a handsome creature of the night. I wanted one. The shotgun barked, the genet fell.

CHAPTER 15

A Horn and a Half and the Full Monty

This morning Spyker, Cyril, and I left for the unfenced area. We needed a change, in scenery and in luck. No more driving today. Today we'd be on foot. We parked the Rover in the same place we parked the first day at Kameelkop. No sooner had we gathered our kit than Spyker's radio hissed.

"Spyker, Pierre here. I need you. Uncle Doug just shot a kudu. We need your help finding it." Isak was with Pierre. Isak is Spyker's best tracker. This one probably wasn't going to be any fun.

"Go. Cyril and I will stay and hunt here. You're bad luck anyway. Go and help," I said.

I didn't want him to leave. I trusted him. Yet, a wounded animal is something everyone pitches in on. He was needed. He went. But not before pulling Cyril over to the side and speaking sternly to him in Afrikaans. While I'm not sure, I'm guessing what was being said went something like this: "Cyril, take this stupid American and hunt him hard. Hunt him smart. He needs his kudu. Don't get his sorry ass hurt. Don't shoot a small one. For God's sake and the sake of your children, don't screw up."

For the next two hours Cyril and I slowly walked through the rolling hills and into the dongas. Ten steps and glass. Ten steps and glass. When we got to an opening, we glassed hard on the other side, hoping to pick out a flash of gray. Nothing.

Cyril then led me up the highest hill on the far south side of the concession. He figured from up on high we might be able to catch a group moving rather than stumbling into them. The hill was mish-mash of jagged rocks, waist-high grass smelling of cloves, a few scattered acacias, and a loose forest of incredibly tall aloes. Some of the aloes still had the summer flowers on top, beautiful spikes of orange, red, and yellow crowning the palm-tree-like trunk. The view from on top was spectacular.

Across the road in the fenced area, the mountain stood sentinel, jutting into a deep blue sky. Greens and gold cascaded down its face. Exposed black rock appeared as ink blots. The sky above had scattered clouds. Shadows from these moved across the mountain, moved across the aloes and acacias, moved across the herd of impala grazing in an opening 400 yards below us. Giraffe moved through the forest, their heads like balloons floating above the canopy.

Cyril offered me a cigarette, which I took. I leaned back on a broad red rock, soaking up the warmth, watching the clouds drift by, listening to the doves laugh, the hornbills scream, the hoo-pooes, well, hoop it up.

I was still interested in kudu, very interested. Now, however, the day was just too fine. My legs were sore from the scramble up the hill. I was a bit tired. That rock was every bit as comfortable as a feather bed.

"Boss, boss! Kudu!" I must have dozed off in the sun. Cyril was shaking me awake. Like the professional he is, he continued to watch and glass. He had seen kudu.

Below us, and working along the top of the far side of the broad donga that split the lower flats like a jagged lightning bolt, small dots of gray ambled to the west. Through my binoculars I could see those corkscrew horns ascending from two of their heads. "Come, come!"

We headed down and to the west. Scrambling over the rocks on the way down was a lot harder than going up. Cyril kept up a blistering pace. He walked and trotted like an antelope. I did the same, only like a stumbling drunk antelope.

Once back on level ground, that blistering pace turned to a third-degree burn. Taking up a two-track trail, Cyril cut west for a good third of a mile. The sand underneath was soft and quiet. When he cut south into the bush, into the heavy thorn cover, it was still soft, but not so quiet. Cornflakes would have been quieter to walk on. Fallen leaves and twigs littered the ground. Walking here was as loud as on a crispy, heavily frosted predawn morning in the northern deer woods. We slowed considerably.

This is a donga, a big donga. You would probably call it a dry riverbed, which is exactly what it is. The minerals in the ground paint the sand in reds and yellows. It compares well to a small-scale Badlands from the prairie states.

When we came on a game trail heading in our general direction, we took it. On the trails, we made time on the kudu, which, by the way, we hadn't seen from the time we left the top of the hill. When we cut back generally south, it was back to the thorns and the cornflakes. Cyril stopped beside an acacia standing nearly 12 feet tall. "Boss. Wait. I'm going to the donga."

Cyril left to see if the kudu were still making their way along the donga. He returned ten minutes later with a big grin on his face. "They are ahead of us, maybe 300 meters. Still walking slowly. We'll swing back and get ahead of them. There is a nice bull. I'm not sure if it is a great bull."

That was more than he had said all day. His English carried a slight British accent, and I remember thinking that it sounded very prim and proper.

The wind was with us, blowing from the kudu to us in a gentle, steady breeze. We wasted no time. Cornflakes or no, dear Cyril picked up the pace. Thorns now tore into my clothes, my forearms, my face. The chase was on.

The jog through the thorns ended about 100 yards from the donga. A small grassy opening separated us from the edge. We used the scrub surrounding the opening as a bit of cover and slowly worked our way to the edge.

"I know we are ahead of them. Unless they went further into the bush, but I think they are still coming." Cyril set up the sticks between two thorn bushes that reached in an arc meeting each other over our head.

Just a couple of moments later, he tapped me on the shoulder. His long bony finger pointed a bit to the east. I shook my head. I couldn't see them. Still pointing east, he moved it in an arc, which I took to mean that the kudu were inside the bush a bit. They were.

They came up slowly, stopping here and there to browse. Stopping to see if all was right in their world. Their ears rotated sharply, searching for a sound that would send them barking and running. Their noses sniffed the wind.

The donga was nearly 50 yards across. The wind continued its slight steady blow, sending our scent to the north and east. Everything was perfect. Except for the fact that they were coming ever so slowly. The wait was painful.

The kudu were directly across from us now, but no shot was offered. I wasn't going to shoot through trees, even if the kudu horns I saw were big. There were two bulls. One looked to be a shooter.

There was no way we could move. We watched them as they marched by us in the brush on the other side. Then a calf angled to the edge, followed by a cow. They made it to the edge and started down into the dry river bottom. They were now only 100 yards away. If they brought the others with them, this would be very cool.

It was very cool. Four more cows and a calf joined the first two. All walked down to the river bottom. Then, one by one, they started up our side of the donga and disappeared behind a cut in the bank.

We waited silently there for five minutes before Cyril again tapped me on the shoulder. He had a big smile on his face. A nod of his head toward the other side sent my eyes following. A kudu bull, the smaller of the two, was coming out. He followed the cows and calves down into the river bottom and disappeared as they did.

"Boss Dan, the big one is there, too. He's a smart one and is waiting," Cyril whispered.

Maybe he was, maybe he wasn't. He certainly didn't show himself in the next half hour. Cyril shrugged. I just shook my head. This was almost funny. So close. Oh, so close. I actually laughed. I wanted to cry . . . until I shrieked, which made Cyril roll to the ground in laughter. A huge spider, one with a shiny, fat, black body the size of a half-dollar with ugly black legs and yellow rings—it was dangling off the brim of my cap no more than two inches in front of my face. I do not like spiders. Not one bit.

I swept my hand in front of my face, which put the spider squarely on my cheek. I slapped my cheek, which hurt like hell and pushed it onto my arm. Finally I got it off me, dancing and prancing like an old lady seeing a mouse in a cartoon.

Once he recovered, which did take some time, Cyril told me, "Dan, the whole time we were watching that young bull I watched the spider come out of thorns and drop on your cap. Then I watched him move all over your head and neck while we waited for the big bull. I thought you were just very good at ignoring him as you didn't want to make a sound or move."

"Christ, what kind was that?"

"We call them bread and butter spiders. They're harmless. Big, but harmless."

Harmless, my ass! The thing gave me the willies. I demanded a cigarette. Now that British lilt to his voice sounded aloof.

It was almost three hours from when Spyker left us. Both of us were getting hungry. We headed back through the thorns, Cyril cautioning me whenever we came near a spider web, which he thought hilarious. Once on the trail we walked back toward the west end of the property. Spyker was just pulling in when we came to the gate.

"Uncle Doug got his kudu," he announced. "Be nice to him; it only has a horn and a half, and he feels like shit."

Thoughts of Ruark throwing his deformed kudu horns into that river in Tanzania in disgust washed over me. I felt sorry for him. Christ, what a deal. But, not make fun? What's a buddy for?

Back at camp I walked up to Doug. "Well done, sir. A horn and a half for a leg and a half." The room got quite silent.

Doug looked up at me, raised an eyebrow, picked up a crutch, and proceeded to belly laugh. That broke the ice.

Yes, it was true. Doug was initially not a happy camper. He was a bit miffed. Make that pissed. Neither he nor Pierre could see the broken horn through the tangle of bush surrounding the kudu's crown. They could just see that big beautiful horn. Doug shot. The kudu fell. Then it ran some.

According to reliable reports, Doug was crushed when the kudu was found and it was discovered that the right horn was broken off just above the first curl. Like me, he desperately wanted a kudu. He thought the gods mocked him.

When Doug saw the bittersweet humor in it all, he rejoiced. He was able to recall the morning, light dappling through the acacias and dancing across the kudu's sides. He saw the kudu stretching out that thick neck of his, reaching to get that tender leaf or bud. When he did this, the bittersweet turned into simply sweet—the simply sweet beauty of the entire day and of the kudu.

Doug and his brother, the kudu. I mean it. They are related. See Doug? He's got a leg and a half. See the kudu? It has a horn and a half. Pretty fitting, don't you think?

After brunch I found out that Mary wanted to go on a game drive. Dave wanted to go sit on the waterhole again. So Spyker and I drove Dave to the waterhole, dropped him off, and proceeded to take Mary on a game drive.

Okay, I'm not always a happy-go-lucky guy. Hell, I wanted to hunt. I wanted my kudu. Any time spent doing anything less than hunting for my kudu was a waste. Spyker must have sensed my thoughts. "Dan, we'll be out after that kudu soon," he said. "C'mon, this will be fun."

God bless Mary. And Spyker. Five minutes into the game drive, which took us to the eastern side of the fenced area, and I was enjoying the drive every bit as much as Mary. The sky was bright. There was a nice soft breeze.

Ostriches sauntered on the edge of the forest. Impala leaped for the sky when we got too close. Blesbok rocked and rolled. Two zebras zipped by in a show of who was faster. This drive was perfect. My head was back on straight. Certainly I wanted the kudu. I'd get it, too. Maybe. When the time was right. Or not.

Termite mounds littered the grasslands. Small dongas slashed across the plains. Then a springbok leaped out of the grass no more than 10 meters from the Rover and ran 50 meters before stopping and lying down next to a termite mound.

Something was wrong. It didn't run like a springbok. The springbok was a female. The females are also horned but much less showy than the rams. The female sports thin, spindly horns that don't have the distinctive lire shape of the rams.

Spyker tried to walk up on it, but whenever he got close the antelope ran away. Not far, but away. After three tries the springbok took off over a grassy hill and disappeared.

"Mary, do you want a springbok?"

"Dave already has one, so no."

"Mary, we have to shoot this one anyway. It's hurt. One of us has to shoot it."

"Mary, come on," I said. "We were with you when you took that hartebeest. We're with you now. Spyker is offering you a springbok. Take it."

"Is it really hurt?"

"Yes, Mary, it is. It is hurt bad. I can't tell from what, but it is slowly dying. We need to take it out."

"Well then. Okay."

Spyker and Cyril looking for that springbok, the one that seems a bit off.

This was great. We found the springbok just over the rise. Like each time before, it ran off as we got close. This time, rather than lying down, the ewe stood broadside to us at about 80 yards. Mary got behind the sticks and, just as she had done with the hartebeest, squeezed the trigger just so. The springbok fell over, its coat blending into the golden grass.

We got up to it just as the flare of fur along its spine lifted, then fell as its spirit left the earth. "Well done, Mary, well done," said Spyker.

I hugged her. "Nicely done."

"Guys, I'm shaking again." And she was. She was shaking a lot.

"Mary, that happens all the time. Don't worry about it."

"But I'm shaking as much as the first time. It shouldn't be that bad, should it?"

"Mary," said Spyker, "it happens all the time with every animal. Enjoy it. It's a free drug. Adrenaline."

After the photos were taken and Mary went back to the Rover, Spyker and I found an ugly ulcer located between the two hind legs. It was green and black and blue and red. Infection ran up and down the insides of both rear legs from the groin to the knee in bright red seeping lines. Poor thing must have been in some sort of pain. Besides taking a ewe to keep Dave's ram happy on the wall, Mary put a quick end to what must have been a slow, miserable death.

When we met with Dave, he hugged his wife and admired the springbok. Then he said, out of Mary's earshot, that he would talk to us later. I'm quite delighted to report that later never did come.

Doug and Marge and the rest of the party were still back at camp. Doug and Marge taking a power nap, the rest drinking their third gallon of coffee and having a smoke. Still in the glow of Mary's success, I grabbed a Coke Light and lit one up myself, from Spyker's pack. Then another from Pierre's.

No more problems for the springbok. Mary took it cleanly and is all smiles. With the second bullet she ever fired from a rifle, she took the second animal she has hunted. Dave and Mary are quite a pair. A pair of blesbok and now a pair of springbok. Dave didn't think the springbok was such a good idea. He wasn't with us, so his opinion didn't count.

"Dan, you and Spyker should head out. Take Clinton and Isak with you. It's early, but you never know."

It took all of ten seconds, and we were loaded and headed off down the trail through the acacias and thorns to the grassland border. Impala, including a massive ram, just walked out of the trail when we came by. An ostrich swiveled its head watching us go past. Then a quick turn to the left and on up Ball Breaker Hill.

Rocks bounced underneath. Our asses bounced off the seat, which bounced off the frame, which bounced off the bowling balls we were driving over. Clinton drove, and, according to the tonal qualities of words in Afrikaans being spoken by Spyker, who for the first time was riding in back instead of driving, he was not doing that good of a job in missing the big rocks. Actually I think it was one of the smoothest rides I've had up that hill.

Spyker slapped the hood softly. "Clinton, stop!" he whispered harshly. Grabbing his binoculars, he scanned into the bush on the right. "A waterbuck. Damn. Okay, go." And off again, bouncing all the way up. Almost.

There's a little step on this trail. Well not so little, really. Maybe 20 inches tall, it stands straight up and comes in a portion of the trail that is quite steep. The Rover didn't make it the first time. Clinton snubbed the clutch. Nor did it make it up the step the second time, another snub. Clinton then coasted down the hill 10 yards or so, wound the revs up to a high squeal, and released the clutch in a sudden lurch.

When we hit the step, we bounced. We bounced up and backwards. The tires grabbed again, and, still spinning quite nicely thank you, we bounced up and over.

If your tongue had been between your teeth, you'd no longer have had a tongue. We did need to repack and rearrange the gear in the back.

Ahead I could see the opening that marked the entrance to the high plain. And a kudu walked through my view across the road from right to left. Maybe a professional hunter has a sixth sense, I don't really know. What I do know is that Spyker grabbed my arm and pulled me out of the Rover. Isak handed me my rifle, and Spyker and I trotted off to the left through a scattered growth of scrub and small acacias. We weren't 50 yards from the truck and heading toward a steep ravine. "Dan, here they come."

A group of kudu began an entrance from the right. I saw a bunch of cows, and I saw horns. The cows I had a good view of, the horns were just that, horns. Everything else was hidden in the acacias and small knob.

We could tell they were nervous—noses high in the air, moving at a stately trot from right to left and coming toward us. I could still see the horns, and Spyker could too.

"Dan, it's him. The one from the first morning. Get a bullet in him, get it in him somewhere in the body. We'll find him."

The bull disappeared, as the cows did, behind another knob. The cows came out, still trotting, noses still in the air. No bull.

Then, just on the left edge of the knob, I saw movement. It was a nose, followed by a face and the horns. It was lower on the hill than the cows. I saw the horns. "Him, you sure?"

"Dan, when he clears, take him. It's the one we want."

He never really cleared. He continued low, the brush and grass covering his body. He must have come on a small tussock, hidden by the grass. I could see the upper third of his body just 80 yards away. The crosshairs settled on his spine.

I don't remember the trigger pull or the push or the noise. I remember seeing the kudu fall over through the scope and, still in the scope, saw the legs come up through the grass and go back down.

"Spot on! He's yours! Dan! You have a kudu. A real trophy kudu!"

Isak and Clinton came running from the truck. They were on us before I could walk more than a few steps.

"Dan, go and see your kudu." I looked back and saw Spyker grab Clinton and Isak. "Let Mr. Donarski walk up on his kudu by himself. He deserves it. He earned it. Dan, mind the horns, and the legs. Come in from the back."

I didn't realize it at the time, but that gesture of walking up on my kudu alone still means the world to me. Hunting, for me anyway, is highly personal. Certainly I like to share it with others. But, at the same time, it is I who killed; it should be I who gives private thanks.

He was beautiful. Larger than I thought, more majestic, more everything. The horns spiraled from the top, his head heavy and black, tipped in nearly three inches of ivory. He sported a heavy mane, a full beard, and white stripes cascading down from his back.

"Uh, Dan, can we come see him now?" I don't know how long it took Spyker to ask that question. The time was right: I had already wiped my eyes (more than once), I had given thanks, and now it was time to share.

That's my kudu lying in the grass. Finally. And that's me making sure it isn't going anywhere but on my wall.

"Christ, yes! Someone grab the cameras."

Clinton and Spyker scrambled down, followed by Isak and the camera bag. Spyker slapped me on the back. Clinton hugged me. Isak whistled and gave me a big thumbs-up. Isak went over and stroked the kudu's horns. Using his hands, he measured the length. He stroked its fur. And then he came over, "Boss, kudu is good." And with that he grabbed my hand and shook it with a big grin on his face.

"Clinton, go back to camp and get some help. And Clinton, do it quick and be sure to bring Mr. Donarski his scotch. This one we'll toast here."

Isak and Spyker got busy hacking down brush and grass so we could get some good photos. They also had to hack out a primitive path to get the Rover down to the kudu.

I went off to the side and wiped my eyes again. This kudu came easy. The hunt, the number of days searching for a kudu, was long and both emotionally and physically hard. I had walked many miles. Climbed more than a few hills. Yet as far as a single hunt goes, this one early afternoon hunt was easy. Sweat didn't break. Breathing wasn't labored.

On the first afternoon at Kameelkop, I remember telling Pierre that I really hoped I didn't see a shooter that day because it would be almost like cheating, too easy. That I wanted my kudu to come hard. I wanted to earn it.

I remember Pierre giving me a quizzical look. Then he said something like, "Never pass up on a good kudu. Some come easy, some come hard, some not at all. Dan, don't be foolish. Don't spit in Africa's eye."

Maybe the gods mocked me those many days and miles. Maybe I had given off bad karma and jinxed myself up until now. All I know is that I worked my butt off for kudu, and when it came, the kudu was well earned.

Those are pretty impressive corkscrews. A quick hand measure says they go 54 inches. All I know is that they are the end result of a lot of miles and a lot of sweat.

Pierre and the others arrived 30 minutes later. The scotch arrived, too. I like my scotch chilled. This was warm. Still, it was the best scotch I have ever tasted. It was taken directly from the bottle.

Francois Heynes, the land manager of Kameelkop, and his wife, Petra, came up with the rest of our party. "Dan, that is the largest taken off this land in over a year. A very fine kudu."

In a heavy Afrikaans accent, Petra came up, hugged me, and said, "Dan, I told you the very first morning that the proof is in the salt. After you saw him that first day, you thought you had him. Now the proof *is* in the salt."

I just smiled. Then I saw the well-fitted T-shirt she was wearing. Emblazoned broadly across the chest were these words, "Out of your league." I chuckled. My smile grew wider as I simply said, "You, my dear, are absolutely right. On both counts." Then I hugged her.

When the kudu was loaded into the Rover, Spyker and I grabbed up Isak and headed for the skinning shed. Everyone else was going hunting. After dropping the kudu off, Isak got to work.

"Spyker, let's go for a drive and get some photos. I'm done hunting today, maybe done for good on this trip. Besides, the scotch doesn't mix well with guns."

We drove along the hills heading to the west where the grass meets the bush. A group of four huge eland bulls simply watched us pass from 20 yards. We passed the dam with the blind and a huge warthog squirted up the hill. Kudu cows tracked us with their ears and eyes. Eventually we made our way up the backside of the high hill and onto the plateau.

"Let's go see what we find on the east side, where the small river cuts through the grass. We should stretch our legs a bit."

I followed Spyker through the grass to a ridgetop overlooking the small river valley. There was a small hill just off to our right. Trees shaded us. There, across the river and on the opposite hillside, was another kudu bull.

He was lying down in the grass no more than 250 yards away. "Dan, it is a good thing you shot the one you did when you did. This one is a shooter, too, but not so big. Yours measures 54 inches, this one goes 50, maybe 51."

Spyker slid a couple of cigarettes out of his pack and passed one over. We sat on a rock and just watched the kudu resting in the bright afternoon sun. He was a solid mass of gray on a sea of green and had not a care in the world. A stalk here would have been easy.

Francois Heynes, the land manager of Kameelkop, and his wife, Petra, came up to join our party. Petra was a firecracker, out of my league. Yours, too.

The scotch whisky was a toast to my kudu. And, yes, the gun was put away before the bottle was given to me. And, no, it wasn't full.

Thirty minutes or so later, I got a whiff of something. It was sweet. Not sweet like the blackjack grasses or the flowers from the remaining aloes, but sweet. "Smell that?" I asked.

Spyker sniffed. "That's kudu." A minute or so later a group of three cows walked down toward the river no more than 20 yards away from us. The bull saw them, too. And he wasted no time in getting up and coming over to meet them at the river. Once they walked off, we did too.

Around the knoll I smelled something a bit stronger. "Okay, this is different, Spyker. It's heavier but still sweet." On the backside were a group of waterbuck cows. The bull, and it was a huge one, was a good 100 yards away. "Dan, that nose of yours is getting good. You're right; waterbuck smells a bit stronger."

"Do you want to sit up here and wait for sunset like we did a few days ago?"

"Let's go back to camp early instead. I'll get cleaned up, pour another drink, and watch the sun set below the mountain from camp."

There was a half hour or so of sun left when I had my drink and pulled a chair out to watch the end of the day. In the ever-lengthening shadows of night, the sounds began. Laughing doves called. A pair of ducks came sliding into the dam. Impala came down for a drink.

When the sun reached the top of the mountain, the surface of the dam was as orange as a maple leaf in fall. The sky streaked in lazy horses' manes of yellow and orange and red. With the sun behind the mountain, the dam's surface turned to mercury and the mountain into a black sheath. The colors slowly faded, taken over by stars. Bats swung on insects in the sky. The nightjars sang. Somewhere from the bush on the other side of the dam, an owl hooted.

CHAPTER 16

For the Birds

Dinner last night came as a "brie." Think barbeque but using honest wood rather than charcoal from a bag or that disgusting propane. Francois and Petra joined us. So did a fellow by the name of Edgar. Edgar is a farmer in the Winterton area, about an hour or so from Kameelkop. Seems Edgar, Pierre, and Spyker go back a ways. The hard jibes one gave to the other only provoked harder and sharper ones.

Over dinner it became evident why Edgar was joining us. We were to accompany him in the morning for a bird hunt. Dave, Doug, and Margaret all hauled shotguns with them. Pierre had arranged with someone for me to borrow one as well.

I don't remember much of the night, the time spent around the fire in the cool night, nothing but the fine food. Maybe the drink, or drinks, maybe that kudu, but I woke up feeling no ill effects.

We drove into Winterton just as the sun was breaking the horizon. Edgar met us at the one major road junction, and we were off to the farm. A big fellow by the name of Richard was with Edgar.

First up would be some waterfowl action on one of his dams. From the start I knew this would be different than the waterfowling I do in the States. The morning was quite cold. Fleece was needed, as were gloves. Steam was coming off the water in a white haze. There was no breeze.

Birds were on the waters of the dam already. The dam was small, no more than a few acres in size. More birds slid in, coming in groups of twos and threes. In the early light I could tell there were at least three species using the dam, along with some type of goose. The geese swimming around were multicolored. Lots of white. Some green and mahogany. Touches of gray. I found out later that these were Egyptian geese, or gyppies for short.

Of the ducks, one had a distinctive white face. This was the white-faced duck. Another had a very yellow bill with the rest of the bird looking a lot like a hen mallard. Easy name on this one, too—the common yellow-billed duck. The third had a distinctive red bill. Like the white-faced one, it also had a long neck. I like easy names that make sense; this one did, too—the red-billed teal.

Another beautiful morning show from the grasslands. Those mountains were washed in rose water.

The birds continued to stream in as we walked to take up positions along the dam. Doves and pigeons swept overhead. As we moved closer to the water, the birds didn't flush. Rather, they just moved to the other side or the middle of the dam. Sheesh, this was going to be easy. Not.

Edgar walked to the other side when he saw everyone was in place. Then he clapped his hands, which sent the birds jumping into the air.

The ducks climbed high for the most part. Dave had one come in low and he crumpled it right on the edge of the water. Margaret followed with another. And that was all the shooting from the 100 or more ducks that were there. And the geese? They climbed high and flew to the west.

Edgar came running over to where Dave and I were on the dam wall. "Stay ready! They'll be coming back in a few minutes." Then, "Dan! Dove. Take him!"

The dove came in along the water, met the wall, and climbed. And then crumpled, landing right at my feet.

Moments later, high in the sky, ducks were circling. Like the mallards I was used to, they circled and ever so slowly dropped closer. Once satisfied that all was clear, they cupped wings and started to settle in.

Over the course of the next hour, ducks came from on high, winging in from the east. One shot here, another there. When all was said and done, it wasn't a big game bag, but it was varied. The three species of ducks plus one more, called a Cape shoveler, which looks like a brother to our northern shoveler. Two species of doves, red-eyed and Cape turtle. And a rock pigeon.

It ended as quickly as it started. Some birds were still on the water, but they wouldn't fly or leave the safety of the middle. Pierre called a halt and all met back at the trucks.

"Now for some upland gunning. We don't have a dog, so we'll have to push them. There's plenty of birds, so we'll get some shooting."

The grasses were high, most reaching above 6 feet. They were filled with seed heads that stuck to our hair and covered our fleece in a thick coat. The birds we sought are called Swainson's francolin. In South Africa they are also called pheasant. About the size of a ring-necked pheasant, maybe a touch smaller, they have no distinctive tail. Their color is drab. The male's plumage is a dark charcoal brown, the female's a bit lighter. Around the eye there are no feathers, only a bright red patch of skin. The males also have a red bald patch just below the chin. The spurs, just up from their three toes, are formidable.

The first one jumped up just a few feet between Margaret and me. Margaret crumpled it well. Then it got tough. Walking through the tall grass was not easy. It got much harder as we made our way down a small hill and found ourselves sinking past our ankles in a thick mud, compliments of a seep spring. Vines grew here as well. Thin and tough, they wormed their way through the grasses, grabbing our legs and feet.

After 30 minutes of only seeing birds flush far in the distance, we cried uncle. And then had the extreme pleasure of going back through the muck and the vines and the grasses. We did not give up, however.

I walked over to another patch of grass and stepped in. Two more steps and a francolin popped up, flew 15 yards, and promptly died in a cloud of feathers. When the bird was in hand, the spurs found my palm. They went like needles into that soft skin directly in the middle of my hand.

The bird in hand is much more handsome than in a photo. Each feather has a distinctive darker band running down the shaft of the feather. Subtle differences in color can be distinguished, and the neck appears almost to be of one color, like a feathered collar. In reality it is just that the feathers are smaller, so the dark main shafts are closer together. The belly feathers are certainly lighter than the back, like the bird was getting a tan on his back, keeping the belly in softer tones. The red around the eyes and underneath the chin aren't a hint of red; they define the color itself.

Not a bad morning of bird hunting. There are Egyptian geese, a few duck species, and a couple of Swainson's francolin.

A fair-size river ran through the unfenced section on Kameelkop. Big, prehistoric-looking lizards scattered from the sandy banks when we came near, disturbing their sun. Easily three to four feet long, I'm told they are mighty fine eating by the Zulus. I'll let you try one first.

Without a bird dog along, the hunting was a lesson in walking and hoping. More often than not, the birds ran ahead of us, like pheasants in the prairie, and only launched when they came to some sort of obstacle. With the grass patches so large, as in hundreds of acres, and with only four gunners—Dave and I, Margaret and Richard—doing the drive-and-block was out of the question. Another thirty minutes of frustration and we hiked back to the truck.

"Want to have some fun?" said Richard with a fiendish grin.

"Always," I said.

"Good. Now it's time for some varmints. The place is overrun with red meerkats and crows. I've got my .223 along. Let's go."

This wasn't any old .223. It was match-grade all the way from stem to stern. The scope on top maxed the power curve at 25. You could see next week through that scope.

Richard handled that gun like a virtuoso. Meerkat at 350 yards? Cloud of fur. Crow at 290? Black feathers drifted in the air. And that was almost freehand, as only his elbows rested on the hood of the Rover. The barrel held by only his hand, the stock only by hand and cheek.

It was another matter for me. I couldn't get the scope to quit dancing from mud clod to meerkat to mud clod, now at the highest power setting. Turning it down to 15 helped simmer down the dancing. My bullet only kicked up dirt just to the right of the lucky meerkat's head. At 10-power the meerkat disappeared in the crosshairs.

Anneli called for Pierre on the radio. It seems she had a plan for our lunch, and it was time to head for town. Richard asked me to ride with him. On the way I learned that he was Anneli's brother. And I learned that he liked to ask some questions. Seems Doug had mentioned to Pierre that I used to be in the Army as an officer, and that once or twice I tasted the copper penny. Pierre, in turn, mentioned it to Richard.

SAFETY IN SOUTH AFRICA

Before you read the following, ask yourself this question: Would you not go on an elk hunting trip in Wyoming because there was a nasty riot in Los Angeles or gang violence in Detroit? (No offense to L.A. or Detroit; I could have picked any major city in the United States) The entire point of the question remains valid. Big cities everywhere are more than slightly troubled by crime. South Africa, and her major metropolitan areas, is no different.

The following is taken directly from the U.S. State Department's Web site (April 07):

Although the vast majority of visitors complete their travels in South Africa without incident, visitors should be aware that criminal activity, sometimes violent, occurs routinely. Notwithstanding government anti-crime efforts, violent crimes such as armed robbery, carjacking, mugging, "smash-and-grab" attacks on vehicles, and other incidents are regularly reported by visitors and resident Americans.

Crimes against property, such as carjacking, have often been accompanied by violent acts, including murder, when victims resist or are slow to respond to attackers' demands. South Africa also has the highest incidence of reported rape in the world. Foreigners are not specifically targeted, but several have been the victims of rape. Victims of violent crime, especially rape, are strongly encouraged to seek immediate medical attention, including antiretroviral therapy against HIV/AIDS. Questions about how to receive such treatment should be directed to the nearest U.S. Embassy or Consulate.

Criminal activity, such as assault, armed robbery, and theft is particularly high in areas surrounding many hotels and public transportation centers, especially in major cities. Theft of passports and other valuables is most likely to occur at airports, bus terminals, and train stations. A number of Americans have been mugged or violently attacked on commuter and metro trains, especially between Johannesburg and Pretoria. Several American travelers also reported theft of personal belongings after strangers whom they invited into their hotel drugged them. In at least one instance, the American died after being drugged and robbed in this manner.

There is a serious baggage pilferage problem at Johannesburg and Cape Town International airports, particularly travelers changing airlines and those flying on smaller airlines—passengers flying on major international carriers may not be affected to the same degree.

Travelers are encouraged to secure their luggage with Transportation Security Administration (TSA) approved locks, use an airport plastic wrapping service, and avoid placing electronics, jewelry, cameras, or other valuables in checked luggage. Make an inventory of items in checked baggage to aid in claims processing if theft does occur.

In the Western Cape, police resources have been strained by continuing gang conflicts and vigilante violence in the Cape Flats area of Cape Town. Travelers may wish to contact the nearest U.S. Embassy or Consulate before embarking on trips to these particular areas.

Armed robbery of cash-in-transit vehicles and personnel occur throughout South Africa and peak during December and January due to the increase in cash flow from commercial stores to banks. These attacks have also included incidents at major malls and in large grocery stores. Individuals should raise their level of situational awareness while in the vicinity of cash-in-transit vehicles and personnel and avoid areas where they are located to the maximum extent possible.

Credit card fraud, counterfeit U.S. currency, and various check-cashing scams are frequently reported. Do not accept "assistance" from anyone, or agree to assist others with ATM transactions. Travelers should try to avoid using ATMs after bank business hours or in remote locations. When giving your credit card to a store or restaurant employee for processing, do not let them take the card out of your sight. Visitors should also beware of telephone or e-mail schemes, which attempt to win the confidence of an unsuspecting American who is persuaded either to provide privileged financial information or travel to South Africa to assist in a supposedly lucrative business venture.

Wow. Pretty scary stuff, and I'm not sorry if I sound glib. Is crime a problem? You bet. Should you be vigilant? Yes again. But crime is a problem all over and if you are not vigilant at all times then you, sorry to say, are a Pollyanna. There are bad people out there. Be on guard always.

That being said, most of the crime problems in South Africa are in the major cities. On safari you probably won't see much of the major cities except to fly in and depart from them and, of course, the drive through them each way. You won't be driving yourself, either. Your professional hunter or outfitter will be doing the driving.

SAFETY IN SOUTH AFRICA

Where you are going to be staying is in the bush. Crime there is very low. Bush life is a hard life, and crooks want the easy life. They generally stay away. Yes, certainly keep your valuables tucked away or turn them over to the PH for safekeeping. Don't flash money around and keep guard on your credit cards and passport. You should be doing this wherever you travel, not just in South Africa.

Years ago the bush did have its share of major problems. Farm raids where farmers and their families were killed by bands of marauding thugs were not exactly uncommon. These were brutal attacks, and you can still see evidence of that past. Farmhouses are generally behind high fences, and these are more often than not electrified. Barbed wire will be seen as the top strand on many of these.

Farm raids now are quite rare. Certainly some still take place, but they are very few and far between. In safari camps this is particularly true, as the bad guys know the good guys carry guns and know how to use them! And, that's where Richard and his friends come in.

Some things we talk about, some we don't. But when you are in the company of a fellow who is asking the right questions, it becomes evident that he gets his news and opinions from experience and not the talking heads on TV, the wish-I-were's and wannabes, or the newspaper and magazine writers who get everything right but the facts. At any rate, I answered most of his questions. And then asked one of my own, "You seem to be in tune with military stuff, and you damn sure can shoot. Have you played as well?"

Richard chuckled, "I still am. A major in the reserve forces. Unlike your reserves, we get called out for special duties when the shit is flying, normally in our area, but it could be throughout the country. Most times it is only for a few days to take care of a problem."

There, it has been finally said, sometimes shit flies in South Africa.

Driving back into Winterton, the once-quiet town from just a few hours earlier was filled with people. This was a Saturday, and a Saturday when people from the outlying hamlets came to town to shop in a bazaar set up at a dusty crossroads, and to collect any payments or subsidies the government thought they were entitled to.

The bazaar was by no means fancy. Some people had simple tables on which they displayed their citrus, nuts, and vegetables. Others had their wares lying on the bare ground. Colorful skirts and blouses swung in the breeze. Music blared from more than a few boom boxes.

Young men stood off to the side eyeing young girls. Mothers hustled little children along. Fathers, like they do most places, hung in the background just wishing it were over. A few played games such as dominoes; some played a game of stones and sticks that I had never seen. It was a very typical farmer's market with the addition of colorful clothes for sale. Heck, there was even a barber with a rickety stool cutting hair with an old pair of scissors.

In the airport, when you land, after you go though immigrations and customs, and in the very few minutes before you hook up with your professional hunter or outfitter, is when you will be most vulnerable. Do not leave your bags unattended. Don't look lost. Act like you know what you are doing.

South Africa is not, of course, the United States. I'd be a Pollyanna to think so. But, it is not the dangerous place many make it out to be. If you stay on guard and vigilant, you will be fine.

If you still have some qualms about traveling on safari to South Africa based upon safety issues you've either heard or read about, then do some investigating on your own. Pick up a paper or go online and read the crime reports coming out of any big city in the States. Now go online and read the Johannesburg paper.

Now ask yourself the question we started with. Would you decide to not go on an elk hunt in Wyoming because of problems in any large city in the United States?

Our group headed for the Dutch Reformed Church a few blocks distant. The church was having its annual fete, or festival. Inside the meeting room tables were set up with kids' toys and candy for sale. Some farmers were selling nuts and vegetables. A butcher was hawking cuts of meat.

Outside on the church grounds, kids ran around playing and asking their parents for more money to purchase another soda pop or juice, some more candy, and, please, just one more toy. And, oh yes, the inflatable moonwalk device was blown up, and the kids were bouncing and laughing. I was really beginning to miss my kids.

Something you won't find in the United States is a concession where the kids could pay a price and drive an all-terrain vehicle. These weren't kid-size; they were full-size units. They tore around the grounds on a semblance of a track. Lawyers in this country would have had a field day, not to mention the folks at family services.

Lunch came in the form of kabobs, specifically lamb kabobs. Thick chunks of lamb, tender, cooked no more than medium rare on a wood fire, marinated in a variety of herbs and spices. I had six. Okay, I won't lie—I had eight. I had none of the vegetables. Why waste hunger on that when there is plenty of meat?

After lunch we headed back for the vehicles and took off for a big gift complex in the country. Think of a mini mall, but much more appealing in design and offerings. A dozen or more shops hawked everything from simple T-shirts and cheap souvenirs to exquisite baskets and jewelry, carvings, and paintings that were at times frightening in price to my miserly pocket. The bar did serve cold beer.

Anneli then guided us to Ardmore, a tucked-away artists' colony in the foothills of the Drakensberg Mountains. Here traditional and modern Zulu art and handcrafts are celebrated. Two baskets, one constructed as they were in the late 1800s with dull, plant-dyed colors, and another from this time with brighter colors and gold-

The church fete. With all the children playing, it made me a bit homesick for my kids.

finished thread, found their way into my bag. Now nearly 3:30 P.M., it was time to get back to Edgar's for an evening waterfowl shoot.

The shooting started slow. The sun was just above the Drakensbergs when the ducks and geese started to fly back to the dam from their afternoon of feasting in the fields. I already had the ducks I wanted, so I was looking for geese. Geese fell. Egyptian geese, to be precise, fell for everyone but me. Until the sun wasn't much more than a memory, I had no shots at a gyppie.

A small group came in high over the dam wall. I was near the opposite side. Too high for the wall gunners to shoot, they cupped their wings and started to settle in. Gliding half the length of the dam, they swung a bit left. The lead bird crumpled.

I'd be lying if I said I saw him hit the water. I did see him crumple against the dark purple sky. I couldn't see him as he met the horizon and landed with a loud sploosh on the water.

Dave must not have been seeing too well either. He ended the day with a double, two birds of different species. Blinded by the setting sun, these birds came in from the west with wing beats like waterfowl. They weren't waterfowl, not the waterfowl we were after anyway. (They did make great fly-tying materials, though.)

On the drive back to Kameelkop, we could smell smoke. To the east an orangish glow came up behind a hilltop. It smelled like a grass fire. A few miles further down the road we could see long fingers of flames licking up and down the hillsides. It was a grass fire. A big one.

Farmers burn the grasses in late fall and early winter. Burning them puts more nutrients into the soil. It also keeps fence lines clear from vines and shrubs that will eventually crumble them.

Not all fires are set intentionally by man. As in the plains and high mesa areas of the United States, an errant cigarette can start up a fire in a hurry. Some fires are started by lightning. Others start spontaneously. The grasses are stone-dry. It doesn't take much. Once one gets going, it is a beautiful and dangerous living thing.

This fire was just that. Beautiful and dangerous. Its flames licked up into the night sky, eating it away like an infection.

CHAPTER 17

Screwing the Pooch

 ast night was awkward. Words were left unsaid. Upon returning from Edgar's farm and having drinks by the fire and dinner in the lodge and more drinks by the fire, only small talk was heard. Truth be told, there was more silence than words.

A few knowing nods between friends. A raised glass in salute for times spent. And more than a fair share of empty stares into the embers. These were private memories, at least for now.

Everyone slept in this morning. No one prearranged it. I'm sure Pierre and his staff were up at the normal early hour and had the coffee ready, eager to get the show on the road. But, outside of the paid help, we all stayed in our chalets until the sun was well above the horizon.

Dave and Mary had their bags packed, and the camp staff was toting them to Anneli's car. They were leaving today. They were dressed in traveling clothes. Their trip was over. That sucked. It sucked for them because they would not finish the trip with us. It sucked for us for the very same reason. Dave and Mary have been friends with Doug and Marge for a good many years. While my relationship with them is nowhere near as strong, over the course of the past two-plus weeks it had become solid.

The breakfast table was quiet. Every now and again someone would wipe an eye. Maybe blow a nose. There must have been a lot of pollen in the air.

Mary, that prim and proper lady, had become a huntress. She experienced the drug called adrenaline. Even her legs had grown stronger. When this trip started, her steps, even with the cane, were faulty. Now, for whatever reason, and I like to think it was pure African magic, she walked much stronger. Dave had fulfilled a child-hood dream—hunting in Africa. Together he and Mary walked the savannah, they toured Cape Town, they celebrated life, together.

Walking to the car took longer than necessary. Some force kept us from getting there quickly. No one wanted to see them go. Sure, all good things must come to an end. But that's fatalistic. It is not living the moment.

Most of us had sunglasses on. The sun was brighter than normal. Those who didn't had eyes glassed over, even a tear or two streamed down due to the brightness. Or something. Parting company is not such sweet sorrow.

I can't remember who it was, probably Dave, Mary, or more likely Anneli, but someone finally put a stop to the farewells and moved Dave and Mary into the car. A last wave and the rest of us walked back to the lodge. Not looking back. Not daring to. Eyes were wiped, by whom I will not say, but they were wiped.

But now it was time to get back to the hunt, to the hunting. It was mid-morning. I had no real plans. Heck, for all practical purposes my safari had ended with the kudu. The only thing I was even mildly interested in hunting was a warthog.

Warthogs are cheap when it comes to trophy fees. They're so ugly they're cute. Just about every time Spyker and I drove by a certain waterhole, a big-bodied hog, one with impressive teeth that stretched past 25 centimeters in Spyker's estimation, squirted away through the bush. It was evident that this warthog liked this particular waterhole.

"Spyker, how about we set up a blind on that waterhole. You can leave me there, and maybe I'll get a crack at that pig? What do you think? That way you can help Doug and Marge with the critters they still want."

Spyker agreed, and after grabbing a few bottles of water we were off. Like Dave and Mary's blind, this one was built around me. Using a big acacia as an anchor, Spyker built a stubby U-shaped affair with a back that I could push over if I needed to get out in a hurry. Once he had me sealed, the fine-tuning began.

A cross piece went across the length of the blind. I placed my rifle on it, and Spyker carefully cut away a shooting port. He made sure I could swing the gun. Made sure that I could see through the scope. Made sure I had water. And then he left, saying he'd be back midafternoon and uttering these cautionary words, "Dan, you have shot some truly big animals. Real trophies. Don't mess up on a warthog. We want the one with big teeth. If you don't see him today, we'll find him on another day. Remember, the males have four warts. You want to see those before you shoot. And for God's sake, don't look for simply teeth. You want the teeth to curl around the snout. Be careful, their gray beard can look like teeth if you only look quickly."

The blinds are built with what is at hand. At hand here is thornbush, coming in all sizes.

Yeah, yeah, yeah. "Go help Doug and Marge."

Within minutes the hornbills, hammerkops, bee-eaters, and more than a few species of doves all came back. These were joined by a mother warthog leading five piglets that couldn't have been more than a few weeks old.

Already they walked with their tails up like a radio antenna. Mama hog walked, and the piglets ran to keep up. At the side of the dam to my right, mother went down for a drink. Piglets went down, too, but they tumbled down the steep bank, ass over teakettle. After drinking for a few minutes, they skirted the edge of the water and left from the other side.

Impala came close but didn't come in. I knew they couldn't smell me, the wind was from the wrong direction. For whatever reason they just continued to walk through the bush. A huge eland cow came in from behind. She may have gotten a whiff of human as she left in a bigger hurry than she came.

A half hour passed. No more four-legged critters. Plenty of birds kept me occupied. Flashes of color streamed through the branches as they took wing. Their songs competed with one another for soloist recognition. From the mountain far behind me, a group of baboons roared.

There's something about sitting at a waterhole by yourself and watching what develops. It's the same feeling, almost hypnotic, as one gets sitting on the edge of a river or the ocean's shore and simply watching the water and hearing it hiss against the sand or move over a fallen tree. The world stops for an instant or two.

Another group of pigs came down on the opposite side for a drink. They were all females. A small male came in behind them. The four warts were easy to see, but his teeth were so small you could barely see any ivory coming over the lip.

Something spooked them and they scattered away. That something was a big pig. He had four warts, a big body, and teeth wrapped around his muzzle. It was my pig.

My pig, however, didn't even stop for a drink. At a quick pace, at a run, he dashed to where the females had been drinking, stopped for a microsecond and then dashed into the bush where he slowed down. I saw him circle back through the bush as he trotted from right to left. I lost him as he settled into a walk still going away.

A loud squeal erupted from just beyond where he disappeared. Through the bush I saw a warthog coming toward the water. It was the big one. I saw the warts, I saw teeth. When he got to the water's edge, I squeezed the trigger and the warthog fell over stone dead.

I felt smug at getting the pig all by myself. No professional hunter pointed him out. None but me judged his trophy status. Nope, this was all my doing. I enjoyed that walk to where he had fallen.

Except for that fact that it wasn't the "him" I expected. Yes, it had a big body, every bit as big as Mr. Teeth's. Yes, it had four warts and a very long, grey beard, but the teeth, damn those teeth! They were no longer than 10 centimeters. That may even be a stretch. I took a, well, a shitty little pig! It didn't matter that his body was big. His teeth were embarrassing. I felt like a fool. I was a fool.

Spyker and Francois came by about 45 minutes later to pick me up. I was embarrassed to show them the warthog. "Guys, I'm sorry, I screwed up and shot one with little teeth." I described how the big one came in and then circled out. How

WHAT MAKES A TROPHY?

People use the word trophy in many different ways. Some use it as a comparison to others, as a testament to their manhood, or womanhood for that matter. For me a trophy describes the hunt itself. It must be well-earned. It must be a mature animal. It must at least be a representative example of a "nice" animal.

Yes, that is very vague. It's meant to be. A trophy entails the setting where the animal was taken and how it was taken. When the gods smile upon you and you have multiple animals to choose from, or compare to one another, it means you consciously decided to take that particular one instead of any member of the species. Maybe the phrase conscious decision is the key here.

Some measure their animals by the books in a "mine is bigger than yours" mentality. In all my years of hunting I have never had an animal officially measured. I'm told a few would "make the books." To be honest I could give a rat's ass if it's the 209th best ever shot or the fifth best. Certainly it would be cool to have the biggest because then I wouldn't need to work any longer if my newly hired attorney and financial advisor knew their jobs well. (At least that appears to be the case in the white-tailed deer world.) It's a good bet that I'll be working for the rest of my life.

That doesn't mean that my trophies aren't the best. They are. They are better than yours for the simple reason that they are mine. I made the decision to pull the trigger and kill that magnificent animal with the funny-looking horns. It was I who immortalized his spirit. It was I who hung him on my wall. I hung him there not to say "lookie what I killed," but rather to say, "look at that beautiful beast; he will live forever and inspire many to ensure his kind still walk the earth."

Your trophies have no emotional attachment to me except possibly in a dream of what may be. Mine do have a deep attachment. So do Doug's, Marge's, Mary's, and Dave's. They are the best ever. They are the best because I was along for the ride, I was with them. Inches don't always matter; memories do.

Something that I found to be a real test of observational skills was to look at an animal and ask Spyker or Pierre if they thought it was shooter. I'd ask that question after I determined it to be or not to be. Early on I was calling critters shooters that were mere puppies. Toward the end of the safari I was getting closer to a 75 percent correct call. I should have studied more. Which is a big hint that you should study before you go as well.

Just what should you study? Everything you can get your hands on. Look at photos in magazines, as most art directors of the major hunting rags won't print puppy pictures. Check out, or better yet, buy a few books on hunting

African wildlife that have a lot of pictures. Study the pictures and the horns. Look at how the horns measure up against the length of the animal's face. How they go to the ears or beyond. How they turn in and then flare back out.

Go visit a taxidermist who does a lot of African work. Ask him to call you when he gets a shipment of horns in. Even better, have him call you when the mounts are done so you can see the horns in relation to the face and ears. Then pay him something for his time when you visit—as long as he shows you what, in his mind, constitutes a trophy animal. Consider yourself in heaven if he has a couple examples in each of a few species to compare to one another.

Rent or buy some videos of African wildlife or African hunting. Chances are the hunting videos will have the substandard animals edited out. That's why I like the standard *Mutual of Omaha's Wild Kingdom* type videos. You see lots of animals in a lot of species. Take a trophy picture from a magazine and compare it to what you are seeing on the screen. Practice calling an animal a shooter or a passer. The more practice you have, the better you'll be able to judge. I only wish I had taken my advice before this trip. It would have saved a lot of doubt about Spyker telling me not to shoot that particular animal when I was ready to squeeze one off.

There are two record books out there if you are into that sort of thing. Someday I may be, but right now I could give a hoot. Those two are the Safari Club International Record Book, and the Rowland Ward Record Book. These separate record books are not equal. SCI, which is the one most Americans will be familiar with, uses a formula generally based on length, width, and mass. Rowland Ward is a much older record keeping system and, for the most part, the one that most professional hunters still judge animals against. This one uses a more simple length methodology generally based entirely on length.

If you are into measuring your animals, that is fine and dandy. I invite you to look at the requirements for each as it pertains to entry into their book. You will certainly learn something, possibly something valuable. Where the animal was taken is noted in the record books, and if you are looking for that bruiser, you will see that some critters grow bigger in one part of the country than they do in another. This is particularly true for spingbok and oryx and red hartebeest, which seem to grow biggest in the Kalahari. Nyala are generally best in KwaZulu-Natal. Kudu and bushbuck in KZN and Limpopo. Remember this is generally. Good animals are where you find them.

In the end, however, it is all about you and what you desire. When push comes to shove, I would submit that any animal well earned and fully mature is a true trophy. Your memory of him makes him so.

That's Spyker leaving me alone in a blind at a waterhole. The plan was for me to take a big-toothed warthog that frequented the water. I thought Spyker was smarter than that.

Here's the warthog I shot instead. Small-toothed bugger. I didn't even want a photo, but Spyker insisted. I'm glad we took some, if only to remember what it feels and looks like when I screw the pooch.

I heard the squeal and watched as this guy came down and how I made sure it had four warts and on and on and on.

I didn't even want my picture with this thing. Francois and Spyker said photos were necessary, and now, with hindsight, I'm glad I have them. If for no other reason than to remind me of my screw-up, I'm glad I have them.

They did, after the photos were taken and the pig loaded into the Rover, start to needle me a bit. I deserved it. The needling wasn't so much in words but gestures. Gestures like their thumb and forefinger held close together indicating how big the teeth were. Like throwing their head back, indicating the pig in back, and then a sheepish shake of their heads. They let me have it but good. I deserved it all.

The rest of the afternoon we drove some and we walked some. Only the colors of the bush, the smell of the grasses, the songs of the birds are remembered vividly.

I'm not sure why I was so down on myself. I deserved some of it, but this was down, as in way down. Spyker and Francois saw my mood and let me stew. I don't know if their silence was because they were enjoying it, or enjoying my plight, or afraid to say a word in the off chance I'd explode.

We found ourselves, just before the sun set, on the broad grassy plain where Mary had taken her springbok. The grasses glowed in the falling light. Halos of neon surrounded the trees in the distance and the tops of the grass, and covered the hills to the west. Guinea fowl scampered over the sandy trail. Up on a hill, still bathed in the last light of day, a group of zebra marched across a high golden hill marked by the odd clump of brush. The white of their coat had turned to pure glimmering gold. The black stripes running like blood from the top of their backs.

Warthogs don't read surgeon general's warnings, either. This one enjoyed a pipe just before making it over to say hi to the fellas in the skinning shed.

Back at camp I gathered all my gear from the Rover and went to clean up. Sitting on the bed, with the shades to the window pulled open, I stewed in the dark. I couldn't believe what I had just done that afternoon. I'd shot a small pig.

Through the window I could see the moon upon the water on the dam. It was a still night; nothing scratched the surface of that mirror. The mountain in the distance was lit up in the purple haze of the moon's glow. Jupiter, even in the bright night sky, glittered like a lone diamond.

Every now and again voices drifted from the lodge down to my chalet. Through the side window an orangish glow and vague shadows came from the fire circle. Scattered laughter. I watched a spider drop down along the window. Even his web shimmered. As much as I detest spiders, I didn't squish him when he came to the windowsill.

Footsteps padded down the path to the chalet. A light switch clicked and there was Spyker. First with a grin on his face, which was quickly replaced by a bit of shock. I must have been a sight.

Sitting on the edge of the bed, I wore only a T-shirt, boxer briefs, and my socks. The bed's lightweight quilt was pulled around my slumped shoulders.

"Uh, Dan, sorry for the intrusion. We were wondering if you had fallen asleep and were missing all the fun. I brought you this," as he handed me a drink. At least he didn't come empty-handed. "Get cleaned up. Some of us are getting hungry, and Moses isn't going to cook the meat until you get up there."

"I'll be up in 10."

Don't Spit in Her Eye

t's amazing how something as simple as a shower can chase away a bad attitude. It's almost like the soap and water are cleansing the inside as much as the outside. After the shower I felt much better. Thinking about the piglet even brought a slight smile now rather than a frown in disgust.

I found the spider while I was getting into my clothes. I killed it. A very satisfying slap from my sandal left the spider in a rather nifty wet spot on the tiled floor. He was pancaked.

"Dan, my boy, nice warthog!" This from Pierre, who found himself doubled over in laughter at what must have been a very stupid looking facial expression from me.

"Yeah, Dan, great pig. Tell us, please. How you were ever able to get that particular one?" This from Doug, who had more than enough elfish twinkle in his eye.

"Yes, Dan the warthog slayer! A salute to Dan!" This from Spyker, followed by a chorus of "hear-hears" by all.

I bowed to the gathered masses in appreciation of their praise. "Thank you, it was interesting. It is some kind of pig. What kind I won't say, but some kind." This brought more laughter. Brought slaps on the back. Clinton brought me a scotch.

I coughed a bit at the first sip. "A good stiff one, Clinton, thanks."

"I figured you'd be needing it."

"You figured right on that one. How 'bout another?"

At dinner I retreated back into myself. I wasn't feeling sorry for myself or the pig any longer. I was thinking of money, as in—do I have enough to do something else? The answer was realistically a resounding no. This was Africa, however, and the one trip I would be making.

I remembered Pierre telling me early on "don't spit in Africa's eye." I did, seven days earlier, when that reedbuck erupted from the tall grass on a plateau. I passed on the shot against all sorts of pleading. An unquenchable and possibly unhealthy desire for a kudu had me in tunnel vision. That reedbuck was thought about each time we struggled to the plateau. Passing on that opportunity haunted me. It was kudu I was after, and a budget I was concerned with. So be it.

166

My final animal was to be a warthog. That was that. I screwed the pooch on the pig. That was certain. That was still troubling. Most troubling was that it was the last animal I was to shoot. The last. Meaning that it was the one I would remember best, probably. Meaning it was the one that Pierre and Clinton and Spyker would remember best from my safari with them. That's what really pained me.

This safari had produced some amazing trophies for me. They were trophies beyond my wildest expectations. It had also produced friendships based on mutual respect and true professionalism. Yes, the staff was working for me, but I was also working for them. I wanted them to be as proud of my trophies as I was. Except for the pig that was true.

Moses was bringing around dessert when I lost touch with the rational and entered into the irrational. "Hey, Spyker? Remember that reedbuck?"

"Yes. Why?"

"The reedbuck, let's hunt him tomorrow. That is if Pierre trusts me to wire him the extra money when I get back." The room got silent.

"Dan, the money is no problem. The problem is you won't find him. He is but a ghost now. You had your chance," Pierre said, shaking his head.

"Pierre, I need redemption. I at least have to try. Him, that *one*, none other."

Pierre got up from the table walked over, grabbed my plate, and commanded, "Then to bed with you, boy! It's an early call for reedbuck. It's a dreamer's prayer that you'll be after."

The next morning Clinton woke me at 4 A.M. At 5 A.M. we packed up the Rover. Spyker leading the way from the driver's seat. Cyril and I in the back.

It was a cold morning. The moon had set and now a million stars danced across the still black sky. Going up Ball Breaker Hill, I felt unseen branches whip at my face. My cheeks stung from the wind and the cold. Once on the plateau we could see the faint gray of dawn's approach to the east. We stopped here.

Spyker climbed up onto the back. Cigarettes were passed around. "We'll stay here until we can see. We don't want to spook it in the dark. There will probably be one chance only, that is, if we even get that one chance."

Dawn took forever. When the sun was still under the horizon, in that faint glow of first light, we started to make out the shadowlike shapes of trees. We could make out slight rises on the ground and the differences in the height of the grasses. A few minutes later a heavy frost covered the ground like a thin blanket of snow. Ice could be seen stretching out from the sides of the inky waters of the dams in ragged edges. We could see maybe a few hundred meters.

When we could see 500, Spyker climbed back in the cab and started to drive very slowly along the trail heading east. Just as we came around a small clump of trees and turned a bit left, I saw shapes in the grasses in a small shallow valley about 700 yards away. When I pointed them out to Cyril, he grinned. I tapped the roof.

Spyker climbed up on the back. We glassed them well. A ewe and two fawns feeding, slowly making their way toward the small creek at the valley floor. "Dan, that ram is around here," Spyker whispered. "He's here. Somewhere."

We continued to glass the valley. Cyril grabbed Spyker. "Boss, far over there!" he whispered, pointing across the valley and the other side of the creek.

There, on the other side, a grey hump could be seen, looking more like a long gray boulder than anything. It was there, and it was out of place. There were no boulders on that hillside, only grass and few small trees. Then it moved. Boulders don't move.

"Dan, you son of a bitch, no one gets this lucky. That has to be him. It's his territory."

In the tall grass we could only see his back. Whatever it was, it was feeding, and never lifting its head.

Spyker grabbed the shooting sticks and we started the stalk. The going the first 100 yards was easy. We were able to use small trees and head-high grass to keep out of sight. From the truck Cyril kept a watch on the animal. It still feeding. Sunlight now lit up the top of the mountain to the west. Gray light covered the valley.

Then the grass got waist-high and we were forced into an agonizing crouch. The animal, and now we can say it was a reedbuck, was still feeding, its head still down.

At 275 yards Spyker and I stopped. Our waist-high cover was now not much more than bare dirt. No cover stood between us and the tall grass along the river. From here I could see most of the reedbuck's body. More importantly I could see his chest.

Spyker whispered, "I'm going to whistle. He'll lift his head. If I say shoot, then shoot. Let me know when you have him dead in the scope." I got settled behind the gun, using shooting sticks as support.

"I've got him."

Spyker whistled. The reedbuck lifted his head. "Shoot him!" he hissed.

"Are you sure it's him?" I saw what I considered good horns, but I wanted to make sure.

"Damn it! Shoot the bloody thing!"

Through the scope I saw the reedbuck tumble, disappearing into the grass. Nothing moved in the void he made. We heard Cyril give a whoop.

As we walked up to him, his horns grew even larger. Tall, wide and heavy, curving up and then out, they taped at an even 17 inches long. His hide was buff colored, like that of a mule deer and his body about the same size, too. His tail was broad, and a bit darker on the top than the rest of the hide. Underneath the tail was as white as snow, looking to be an exact replica of a white-tailed deer.

"Now, dear Spyker, what's that about spitting in Africa's eye?"

"Dan, you are a very lucky man. This is one huge reedbuck. I know I've never seen bigger. Well done." Then he got serious. "Dan, whether you know it or not, this won't be your first and last safari. You'll be back, and you'll want to hunt dangerous game like buffalo and leopard. Never ask if I'm sure. When I say shoot, you damn well better shoot."

Then he laughed and slapped me on the back. "Stay here, I'll get Cyril and bring the car."

Here's my redemption from the warthog fiasco: one uncommonly big mama mojo of a common reedbuck. I learned never to ask, "Are you sure?" with this one.

Thirty minutes later he arrived with the sun. Just as he was pulling up to me, the sun danced on the top of the grass and in seconds washed across the ground. The melting frost had the grasses in a deep, wet, and shiny green along the river. The sides of the valley, in the slight breeze and the dried grasses, looked like a slowly flowing carpet of molten gold. The western slopes were still in shadows.

As we were taking photos, the soft pluumph of a distant rifle shot was heard. After loading the animal in the Rover, we slowly headed back to camp. This time we instructed Cyril to drive very slowly. Spyker and I sat in the back, smoked a cigarette or two, and simply watched the early morning unfold into a gloriously rich day.

At the top of Ball Breaker Hill, Cyril got a bit nervous and asked Spyker to drive. This particular hill would give anyone pause. Going down was every bit as hard as driving up, probably harder.

We didn't make it all the way down. We couldn't. Pierre's Cruiser was blocking the path. Doug was just walking away from the truck when we pulled up. He had the biggest grin on his face that I had ever seen.

"You guys are a bit late. I shot another kudu. This one has both horns. It took Isak about 45 minutes to find the thing. I haven't seen it yet; they just yelled for me to get my broken-legged ass up this damn hill. "

Now, you should know that the farthest Doug had walked since his surgery may have been 50 meters or so at one time. For the most part the ground was level on his prior foot travels. Not this time.

Think about that for a moment, won't you? Here's Doug, using two crutches, walking up a rather steep hill. A hill covered with knee-high or better grasses. Scat-

Doug and Pierre with Doug's second kudu. You'll notice this one has both horns. You won't notice the blood from the rocks and the thorns on Doug's toes as we cleaned him up a bit for this shot.

tered rocks, and rather sharp ones at that, reached out at that cast. Thorns in the trees and, oh yes, thorns along the ground as well. All that, and Doug's little pig-gies, his toes, exposed to them all. I think they found most all of them, too.

He didn't complain, not too much. A few ouches and whoas and shits and damns, all serviced through clenched teeth and a set grimace, and one hell of a lot of determination had him up the hill and sitting behind that big kudu bull. This one had both horns, with a wide spread and heavy bases.

Doug's eyes were glassed over, as were Marge's. "Happy anniversary, Doug," she said and then kissed him. "Don't expect anything else," with a lot of emphasis on the word "anything." I still wonder if she meant another kiss, another gift, or just what "anything" might have meant.

The group had spotted the kudu just off the road to the right and more than a little hidden in the bush. Doug's shot was a rear-quartering shot. As we all found out later, the bullet hit the kudu farther back than he wanted, hitting the kudu in the upper ham.

There was no blood found anywhere near where the animal had been standing. Doug started to doubt his shot. Doug's no slouch with a rifle; where he aims you can bet on a hit. Pierre sent Isak in a wide arc where the kudu had run. Then a slightly wider one.

A whistle brought Pierre to where Isak was stooped over in a patch of grass. It turns out that Isak had noticed something not quite right with the way the grass was laying. He told Pierre that the animal was hit, that it was hit in the rear right leg. He took up the trail following what he could see, and no one else could. Nearly 30 minutes later, after crossing over a broad knob, he spotted the kudu lying dead in the grass. The whistle brought up Marge, Clinton, and Petra.

There was no way to get either of the hunting cars near the kudu, and there was no way we were going to drag him to the cars. Clinton ran back, grabbed the Cruiser, and sped back to camp for some more help from Francois's staff.

Once the work crew arrived, the work began. The kudu was chopped in half, lessening the weight. Poles were cut, and straps from the kudu's skin were used to lash the halves to the poles. With a yell of "La Fontaine!" from Clinton, the staff hoisted the load upon their shoulders and slowly started the walk first up the knoll, then down the other side. More than a few rest stops were taken. Half a kudu, carried by four men, is still half a kudu.

Doug didn't say a word as he followed along behind. His smile was enough to keep the rocks and thorns away from his toes. Only when we got back to the trucks did we mention the reedbuck. I'm not sure what the others expected us to shoot sizewise, but when Clinton let out a loud "Damn!" the others came over.

Pierre looked at the reedbuck and then at me with a huge grin. Then back to the reedbuck, measuring the horns with his hands. "Dan, I don't believe it. That is one mojo reedbuck. He's huge!"

You don't drag a kudu like you would a deer. You get as close as you can with the hunting car and then cut it in half.

Isak and the other trackers and skinners came over. Each whistled and shook my hand. Marge gave me a hug, Doug shook my hand.

We lingered over breakfast on our return to camp. Moses had made up some special pastries that were hot and flaky and full of fruit preserves. We told and retold our stories of the morning, and celebrated our fortunes.

Now I was done. There was no way I could shoot anything else. Doug and Margaret still had a number of holes to punch on their tickets, so a serious planning session started. Doug lit his pipe, Spyker, Pierre, and I lit cigarettes, and I still had a pinch of Skoal between my cheek and gum. That was a bit much—I took the Skoal out. Moses set a pot of coffee in the middle of the table and a teakettle next to Doug.

Doug still wanted an oryx. He wanted a warthog and not one like mine. Margaret started the trip wanting a waterbuck and reedbuck if either came by. Now she really wanted a reedbuck. A flip of the coin decided the afternoon. It was to be Doug's for oryx. We'd work the high plain for them. Spyker and I going up high, Doug and the rest staying in the grasslands. Radios would keep us in touch. If Spyker and I came upon any, we'd let the others know. We did, too.

Spyker and I left a good hour before the others and drove to the far side of the mountain and up to where the rock was shattered by lightning. Kudu mocked us. They were all over the place. Mostly females and young males, with a few marginal shooters thrown in for good measure. Like the impala just below camp, they seemed to know that they were now safe.

After glassing from the rock we moved to where a long rocky ridge rose up from the high plain. Getting out of the truck, we heard a gunshot far in the distance from the direction of camp. Spyker called Pierre on the radio. Doug had his pig. It wasn't small, either. They were taking it to the skinning shed and then would head up onto the grass. Twenty minutes later a pair of oryx, also called gemsbok, rose up from the grass underneath an acacia.

"Pierry, Pierry, Pierry," Spyker called.

"Yah, Killi, what?" Over the course of the safari, while on the radio, people's names changed. Pierre often became Pierry. Spyker became Killi. Both would be called Lolli, or MaLolli. Other names, too, but not that complimentary.

"Pierry, da gemsdabokken gefeldt da hagenstaus."

"Where?"

"Daqr hagenstraussder"

Okay, most of those words were made up because I can't spell Afrikaans, much less pronounce it at all. Basically Spyker told Pierre we had gemsbok in sight, that they were about 500 yards below us, that we were on the rocky ridge, and that Pierre's group should get into high gear and get up on the plain to shoot one.

"Twenty minutes," came the reply from Pierre.

Something like "hurry it up" ended the radio conversation.

The gentle wind was blowing from the gemsbok to us. That meant that our scent wouldn't scare them off. As luck would have it, we could even see the tan Cruiser pull onto the plain where it stopped about a mile away. Unfortunately the gemsbok were moving directly toward us.

"Killi, where are you?"

"The bonnet is pointing right at us. We're on the ridgeline in the rocks about a mile from you. The gemsbok are below us about 200 meters now. They are slowly walking and eating in a patch of acacias. You have to hurry," Spyker whispered.

We watched as the Cruiser made its way along the trail. Every now and again the gemsbok would look back at the noise of the car, or maybe the smell of exhaust. Then they started a slow trot away from the Cruiser, getting closer to us. Underneath a broad flat-topped acacia, halfway up the ridge we were hiding on, they laid down. Their heads turned to watch the vehicle.

"Pieery!"

"Yah"

"Da gemsboker, 40 meters from us," he whispered.

"Ya Killi. Wait." We watched as Pierre got out of the Cruiser and searched for the gemsbok, and us.

"Okay, Killi. I see you and Dan. Da gemsbokkers? Where?"

"Forty meters below us and to our left. Next to the tree."

"Yah, got em."

We watched as Pierre climbed back in the vehicle and put it in reverse. That was comforting. If Doug was going to shoot from where it was stopped, we'd have been playing catch with a piece of lead. Sure there were rocks we could get behind, but as someone who has heard the whistle/crack of a bullet zinging overhead, I didn't really need to hear it again.

Pierre maneuvered the vehicle around, turning back the way he came. Then he turned off the trail and into the grass. He wasn't getting any closer; rather he was running a straight line toward the ridge, and parallel to the gemsbok. Then he came to a spot where the gemsbok were straight out the left-hand window at about 350 meters.

One of the gemsbok stood up when the vehicle stopped. The other stood when the Cruiser door was opened and Pierre got out and helped Doug down from the back.

Doug got on the sticks. "Killi, Uncle Doug is going to shoot."

We hunkered down behind a big rock and heard the blast. We also heard a zing overhead. When we looked for the gemsbok, they were heading up the hill, and if they made it would pass to our right. Another shot came and the rear gemsbok staggered. We didn't hear the zing this time, and weren't disappointed. I watched and then ducked as Clinton raised a rifle and popped off two rounds at the fleeing animal.

"Pierry, have Uncle Doug unload please. Big bullets flying close."

We kept an eye on the hit gemsbok. It left its partner and headed into a draw just below the ridge. Radio calls went back and forth, as we could see where the animal went and Pierre's group could not. All of the calls in excited Afrikaans.

Clinton started to run after the gemsbok. From my perch I could see that Clinton saw the gemsbok. He yelled back to Pierre in Afrikaans, and fired another round. Then he yelled something else, again in Afrikaans. More radio calls between Spyker and Pierre.

Doug couldn't see what was going on. He couldn't decipher the Afrikaans being shouted or over the radio. It must have been too much for him. In a break from the yelling and radio calls, I heard a very loud and commanding shout from him, "Would someone *please* speak some fucking English!"

From the radio and from the yelling, Pierre had learned that the gemsbok was down. I watched him as he put his arm around Doug and shook his hand. That's when Doug let out a hearty "Yes!" Doug had his oryx and it was not yet three in the afternoon.

When we had the animal photographed and loaded in the Cruiser, Francois drove up. He pulled Spyker and Pierre over to the side. I could see some grinning from Spyker.

Pierre announced that it was Marge's turn and that reedbuck was next. He also said that Spyker and I had other work to do. "C'mon Dan, we've got to be going. Just the two of us."

When we pulled away Spyker told me what our work was. "Dan, Francois says that your reedbuck and kudu are the biggest of the year. The reedbuck is the largest he's seen. He needs meat for his family and wants us, you and me, to shoot it. We're going across the road to the unfenced area. We'll be looking for impala, reedbuck and kudu, duiker, maybe a warthog if it's a young one."

"Uh, okay. I know that cull animals are much cheaper. I can do that if the price is right."

"It's right, Mr. Donarski. We're shooting for free. And while we're hunting for meat, if it's a trophy it still gets shot." That was too cool. I could still hunt, and hunt with a true purpose, and no worries about pocketbooks.

We took a different road, a grown-over trail really, into the unfenced area. A road that went through a cluster of a dozen or so thatched huts. Some were certainly still in use, some not much more than a memory. One was made of concrete blocks; the others looked to be of mud and dung. A young girl, not more than two years old, peeked from out of a doorway. Then another, about the same age, peeked out from the other side.

In a rush, two cur dogs ran out of the house barking and snarling. A lady of about 40, her face covered in a white paint, walked out and hushed the dogs. In Zulu she and Spyker started to talk. Then she walked into the concrete block hut, the dogs trailing behind.

Another lady, maybe in her late 50s, came out. She looked rather stern, and perturbed that we had disturbed her family. Spyker and I smiled; he greeted her in Zulu and I said hello. Then she smiled.

She wanted to see what was in the backpack and when I showed her my cameras she beamed. She yelled something back to the house, and a young boy, maybe 14, came out followed by what I guessed were his sisters, both a few years older. The painted lady was next, followed by the young children we had seen peeking out from behind the door.

Mama wanted pictures of everyone. She wanted each one individually and all together. Most, however, she wanted me to take some pictures of her new kitchen cabinets, bright blue and made of aluminum. Mama asked through Spyker if I would send the pictures to her. One of the older girls wrote their postal address down on a piece of paper. This was the Mogadelasha family village. (When I got back, that was one of the first things I did.)

The Zulu village outside of Wasbank. After a short time the family proved very friendly.

The older girls were coyly shy. At first they were reserved for their pictures, and then they started to get a little giddy and camped it up for the camera. I can still hear their giggling and laughing. I had some Hall's cough drops that I passed around along with some hard candies. The hard candies went over better. Seems that menthol eucalyptus was a bit strong for them.

Spyker asked them about the animals we were looking for. Mama got very formal; she seemed proud to be asked her opinion, and pointed this way and that, showing him where we could expect to find some animals. When we drove out of the village, they stood in a straight line and waved good-bye.

In the last hour or so of light we never saw anything more than a duiker. That duiker was a good 250 yards away. Duiker are small antelope, maybe 30 pounds. We saw only its head above the grass. When I squeezed the trigger, we saw it dive away unscathed.

Chases Through the Grass

inner and the fire that night were more than a little joyous. We celebrated and toasted the reedbuck, the kudu, the warthog, and the oryx. Sleep came easy that evening.

Clinton's knock on the chalet door came as a surprise. I had slept like a baby, but was still quite tired. Normally I was awake well before he tromped down the path to my chalet. Heck, normally I was up at the lodge having coffee before he started to make his rounds waking the others. This time, however, it just seemed to come so early.

Over coffee it was decided that this day would be all about Margaret. Waterbuck and reedbuck. The same basic plan as with Doug and his oryx the day before.

During our hunt at Kameelkop we had seen a few waterbuck. Spyker and I had observed one very good bull and a number of cows on the east end of the property. In Pierre's travels, his group had seen a nice bull off toward the west where an old abandoned homestead was becoming part of the land. Each of us left to go look were they had been.

There's something about waterbuck. It's said that kudu are majestic animals. If that is the case, then waterbuck—the good bulls anyway—have a regal air to them. The bulls carry those tall swooping horns proudly. When they trot away, their horns are held high and stiff, like a young girl practicing to be a model with a heavy book balanced on her head. When they run away, they run in a loping motion. Their bodies almost still, only the legs stretching out and then coming back in for the next stride. They're smooth, like a racehorse, in their fleeing.

A waterbuck's coat is grayish and appears quite curly. Their coats have a distinctive odor that most liken to turpentine, and the coat feels a bit oily. Some say the meat is unfit to eat, others love it. I know how they look because I've seen these things. I've smelled them, too, and to me they smelled a bit musty sweet. I wanted to feel one.

We took Cyril with us, this time driving onto the grassy plain filled with dongas and termite mounds where Mary took her springbok. We crossed the creek that ran down through impossibly thick bush from the high plateau. Taking up a weak trail, we headed slow and steady up and across the side of a long, high rounded hill where zebras and eland watched us pass. Trees were widely scattered on the hill-

With Cyril keeping a close eye, Clinton brings the gun to bear with a jackal in his sights.

side, giving us a good view of the valley below. To the south and west we could see the plateau open up as we continued our search by diesel for the waterbuck.

The sun had not come up in its normal glorious way this morning. Instead of showy colors, it just sort of appeared. Faint tongues of steam rose up through the bush from the creek bottom like distant smoke. Once in the slight breeze it disappeared, only to reappear when the breeze died. Water dripped from the trees and the grasses. No frost this morning, just a damp chill.

The ewe reedbuck and her two fawns were in the valley below, gray shapes slowly moving through the yellow grass. From up here we could see where my reedbuck had fallen the previous day, the tire tracks still cutting through the grass to where he died.

Just as we headed down the hillside and turned onto the plateau, Cyril tapped the cab. He pointed out the shapes to me and to Spyker when he climbed up into the back. Waterbuck. Eight of them, with one very good bull, were just inside the grass alongside the edge where the bush gets thick and drops down to the creek.

A call was made to Pierre on the radio. They were on their way. From the Rover we waited and watched. The waterbuck moved around a bit, basically just milling around. Then they sat down. Only their heads were above the two-foot-tall grass.

Pierre called us when he was on top of the plateau. We didn't hear him or see him. After telling him where we were, and where the waterbuck were in relation to us, he decided to start the stalk from where he was.

Where he was happened to be was a good 1,200 meters away. A thick finger of bush, maybe 600 yards wide, separated him from the grass he was parked on and the grass where the waterbuck were lounging. Going through the bush would be a lesson in futility. It would be too thick with too many dead branches snapping underfoot. They skirted the bush, staying right on the edge.

We finally saw them as they rounded the bend. Through the binoculars we could see the waterbuck, still 700 meters away. We watched as he pointed them out to Margaret. Now they would have to get inside the bush if they wanted to get closer.

Every now and again we would catch a flash of movement. Spyker held his binoculars on the waterbuck in the grass. I followed the hunters in the bush with mine. The hunters were moving slowly.

"Damn!" Spyker hissed. "He's standing and looking toward them."

"Still too far for them," I said.

"Oh hell! Now they are all standing."

I turned and looked at the waterbuck. The bull lifted his nose, more of a nod than a lift, and the eight waterbuck slid from the grass into the thick stuff.

Pierre and Marge hadn't seen them disappear. "Should we call them?"

"Dan, those waterbuck got a little nervous, not a lot nervous. My bet is that they are just inside the thick stuff. They could still come back out."

Five minutes later they did just that. Right back to where they had been resting. This time, though, sixteen eyes and sixteen ears were boring holes through the air and into the bush where the hunters were walking.

We watched the waterbuck watching the bush. The bull jerked his head and in a flash they were in the bush again. This time they were very nervous; they weren't hanging around. Marge and Pierre either had seen them dash off or heard them crashing. Even without binoculars I could see Marge's shoulders slump and watched as Pierre gave her a reassuring hug, his arm draped over her shoulders.

They started to walk along the edge back to the vehicle. We drove to meet them. After talking through the details of what had just happened, a plan was made.

Both Pierre and Spyker felt darn sure that the waterbuck were still in the area, probably down by the creek in the middle of the thick stuff. Somebody, or some-bodies, would have to push them out for a shot.

Clinton took Isak and Cyril, along with another skinner, and drove them in our Rover to a spot where they'd get out and go into the creek bottom. Then the three trackers would push uphill, through the thick, trying to get the waterbuck to come out onto the plain. As one of the escape routes would be hidden, Spyker and I hiked over to where we had been watching the previous episode unfold. From there we could see down the valley and let them know if they squirted out to the left, instead of the right.

Nothing squirted toward us except a few birds from the upper branches as the boys struggled through the bush. Eventually we could see Cyril on our side of the creek. He was covered in sweat and the leftover morning dew. When he was directly in front of us, Spyker called him up.

He didn't just sit down when he came up on us, he dropped down. Sweat was crusted in white streaks across the back of his coveralls and on his forehead and cheeks. His boots were thoroughly wet and muddy. He tried to roll one of his cigarettes, but his hands were too wet. I gave him one of mine. Don't ask me why, but that perked him up. We waited a good fifteen minutes before leaving to make sure nothing came out behind them.

"Cyril, do you know of any other reedbucks that Margaret might shoot?" Spyker asked.

Cyril smiled a full-toothed grin. "Yes, Boss. Down below there is one that is nice. He's in the grasses where we drove through this morning. I can find him."

"Cyril, are you sure?"

"Yes. Very sure, Boss."

Spyker sent Cyril to catch up with the others. Spyker and I took the long way around, hoping maybe we'd see something in the loose mix of trees where we had watched and smelled the waterbuck and kudu a couple of days ago.

We found something in that loose patch of trees, too. The problem was it was not what we were looking for, and it was dead. I stumbled on a rock and did a face plant into the grass no more than a foot from a dead mountain reedbuck. Grass was pushed down over most of it. A gaping hole, easily a foot across, was just in front of the hind leg. A few rough holes were in the hind quarter.

"Spyker! Get over here, look at this."

When he came over, a different look came over him. His ears went on high alert, and he carefully scanned the area. "What's this?" I asked.

Somewhere in that mass of tawny grass, there is a tawny-colored reedbuck. Somewhere.

This is what is left after a leopard kills a mountain reedbuck. Only in areas where there are a lot of predators and scavengers does the leopard pull the meat into a tree. Here they just cover it with grass.

"Dan, remember that coughing we heard the very first afternoon here? Remember me saying that anywhere else I would swear it was a leopard, but here it must just be a kudu? This is a mountain reedbuck killed by a leopard." He bent down and measured the distance between two slashes on the open hind. "Certainly a leopard, the canines are just over two inches apart."

I had read a lot about leopards and leopard hunting. Leopards are often hunted by hanging bait in a tree. The baits come in the form of whole impalas, warthogs, baboons, or the hind of a zebra. Leopards, when they make a kill, have the habit of dragging the carcass into a tree so that other predators and the scavengers won't get to it. That way they can come back on multiple nights and have a meal rather than going through all the work of killing something every day. "How come it's not in a tree?"

"There aren't a lot of scavengers around, not enough to make the leopard that concerned. As for other predators, they are quite rare, at least ones big enough to bother a leopard. In areas like this they simply cover them with grass to hide them from the birds. You know, we could build a blind. . . ."

"You mean . . . ?"

"Let me work on it. Probably just for photos. Don't say a thing." We hustled back to the vehicles. Hmmm.

When we got to the vehicles, we decided to try for the reedbuck that Cyril had spoken about. At least we decided that Spyker and I take Cyril and head for the flats to look for him. The others would do a slow drive looking for another waterbuck.

Until he jumped up after the group walked past and caught them looking at a termite mound, the reedbuck stayed well hidden.

We weren't on the flat more than fifteen minutes, driving at a snail's pace to miss the termite mounds and pig holes hidden in the waist-high grass, when a reedbuck exploded no more than a foot off the passenger side door. It leaped left and then headed straight away, bounding through the grass, his white tail up, like a picture-perfect escaping whitetail. When he was about 200 yards in front, he stopped dead in his tracks and lay down.

Cyril grinned. "See, Boss. I told you. Good reedbuck in the grass. I found him."

"Did he just lie down, Spyker?"

"Typical reedbuck. These guys think they can hide. Remember that one that jumped up at your feet up on top. You can walk within 5 feet of these things, and they'll never move. They are also very territorial. This one likes it here. We're going to get him."

In the twenty or so minutes it took Pierre to get to us, the grass never moved where the reedbuck was hiding. Margaret, Pierre, and Clinton got off the Cruiser.

"Marge, the shot will come quick. We're going to need to walk right up and spook him."

We watched them move out in front of the cars. Through hand signals Spyker and I guided them to the spot where the reedbuck should be. Nothing. They continued walking, but just a few steps. The reedbuck leaped up behind them, no more than 10 feet away, and headed straight for the vehicles. He passed within 25 feet of us, offering no shots for poor Marge.

Digital or film? Some folks will think that this is a stupid question, as everyone knows that digital is now ruling the roost. Everyone is wrong. Bring both.

True, digital is a very fine system. You don't need to worry about carrying those rolls of film, nor do you need to worry about that film being cooked in some overzealous X-ray machine at some airport. If you are going out and buying a digital camera of any kind, get one with at least six megapixels. As long as you aren't blowing up your shots larger than 8x10, you will be very pleased with the quality of any prints you have made.

Film systems are fine as well. If you are shooting 35mm film, 8x10 prints will come out very nicely. With film you don't need to worry about the techno-gremlins doing weird things to your memory card. Or to the computer inside the camera. You don't need to worry about losing that painfully small memory card.

Besides, if you aren't carrying two cameras on safari, you should be. Things happen. Things break. You need a spare. Bring one, or more, of each. Use them all at every opportunity.

Maybe it is because I know film better than digital. Maybe it is because I am techno-challenged. What I know to be absolute truth is that I am very sure of the photos I take with a film camera as long as the film has been stored properly and hasn't been neutered by an X-ray or two, or three. With digital I am somewhat confident.

Point-and-shoot cameras have come a long way in both systems. Most have a fair to good zoom. Film varieties have gotten downright cheap lately. Digital models have had their prices cut in half with each increase in technology. These are very light in weight and their small size makes most easily fit in a pocket. My friend Doug calls these PhD cameras, or "Press here, Dummy." Like the name implies, you just point them at the subject and press on the shutter button. They are that simple.

Most of the single lens reflex (SLR) cameras have an "auto" feature. When on auto, they're just like PhD cameras. The beauty of shooting these in the manual mode is that you can really get creative with light and aperture and shutter speed. You can do something called bracketing by shooting a photo, then shooting another one at the next lower shutter speed or aperture, and then shooting a third photo at the next higher one than the first. Light meters built inside the camera are not perfect. They are close. To get the best picture you possibly can, always bracket.

When you are shooting film, shoot high-quality film. For slides my choice is Kodak's E100VS. The VS stands for very saturated. This film is "professional" rated, meaning it is a bit pricey. It also has been worth every penny, as the colors are crisp and true to life. When it comes to prints—and unless you have some delusion about paying for your safari with all the photos you are going to take, prints are the way to go—my choice is Kodak's High Definition line. The 200 is magic and damn hard to find. The 400 is very good, and most people won't see any difference between it and the 200-speed film.

NEVER put film, exposed or unexposed, in checked baggage. Those X-ray machines *will* cook it. Put the film in the carry-on. Ask the nice people at TSA to hand check the film. They will tell you that film under 800-speed is no problem, that you should just send it down the line. Don't. Ask them politely again. True, one pass will most likely not hurt your film. It is not true for multiple passes. You are going through at least two on this trip, more than likely four security checks. The more times the film is exposed, the more it will cook.

With digital, don't go small when it comes to memory cards. My choice is the two-gig card. With the digital camera set to capture the images at large format JPEG, I can get nearly 250 images on one card. On this safari, I carried three of these.

Batteries are a big consideration. I don't give a hoot if you just replaced them a few months ago. Replace them the week before you leave and bring along another three sets. If your camera uses those fancy rechargeable batteries, then buy two extra and make sure they are fully charged before you leave. And do not forget to bring the charger and an adapter along.

When it is time to take the picture, move around. Shoot from a lot of different angles. Make sure of your background. Trample down, or better yet cut down, any grass or branches that are in the way. Be very anal about this. A blade of grass that you don't see in the viewfinder will be an ugly yellow or green blur across the face of the photo. If you or your subject is wearing a hat, make them tilt the brim up high so the shadow doesn't blacken their face. If it makes them look dorky, take the darn thing off. When there is time, such as when taking photos of you and your trophy, take the time to shoot the very best picture you can.

Take the photos with the flash on and the flash off. But, *always* be sure to take some with the flash. Yes, even in bright daylight. The flash will cut down on harsh shadows and make the picture better in most cases. The flash will usually not wash out the photo. If it does, then you will still have the photos taken without the flash.

If you are bringing an SLR, you will want a couple of lenses. A good wide-angle lens that goes somewhere in the range of 18 to 55 will serve your scenics and close-up trophy work very well. When the critters are out there a ways, you'll need to go bigger. I wouldn't go any larger than 300, 400 if size matters to you. My lens for this is a 28 to 300. I do carry a 2-power converter as well, since sometimes size matters. But for 99.9 percent of all I shoot, the two lenses are all I use. If you are only going to carry one lens, then the 28 to 300 would be my best advice.

The bottom line is to come prepared. Bring lots of film and lots of memory and lots of batteries. Take a lot of photos. When you think you have taken enough of one particular scene or trophy, shoot a half-dozen more. Shoot until your finger bleeds. You are in Africa, for God's sake! You are going to want more photos than you thought.

Then he did what he did before. The reedbuck went down about 150 meters behind us. The stalk/push/search was on again. And he was found again.

This time he made a leap away when the hunters got within 30 feet or so. Two leaps and he jumped into a donga, came up the other side, and disappeared into head-high tall grass.

When everyone gathered, a new plan was implemented. "Okay," said Pierre, "we know he's here. We don't want to push him again, as he may leave for good. We can come back for him later when he is completely settled down. Let's go back to camp and eat."

We were all pretty tired after our chases through the grass. Petra came by at brunch and joined us. Doug and Marge went off for a nap while the rest of us hung out in the sun on the stone deck of the lodge.

Just after two, we rousted Doug and Margaret. A growl from Doug signaled they were awake. Spyker and I were heading across the road to the unfenced area with Petra tagging along with us this time. We left Cyril to play reedbuck guide with the others. Spyker gave him very strict instructions on the reedbuck and just how important it was for Marge to get the critter in the salt today.

Just after crossing the road into the unfenced area, a small herd of impala ran away through the bush. We continued to drive, looking for a bigger herd that we had seen a few days earlier. The bigger herd had a huge ram as its leader. If we were shooting for meat, then why not try for meat and another trophy at the same time?

We found the bigger group, too. The only problem was they found us sooner than we found them. What we saw was the west end of eastbound antelope. The ram was with them.

No one felt pressured to shoot, so we just continued to drive. We came upon other impala, and once or twice we even left the car trying to get close enough for a shot. While we certainly wanted to help get a supply of meat, the afternoon was just too pleasant to bust our tails in the attempt. Through most of the afternoon we seemed to be on nothing more than a Sunday drive through the country with a few short strolls thrown in to stretch our legs. It was, all in all, a very pleasant way to spend the afternoon.

An hour or so before sunset, we spotted the big group of impala from a good distance away. Petra had, over the last half hour or so, needled us on being the "big white hunter" with nothing to show. She camped it up with tales of Francois and her starving because the big white hunter wouldn't hunt, wouldn't shoot. Okay, that was the gauntlet being tossed. This group would be hunted.

The herd was across an opening broken up by aloe and scrubby acacias. Spyker and I worked around the opening and found the impala quietly grazing away on tender shoots of grass. They were still a good distance away, and there were too many branches in the way to get a decent shot off.

We went into the thick stuff and got closer. We got very close. Forty meters close. Branches were still in the way, except for one impala ewe that was in the clear. It fell stone dead at the shot. I should have stayed ready. As I dropped my gun, the huge ram stepped into the very same opening, looked at me, and dashed away with the rest of the group. All I saw was that fine reddish-golden skin streaking through the brush. We loaded up the ewe and headed back to camp.

Pierre, Cyril, and Margaret are all smiles with the reedbuck. Cyril has a reason to be. He guaranteed it would be there, and it was.

Pierre and the others were standing around the skinning shed when we pulled up. Cyril had his arms folded across his chest. A huge smile broke out across his face, and he nodded his head slowly up and down.

"See, Boss. I got the lady her reedbuck. I took them into the tall grass, and I found it. I was walking in big circles when it got up and ran off. I saw where it went down into the grass across the donga. We hunted it there. The reedbuck stood up when we were close, and the lady shot it dead. Right there it fell. I did a very good job."

Spyker and I both thanked him and congratulated Margaret. I rummaged through my daypack and tossed Cyril a pack of cigarettes. He took one and threw the pack back. "Nope, these are yours," I said and tossed them back.

"Thank you, Boss. Thank you very much."

Doug came out of the skinning shed and went to the cooler box in back of the Cruiser. Pulling out a Coke, he passed it to Cyril.

"Wow, I must have done very good."

"Cyril," said Doug, "You did a marvelous job, very good, indeed. Margaret has a fine reedbuck because of you. Thank you so much." Then Doug gave him one of his patented bear hugs. I thought Cyril was going to float away.

CHAPTER 20

A Fight for the Waterhole

Around the fire last night a thought occurred to me. I was not supposed to be here. If all our prior planning had come to fruition, I should have been home already. I saw Doug's glass was empty, as was mine, and went up to the lodge to pour us both another cocktail. I made these with plenty of ice and Clinton-strength; there was no room for water in the glass.

Getting back I lifted my glass in a toast, "Ladies and gentlemen, I have a toast. To Doug's broken leg!" They all looked at me sort of funny. Doug looked at me with a quizzical eye.

"Folks, look. Right now I should be home in Michigan. I'm not. I'm here in Africa, with you. If it weren't for Doug's leg, that is where I'd be right now. Hell, I wouldn't have been with you guys the last two days, not to mention the couple of days coming up. Doug, don't take this wrong. For me, your broken leg was a stroke of great fortune!"

"I'm glad it was good for something," he replied. "All in all, the leg isn't too bad. Sure it slowed me down. But who the hell cares really. I am still able to hunt, more or less, I'm in Africa, and I'm with my wife and my very good friends. To my leg!" Then he instructed me to pour him another, same way as the first. We all toasted on that leg again. And again.

Morning again came early. This time I could feel why. A few Tylenols and a pot of coffee made most of the still-dark morning better. I did apologize for snarling at Clinton when he knocked at my door. I was no different than the others, though, except for Margaret and Anneli; they both seemed fine. Doug took his morning relief. And tea. And nicotine. Pierre, Spyker, Clinton, and I did, too.

Margaret sometime in the evening decided that maybe she didn't really want a waterbuck. That maybe if they just went out for a drive something interesting would develop. No sense in getting hurried up on our last full day. We lingered over more caffeine.

Through the windows we could see the day growing a bit brighter. Dawn had arrived. And so did something else. We didn't need to take a drive to see something interesting.

Golden grass and spectacular rock formations dot the high hills of Africa.

We all heard a commotion coming from the area near the dam. Some scuffling and clacking, some strange sounding squeals. We couldn't tell how far away it was, but it most certainly was coming from somewhere near the dam.

The boys walked down toward the dam; the girls stayed at the lodge. They shouldn't have. Drawing closer to the dam, the noises got louder and a bit more violent. A fight, or at least a good argument, was taking place. Through the trees we could see flashes of gray, a bit of brown. Yelps and grunts, the sound of something hitting flesh. Splashing in the water. More yelps.

Drawing closer we watched as a huge bull waterbuck, his horns close to that magical 30-inch rating, pounded the stuffing out of a younger bull. The younger one, with horns barely half the size of the bigger one, had heart. I'll give him that.

The big bull would come at him, thrust his horns, and smash them against the horns of the younger and smaller bull. The blow would stagger the youngster but not put him down. Instead, upon regaining his balance, the younger would charge the older and try to thrash him with his smaller horns. It wasn't a fair fight.

At the smaller's thrust, the bull would counter and knock them to the side. Then he, the bigger one, would wind up, grunt loudly, and plant his horns somewhere on the skull or neck of the smaller. That's when the younger would yelp.

When the younger looked like he was giving up, the bull chased him around the entire perimeter of the dam. The two waterbuck were oblivious to the five of us watching from the fifth row, center.

The younger one wasn't giving up; he was determined to show the bigger who was boss now. In the end it didn't happen. The smaller waterbuck, with a gash on his nose and two on his neck, finally ran off. The big one pranced around, making sure that he was now alone. Slowly he took a drink from the dam. He licked at a trickle of blood on his left front quarter.

Stretching out that long neck, he tilted his head back in a stretch that had his horns touching the middle of his back. Then he stretched it forward, his muzzle between his front legs and his horns sticking straight out, parallel to the water. Coming back to the normal position, he tilted his head back ever so slightly, regally, and in the direction that the smaller one had run off, opened his mouth and uttered a loud and drawn out grunt. Then he walked off.

"Uh, fellas? Where's Margaret?" I asked.

"Shit. Margaret. Damn, that was her waterbuck." I really don't know who said that, but I know we all were thinking it. We high-tailed it back up to the lodge.

Margaret was interested, Anneli, too. But neither was overly so. "If I see him I see him. It's too bad I wasn't there. Oh well, it's our last hunting day, I just want it to happen without any plan." I couldn't believe it; if it were me with waterbuck on the list, I would have been kicking myself for not going down to the dam. Now I would have hurriedly gotten my gear together and demanded we leave immediately.

Not Margaret. She was taking things as they come. Be what may. Thirty minutes later we gathered by the hunting cars and started preparing for the hunt. "I want to see the other side of the road this morning," Margaret said. "I have never been over there, I want to see it."

"Margaret, I do too," said Doug. "Don't you want to try for the waterbuck?"

"I just want to enjoy the day, and I want to see the other side of the road."

"Gentlemen," announced Doug, "We're going across the road."

Francois was still looking for some more meat. There really isn't all that much meat on an impala. We would still be hunting, and who knows, maybe a waterbuck would jump out in front of us.

The small group of impala was where we found them yesterday. And, like yesterday, they scampered away through the bush. A pair of warthogs just about flew out of a waterhole when we drove close, their tails like antennae, straight up in the air and dripping water.

The big group was still there, too, on the far eastern end. We separated, trying to cut them off as they juked and jived through the bush, into the dongas, and back into the bush. Eventually Spyker was ready when they were not, and another impala, a small ram, paid the price.

Spyker mentioned the Zulu family when we had the impala loaded up. There was no doubt that Doug and Margaret wanted to go and pay their respects.

Mama and her eldest daughter in the white-painted face were out in the yard herding their small flock of chickens away from the house. This time there was no stern look or questioning glance. Mama gave us a big wave and called out to the house. The whole group streamed out. The dogs didn't even growl at us; in fact they came over, rolled onto their backs, and wanted their bellies rubbed. Mama shooed them away.

Pierre and Spyker spoke to them in Zulu. Mama went into one of the other huts and came out smiling and laughing, holding a covered calabash. She got down on her knees when she saw Doug had his camera out and giggled like a little girl while scooping out some of her own home-brewed Zulu beer. We declined, politely. She, on the other hand, took one heck of a long pull straight from the big calabash. Trickles of a grayish-brown liquid streamed down from the sides of her mouth.

The teen girls went into the house and brought out a boom box. Dancing broke out. When the girls and Mama saw that our professional hunters knew the Gita, a dance full of stomping feet, they left again and brought out a different CD.

Turns out the CD was by a fellow by the name of Johnny Clegg, and the very same CD that Anneli had me buy the day of the bird hunt. They put the CD in, turned it to my favorite song, Impe!, and cranked up the volume. Even the teenage boy laughed at us while we danced with Mama, daughter, and granddaughters. Everyone danced, even Doug, kind of.

The girls then brought out a Zulu war shield. Made of a very tough hide, it was decorated with white paint and chevrons of African wildcat skin. True or not, we were told that it was old

When mama determines you are a fine upstanding member of the human race, she'll break out the calabash. It holds home-brewed Zulu beer. You can have the first swallow—I'm not that thirsty.

when Mama was a little girl, that it had been her grandfather's in the Zulu war.

The Zulu family wanted more pictures. Doug and I obliged them, taking pictures of everything, even the shucked maize tucked away in the little hut in the rear of the compound. Pictures with the girls, the babies, the chickens, the dogs. With the bright blue aluminum cabinets, on the hard couch inside the living area, of their prized cow, and a lot more photos of everyone gathered.

The girls and the young boy kept looking at the guns tucked into the rack on the vehicles. Margaret pulled hers down and, after making sure it was unloaded, handed it to them. Oohs and aahs erupted, hands stroked the brushed metal of the barrel. They worked the action delicately.

Then, without any of us seeing, Pierre went back to the car and grabbed the impala. He brought it over to where the children were holding the gun, and set it down at their feet. They looked surprised. "This is for them," he told us. Then in Zulu he told Mama and her family that the impala was for them; it was our gift for the warm welcome and the fun.

The Zulu family was thrilled when we presented them with an impala for their table.

You would have thought that we had just rescued them from the grave. Mama got a little choked up, and the girls and young man just looked excited. She went to great pains, and I mean great pains, to thank us. She shook our hands more than once. She bowed more than a dozen times, and clasped her hands to her breast and continued to say thank you.

It was hard leaving them, our new friends. They wanted to continue to dance, to have a party. We did leave, in a wave of hands and happy voices that didn't disappear until we were well out of sight.

Spyker and I left the others as they headed for camp. We had something we wanted to look at up over Ball Breaker Hill on that plateau. The leopard kill.

We left the Rover a good 500 meters away from the kill site. We walked slowly, this time both carrying guns. We didn't carry them by their sling or nonchalantly over our shoulder. No, the guns were carried at port arms, ready to be used if needed.

Quietly we made our way toward the mountain reedbuck, careful not to step on twigs or stumble over a rock. When we were within 5 meters or so, Spyker threw a few rocks in the direction of the kill. We saw nothing, and heard nothing.

The kill had been worked over. Recently worked over. Some of the blood from the hindquarter was still very much wet where canines sliced through muscle. The leopard had again covered the kill with grass. The blood smears on the grass were still wet.

We had been close to finding the cat on the kill. It would have been very cool to see it, but a big part of me was damn glad we had not. We dropped Cyril off at the skinning shed. I had a new fleece sweater in my bag.

"Cyril, wait! I want you have this sweater. It will keep you warm on cold mornings." This was said through a choked-up voice.

That's Moses, again. This time in formal cooking attire.

"Oh! Thank you, Boss! This is very nice. Very, very nice." He shook my hand firmly.

Back at camp, like always, there was a huge spread of food waiting for us. This may have been our last day. We may have been half-stepping it when it came to seriously hunting. Moses, however, wasn't half-stepping in the kitchen at all.

After dinner the brutal part of the trip, the proving up, was arranged.

"Dan? Can you come over here?" This from Anneli and she said it again, as she did everything, in that sweet, flutelike voice of hers. She was sitting at the dining table. A ledger book was spread out in front of her, and my name was at the top of the page.

"I know what's coming. Give me a minute, and I'll go get my stuff." My stuff being my cash and traveler's checks.

Anneli went over every day with me. What were observer days, what were hunting days. What animals I shot when and the cost. I expected this process to be like having a root canal done without the benefit of anesthesia. It wasn't any worse than having your teeth cleaned.

I did feel bad about the fact that my cash supply didn't cover everything. Anneli told me not to worry, that Pierre had already told her. In fact, she told me it took a lot of class to mention it before I shot anything else. Some clients don't say a word until the proving up. That, she said, isn't classy at all.

When I was done counting out the money, Anneli counted it back. This was as much for my benefit as hers, I'm sure. Then she wrote out a receipt and, like the hygienist at the dentists's office, told me I was all finished. I half expected her to take that stupid bib off from my chest.

PAYING FOR YOUR SAFARI

Okay, here's where the rubber hits the road. Virtually every safari operator in Africa will not book your dates until he or she has received a down payment on the hunt. That down payment is normally 50 percent of the daily rates. On a 21-day South African trip, and with daily rates of $350, you will need to pony up $3,675, half the daily rate, to secure your dates. On package hunts, something I do not like, you'll have to pony up half the total cost of everything, daily rates and trophy fees.

So, how do you go about paying off the rest of your bill?

Two ways. The first is a bit easier in my mind. A month or so before you leave for your safari, you wire the balance of what you owe to the professional hunter's account in Africa. If you went through a booking agent, he or she will be able to supply you with the details. As you will be shooting some critters, you could also add a down payment on those animals, say half the trophy fees involved. Then, when the proving up time comes, you will have a much "lower" final bill that you will pay in cash or traveler's checks.

The second way to pay off the debt is to take a pile of cash and traveler's checks with you. I don't know about you, but I really don't like carrying thousands of dollars in negotiable instruments with me. It makes me nervous. I find myself continually hiding it, counting it, and recounting it. The fewer dollars I can carry the more relaxed I am. You will be, too.

Now, what happens if you come up short? In a short phrase, shame on you. That makes things uncomfortable for you and the professional hunter. You should be keeping track of what you have shot and what your finances are.

On this safari I ran short. I knew I was going to run short as I shot all the animals I wanted and plenty more. But before I ran short, I talked to Pierre. I highly suggest that if you find yourself getting into the same situation, you talk to your PH before you blast away at that trophy Lady Macbethderbontelle. You'll be glad you did, and your PH will think you are a class act.

In my case Pierre had no problem with me going over. It may have been that he had done business with Doug in the past and trusted him. It could well be that he had grown to trust me. It was probably both, with heavy emphasis on his relationship with Doug.

Then she, like the gorgeous little minx that she is, asked, "So Dan, when will we see you at our camp in Tanzania? It would be a pleasure to have you there." She had to plant that little seed, didn't she? Buffalo, leopard, lion, hmmm.

"Soon. I hope quite soon," was all I could struggle out.

Doug and Margaret were walking in as Anneli was closing her ledger. "Oh good, you're here. Shall we take care of the business, Doug?"

"You mean we have to pay for all this fun? Sure, let's get it over with."

If given the go-ahead to shoot away, don't be a welcher. Within the first couple of days you are back at home, send the money along to the PH. He'll be glad you did and so will you.

Then there's something called a tip. All the brochures say that tips are at the client's discretion. That may be true, but unless your safari goes completely haywire, you are going to want to tip. In the most general of cases, a tip of around 10 percent is the accepted rate. This is paid to the PH.

The PH then divides that tip up among the staff as he sees fit. The skinners and trackers get their share, the chef his, the laundress and other staff theirs. And, of course, the PH keeps a portion. Now, if a certain member or members of the staff have done some truly extraordinary things for you, be sure to mention that to the PH. He will adjust their portion of the tip accordingly.

Some folks feel that giving gifts is an acceptable way of tipping without putting any cash down. In some cases that is true. A great set of binoculars or a scope, a rangefinder, some valuable and tangible item will be most greatly appreciated. Leaving your leftover bullets, while a nice gesture, is generally not considered part of the tip. Same goes with unused batteries, though these will be treated like gold.

The bottom line is: Money is money. You can use it anywhere. So can they. Money rules.

The last thing in the proving-up phase deals with taxidermy. We're going to get deeper into taxidermy in the appendix. What you need to know is that most taxidermists will require a 50 percent deposit before they start to work on your animals. Even if you are going to mount them in the United States, there is still taxidermy work that needs to be done in Africa before the trophies can be shipped. Be sure to budget for this, too.

Basically, if you can afford a good 7-day guided elk hunt out west, you can afford an 8- to 10-day safari to South Africa and shoot three to five animals. With a good guided elk hunt going for around $7,500, that same amount of money will pay for your round-trip ticket, pay your daily rate, and pay for three to five animals.

Without any question, hunting in South Africa is the best deal in the traveling hunter's world. ▪

I left the room so they could do their business in privacy and walked down to the dam. It was a fine afternoon. The sky was blue, the sun was hot, and I was broke. We did have plans to go for an afternoon hunt. It would be one last chance at a waterbuck, or maybe another meat impala. This plan changed to just relaxing.

I saw Spyker walking up the road past my chalet and called him over. "Spyker, our time is short. Could you grab Isak and come to the chalet?"

"Sure. Why?"

Sundowners are another of the fine traditions experienced on an African safari. A cocktail or two while the sun goes down is pure nectar, as seen by the smiles on Spyker, Pierre, and Clinton.

"I have something I want to give him."

A few minutes later they showed up at the door. Isak stood out a ways. "Spyker, could you tell Isak that I would be honored if he came in?" He did just that, and Isak entered the room slowly and with more than a degree of humbleness.

"Spyker, could you tell Isak I would like to give him a pair of my hunting boots? His are on their last legs. These should fit him. If they don't, he certainly can sell them and get ones that do fit." I had tears in my eyes and was thoroughly choked up. Isak had worked his ass off for me, for everyone.

"And Spyker, could you tell him I want him to have this fleece sweater, too. It will keep him warm." I handed him the sweater. "And please tell him that it is my greatest desire to see him again. And that until then I want my boots to still walk in Africa, I want my sweater to keep a good man warm. It's like I am leaving a piece of me here. I wish to leave it with him."

Spyker translated what I said into Zulu, and handed each item to Isak. Isak looked at the ground. He wouldn't look at me. He did put his hand out to shake mine and then, quietly, he left the chalet.

Around 4 P.M. I heard Pierre call for me. Doug and Marge were already up at the lodge. Spyker, Clinton, Cyril, and Anneli were also there. "We're going to have a sundowner. I have the cooler boxes packed and in the vehicles. Grab your cameras."

Okay, this one was set up. I couldn't resist the sunset and the fellows playing at being models.

We drove up on top of the high plateau. The sun was still a good half hour before beginning to set. We parked the vehicles across on the far south end, where the more gentle road heads down through the brush. Camp chairs were laid out. A bar appeared on the tailgate of Pierre's Cruiser. That's when I noticed what Cyril was wearing—the sweater that I had given him. That made me feel very good.

Drinks were poured and snacks were laid out. The sun was beginning to set, and the landscape turned into a dream. The grasses glowed. The sun dripped in pastels of red, yellow, and orange. Halos of light surrounded us. And more than a few tears ran down Doug's and my face.

The tears were certainly due in part to the realization that this adventure was almost over. They were also due to the stunning sunset. It's easy to say so on one's last night in safari camp, but this sunset was the most beautiful and lingering we had experienced during the entire trip. Sublime is an all too easy word to misuse. But in this case, sublime defined the moment.

The sun turned red as it hit the horizon. Shadows grew to giants. Red washed over the trees below us and the grasses behind us. Ever so slowly it began to disappear. Ever so quickly it was gone.

I don't remember the ride back to camp. I don't want to.

CHAPTER 21

Three Hankies

inner that night was again, as always, particularly fine. Dessert, too. The conversations were muted. Punctuated by a few laughs and more than a few memories, but muted nonetheless.

Around the fire after dinner it was all we could do to just stare at the flames. Each of us left to our own memories and our own prayers of thanks to our own creator.

Africa had become a highly personal experience for me. All of it was physically challenging. All of it was emotionally exhausting. All of it was spiritually fulfilling beyond anything I could have hoped and dreamed for. Yes, there was a cost of admission. Yet in the end, it was a bargain from beginning to end.

The morning was harsh. Not from alcohol but from the emotional drainage of the night before. We packed our bags by ourselves and set them out in front of our chalet's door. Someone on the camp staff came by and picked them up without a word.

When it was time to leave and head back for Johannesburg, Doug and I wept crocodile tears. We're emotional saps, the two of us. Our tears started Spyker's, and then Clinton's, Margaret's and Moses's. Only Anneli and Pierre seemed to hold it together, but even they had wet eyes. Maybe not as wet as ours, but they were wet.

You should bring three hankies with you when you come to Africa. You will want one to keep your binoculars and scopes free from dust. You'll want another to wipe the sweat from your brow and the dust from your nose. The third is for the tears that most certainly will fall when it's time to leave. You may, in fact, need two for this last one.

Spyker finally got Doug and Marge and I loaded into the combe. Pierre had Isak with him in the Cruiser. The rest of the staff, inlcuding Anneli and Clinton, were staying behind to shut the camp down.

The drive to Johannesburg was uneventful. It seemed to take forever. Part of the reason was certainly the wish to just get this long good-bye over and done with. Doug and Marge's flight was leaving early in the evening. Mine, well, when I changed my reservations to stay and "help" Doug, I found I had to spend an extra day. All the flights today were filled. Oh well, another night in Africa. That, to be honest, didn't sound too bad at all.

Well sated. Moses again did his magic, with every plate licked clean. Except the ladies' plates—they have more class than that.

We pulled into Jo-Burg just after noon. Pierre had arranged for us to have lunch at Carnivore's. Carnivore's serves wild game meat. Oh, I'm sure you could get chicken if you really wanted, but why bother?

Servers come around Carnivore's dressed in fancy serving clothes. Each one carries a spear. Upon that spear is a big piece of meat. This one has kudu, that one ostrich, and the one coming right behind eland. Or impala, or gemsbok, or warthog or reedbuck, and the list goes on. All of it is cooked on a rotisserie over an open flame. The serving portions are sliced off with a broad-edged knife. You can pass on any and ask for more of another if you desire.

These servers keep coming and coming and coming until you surrender. On each table sits a white flag held up in a small flag stand. As long as that flag is up, meat continues to be brought to your table. When the entire party is done, one member of the party takes the white flag and lays it down on the table. That's the surrender. And for us, Doug is the one who cried uncle. That is something I never thought I would see. Not even in the two full hours the servers kept bringing our food.

The ride to the airport was more than a little interesting. Johannesburg is a big city with real big-city problems. Shantytowns mark the outskirts. Corner street vendors whose clothes are more memory than covering hawk everything. Oranges, avocados, flowers. Bundles of trash bags. Phone cards. Purses, some that looked well-used. Soda pop that doesn't look like the color that initially came in the well-known bottles. Everything was for sale.

The airport was a crush of people. It could be that we had been away from crowds for so long that any gathering would seem busy. I doubt it though. This airport was filled to the brim with people.

Carnivore's, in Johannesburg, serves meat. Lots of meat. They bring it to you on swords.

You can't check in for an international flight until five hours before that flight is scheduled to leave. Sometimes you have to wait for three hours. I really believe it depends on the moon phase rather than policy.

Luckily Pierre had arranged with South African Airways for a wheelchair and special assistant to get Doug through the lines without waiting. This proved to be a godsend, as Doug went from the 100th person in line to the front of the line, Margaret right behind him. SAA even had someone carry their bags for them.

It all happened so quickly that neither Pierre nor I could say good-bye to them. The best we could do was wave from the lobby as they went behind the check-in counter and on to security. I guess that was for the best. Our tears were already shed earlier that morning. More would have been unnecessary.

Pierre and I needed a room. We found one across the street from where I spent that first night three weeks ago. When we walked into the Town and Country Lodge, a very proper, very young, and very pretty black woman in a maroon blazer met us. When she found we each needed a room, she arranged it quickly and professionally. After credit cards were run and the hotel policies explained, she offered us a glass of port. "To welcome you to our hotel." Try getting a glass of port on the house as a welcome gesture in an American hotel at check-in.

The rooms weren't anything special. They were neat and clean, the bed was firm and the sheets pressed, the TV worked, as did the plumbing. I told Pierre I was going to clean up and that I'd meet him at the bar in an hour or so.

After a few beers at the bar, he told me to grab a coat, that we were going to a pub he knew of. A place called News Café. Turns out News Café is a chain bar not all that dissimilar to an Applebee's. What is different is that the eating here is secondary to the drinking, just the opposite from the U.S. chain. Music played a big part of the scene at News Café. Pierre said these places were the most popular with folks our age. Music from the 1970s blared from the speakers. I felt at home. Fun as it was, we left before the party was "really going to start," according to the bartender. We were tired.

In the morning, Pierre had some business to attend to in Pretoria. I hung out in the room and watched some TV. South Africa does have some interesting TV. They have their soaps, their Jerry Springers. I found a movie and watched it.

A lone giraffe peeks out of (and over) a patch of acacias.

Just after 1 P.M. Pierre came back. I had arranged a "day room," so my room was still my room. Basically a day room is like a very late check-out. For about half of the nightly rate you can stay in your room until the dinner hour, sometimes longer. Even if you haven't spent the night.

Say you get into town at 9 A.M. Your flight doesn't leave until that evening. You most certainly do not want to spend the day in that mass of befuddled humanity at the airport. Day rooms allow you to spend the day in peace, in a hotel room.

When Pierre came back to the hotel, it was time for lunch. We found a diner specializing in fish. I ate klipfish, whatever that is. I know klip means rock, as in klipspringer, the antelope. I'm guessing it was a rockfish. African rockfish are certainly different than those I was used to in Alaska. These were very good but quite small.

My flight was scheduled to depart for Amsterdam at 10:50 P.M. that evening. Pierre said he was going to stay with me until check-in at 6 P.M. This was kind of him, but foolish. In five days he would be heading for Tanzania and his hunting concessions along the Ruaha River in the Selous Game Reserve. Each year, in late May or very early June, he drives up fully loaded, picks up a bunch of staff in the city of Dar es Salaam, and heads for the Ruaha.

There he builds his camp. Each year he builds it. At the end of the hunting season, in December, the camp must be burned down, and the concrete pads that the tents and such sit on must be broken into tiny pieces. Africa's rains swallow up the residue, digesting it, and then leaving the landscape as God intended. It must be rebuilt the following June.

He'll be staying in camp until just before Christmas; there will be no breaks. The nearest village is a good four hours away. With that looking him dead in the eye, he certainly didn't need to babysit me.

The green hills of Africa, which seem to drift frequently into the mind's eye of anybody who has been lucky enough to spend time there.

"Hey, Pierre, let's see if I can sweet-talk my way into checking in early."

"Won't happen, Dan."

"Let's try anyway."

Off to the airport. Sweet talking might have worked. Might have if there was anyone at the check-in desk for KLM. A security officer told me that they wouldn't arrive until six, sharp. It was just before two.

Pierre and I went to a small diner in the airport, the two of us manhandling my gear, and grabbed a soda. We made a bit of small talk. But this was stupid. I didn't need a babysitter.

"Hey, Pierre. Why don't you get out of here? I can handle myself. If you leave now, you'll be back in Winterton before I'm even done checking through."

"You want me to leave?"

"Not want, but if you are staying because you think I need some help, don't. I can handle it. I have the papers. I'll be fine. Give Anneli a kiss for me when you get home."

We shook hands and gave each other a hug. I watched him disappear down the escalator into that mass of humanity.

Six took forever. I saw people lining up around five, so I hustled my butt down the escalator and into line. That same security officer was there. "Sir, I will help you when the queue opens. Don't move forward with the others when the queue starts; I will help."

Promptly at six, the uniformed staff of KLM came out in march step, standing at parade rest behind their individual counters. The line first went through a weigh-in process of each bag and then to the counter with a weight tag on each bag.

A small group of rhinos, one of the symbols of untamed wildness of Africa.

I was beginning to wonder if my security officer friend had forgotten me. I was letting a lot of people jump in line ahead of me. There was a tap on my shoulder.

This well-dressed and well-mannered security officer, this fellow who was working for minimal wages, this bright young man, was a capitalist. "Sir, I will help you, and then maybe you can help me."

"Lead on, sir, we have a deal."

My bags were weighed, by him lifting them up and giving a nod to the weigh-master. Then he brought them over to another area and, nodding to the person there, took me to the front of the line and had the big gear bag wrapped in plastic. Then off to the counter.

To the head of the line again. "Excuse me, please, I need to get these guns checked immediately. [You should know that there were at least six others with guns already waiting for boarding passes, but only I was getting this treatment.] Please, sir, follow."

I was issued my boarding passes, and my gear bag left on the conveyor. Then he escorted me into a small room where the guns are cleared to leave. There must have been twenty or more guns waiting to be cleared. He walked over to the uni-formed South African Police officer and said something to him. All of a sudden I found I was next in line. A quick check of serial numbers and I was out of there.

"Sir, there you go, I helped. I saved you a lot of time."

"Yes, you did, and I thank you for that." I shook his hand, and somehow a $20 bill found its way into his pocket.

"Thank you, sir. Have a good flight."

I turned a corner and saw a horrible sight. At least 200, probably closer to 300 people, were standing in line to go through the security X-ray.

I hustled back and saw my helper walking back into the gun-check room. "Uh, excuse me? May I have a moment?" I asked.

"Yes, sir, is there a problem?"

"Not a problem as much as a situation. I was wondering if you could provide me some assistance with this security point. It is very long."

The man put his hands in his pockets and pulled one halfway out. In that hand was the twenty. When he saw it, he looked at me and nodded. "Sir, it would be my pleasure to help a generous man."

He escorted me to the front of the line. When he was getting ready to leave, I tried to shake his hand again. "Oh no, sir. I am very fine."

This place is huge. It holds a lot of shops, at least half are duty-free stores (rip-offs), about a quarter are standard airport shops. The final quarter are shops dealing with African hats, T-shirts, rugs, baskets, even some with zebra skins. You name a craft and they had it. Some were humble, others quite nice and pricey.

The flight to Amsterdam left on time. Somewhere around 6 A.M. the next day, I was no longer in Africa. By 9:30 A.M. I was in Amsterdam.

Getting off the plane in Amsterdam was interesting. It took forever. When I was leaving the plane, I found out why. Armed military were standing in the Jetway. With them were immigration officers. Everyone was asked for a passport. Everyone was asked his or her citizenship. This wasn't cursory. This was a good hard look. I still don't know why.

I never left the terminal. It was as it had appeared the first time, to be very much like a Greyhound bus station. I just wanted out.

When my flight back to Detroit was called, I found myself in a rather long line with the other passengers. Four interview stations were set up just inside the hallway. Each of us was interviewed. At some length. I was given extra attention.

"Mr. Donarski, you are traveling with firearms, I see?"

"Yes."

"Why?"

"Hunting."

"Why?"

"Excuse me."

"Why do think it necessary to shoot animals?"

This was getting ridiculous. It took some doing, but I remained calm, at least on the outside.

"Sir, do you have a rat problem in Amsterdam?" I asked. "No offense, as we have them in the United States. If you do, then you know that you must control their numbers or problems will result. Too many rats is not a good thing. It is the same with other animals. Too many causes starvation and they die badly."

"Oh, I see. So you were doing population control?"

I saw a quick end to this. "Yes, sir, I was. It has to be done." I looked forlorn, or tried to anyway.

"Yes, bad business. Necessary but bad. You are free to go."

I gathered up my passport and the other paperwork and walked away. I did not look back.

The plane left Amsterdam at 11 A.M. We arrived in Detroit through the wizardry of time zones at 1 P.M. Time for the U.S. Customs and Immigration checks.

Immigration was no problem. None at all. The officer even asked me what I shot on safari. When I told him, he just whistled and said, "Someday . . . "

"Someday will never come, sir. Make your plan to do it. Then do it."

None of my bags came off the baggage carousel before customs. None of them. I was searching rather desperately for them. I asked more than one Northwest employee about my bags. I mentioned that as I was traveling with guns maybe they were brought somewhere else. "No," I was told rudely. "All bags are on the carousel. Everything. Your guns are not special. Everything goes on the carousel."

I waited a few more minutes after every bag was taken and hustled off to the customs check. Finding another employee from Northwest, I asked again. This lady was even more rude than the first. "Your bags must be lost. They never got on board in Amsterdam."

"But ma'am, I was told by the flight attendant that my guns were on board, as well as my bag. They handle guns very carefully in Amsterdam." I was told that, too, by a flight attendant when we were taxiing for takeoff.

"Your bags aren't here! They never made it on board. Just get to customs and file a report on the other side." She huffed away. I slinked to customs.

"Sir, is there a problem?" the customs agent asked. I must have looked quite depressed.

"Yes, there is. Seems my guns and my bag didn't make it on the flight in Amsterdam even though I was told they did."

"You are Mr. Donarski?"

"Yes."

"You have a silver gun case and a big brown Cabela's duffel?"

"Yes."

"Then you don't have a problem at all. They were brought here. We have them and you are all set. We just need to check the serial numbers against your 4457."

"But . . ."

"You mean the people at the carousel from Northwest? Clueless. They don't know what they are talking about. All guns are brought directly to customs, as are the bags if there is ammunition in them." I just shook my head.

Everything was there, and in order. I turned my bags over to another person to check in for my last flight. I retreated to the World Club lounge and waited for the final flight.

Driving from the airport in Pelston to my home takes about 80 minutes. I missed my family. I had to continually check my speed. The sun was still up but on its decline as I crossed the Mackinac Bridge into the Upper Peninsula.

There were hugs when I got home. My family kept me up with questions half the night. Finally the kids grew tired and went to bed. I slept the sleep of the dead.

CHAPTER 22

Left Behind

ive days later I e-mailed Doug. I wanted to e-mail him sooner but just couldn't. E-mailing would be the finality of the entire experience. I was still in the afterglow. I didn't want it to end.

Dear Bwana Kiboko,

While it was probably best, handkerchief-wise, that our good-bye was from 30 meters and a mass of humanity away, I still feel something missing. It is impossible at this time to put into words how much I appreciate the invite to come along for the ride and experience Mother Africa. I expected a lot—a mountain—and I got the whole mountain range, even more.

I am emotionally worn out. That is a feeling I haven't had, well, since a particularly unpleasant job for the government. Yet, this time, the feeling is quite different. The outward symptoms are the same, the inner symptoms are strange. It feels empty.

Even Kris sees it in me. When looking through the DVD of photos, she turned to me and said, "This was a one-time deal for you, right?" I answered her that yes, as that is what we had agreed upon. Then she shocked me by saying, "How can it be? This trip has changed you." When I mentioned your plans for a return to Tanzania, she told me that we would work it out. Somehow.

Hell, Doug, I'll flip burgers, I'll shovel shit, I'll wipe snot-filled noses. I'll do anything to go back.

This trip was, and is, a defining moment. There was adventure around the next bend, over the next hill, each and every time. There was magic in each sunrise and sunset, every shadow, every breeze. The breast milk of Mother Earth has an added touch of honey that I have never tasted before. I long to suckle it again.

I am forever in your debt for sharing the experience.

Bwana Palahala

P.S. I trust the leg is improving.

The author and professional hunter Spyker are all smiles thanks to the size of this bushbuck.

The next day I received this in reply.

Bwana Palahala,

Ruark was right again. Your soul does get left behind, or simply refuses to leave. A part of it will never catch up. After reading that part of his book again, I have come to understand that this is okay, even normal. Now that I can put a phrase to the weirdness of it all, it doesn't bother me. In fact it is the most tangible evidence that this philosophical/religious skeptic has ever experienced for the existence of a soul.

And sometimes you come to a turn in the trail. A turn you may or may not want to take. You can't see behind it, but you do take it. And something opens up in front of you that you kind of heard of but never thought you would actually experience. When you are lucky, it defines you as a man, it answers questions in your life. All you really want is more because in some unexplainable way you know you have discovered something great, and you know that things that used to be important don't really matter as much.

The emotional impact of a trip like this is powerful. It is harder on someone who has been set up for it through prior experience. I was set up. You were set up. I can only beam with pride and satisfaction if I did anything to help set you up. I fell hard and fast. To some extent I am still in free-fall. You are, too.

You spoke of debt in your last mail. There is no debt. I gave up nothing, and nothing is expected in return. All I did was receive, which is exactly what you did, too.

A herd of blue wildebeest in the fading African light.

Nothing is quite the same as before. All I want to do is to go back. Everything we ever wanted is just beyond that tree line, or around the curve of the hill. All we have to do is go over and collect it.

Doug, who was a short time ago Bwana Kiboko, and longs to be again

P.S. The leg is fine. It gets stronger every day. I know in winter it will grump and remind me of a hillside in Africa. So what? Scars are the medals life hands out for attendance. Neither you nor I have been truant.

I couldn't let this conversation go. I didn't want it to die, I couldn't. A piece of me felt hollow.

Doug,
It is heart and soul, isn't it? Your reference to Ruark helps a lot. I had forgotten that part of his story. My soul isn't lost; it just decided to stay behind in a place where milk and honey flows, where the lion lies with the lamb. I left some clothes and boots with the trackers so that I would have a piece of me still walking in Africa. I'm glad I left them even more now. With the clothes my soul drifts in the breeze, kisses the tops of the grasses, ruffles the fur of beautiful animals. It breathes the dusty air kicked up by herds of wildebeest and spingbok. The feeling is still strange, but I am getting a better handle on it.

Preconceived notions don't work in Africa, do they? I went for four critters and came back with so much more. My dreams were shattered in three weeks. Shattered because the dream did not do the experience justice. When the pieces were put back in place, I found that one plus one can, and does, equal five, six, or seven. That if it only equaled two, then it would just be another place down the road rather than what it is. It *is* Africa. Africa, where nothing makes sense to the emotionally incoherent and the academically regimented. Africa, where everything makes sense to the dreamer.

Nothing is the same. When good buddies who have an inclination for this sort of thing ask me about the trip, I have only been giving them the short story, that it has changed my life. That's all I say, all I can say. I am still figuring it all out.

When they press me for details, I tell them, yes, I took this and that and the other. But, really, that is not the point. The point is that it changed me, and yes, the animals helped facilitate that change. In the end they were but one player in a cast of many. The playwright isn't through with me yet. Nor with you, thank God.

Okay, I rambled a bit, so be it. It's the way I feel and fuck 'em if the others can't understand.

Dan

Finally this came from Doug a couple of days later.

Bwana,

Once you realize that it is your soul that's missing, and that your poor corporeal body had to leave, but it, your soul, has the freedom to choose to stay awhile, and that it did choose to stay, then it is all okay. It's okay because you know exactly where it is, and you know that it will come home eventually. Right now it's just taking a sabbatical.

And if it doesn't come back, if it chooses to be stubborn and just won't leave, that is okay, too, because you know where to go and find it again. All you have to do is to drag your stupid, drooping, corporeal body back there. It'll be there to greet you with a hug and a kiss. And it will forever be too polite to mention that you were stupid enough to leave in the first place.

My hat speaks the truth.

Once you are engaged in something as grand as this, as you and I most certainly are, it is all reaction and instinct. That is why I kept saying to Pierre when he asked me what I wished to do: "Let's go out and see what happens. I won't spit in the eye of God."

For the right mind Africa is a drug, a fulfillment, a promise, and a prophesy. Africa makes sense to the dreamer. Hemingway was a dreamer, sort of. He got it, sort of. Ruark was a pure dreamer, and he got it all. It made sense to him. Thankfully he could write it all down well enough to tell other dreamers so they, too, could go and hopefully "get it" as well. Dougie and Danny are dreamers. The damn thing got them but good.

Sorry about that, hoss. Ain't nothing ever going to be the same.

Doug

Two Years Later

t at times seems a lifetime ago. At times it seems like yesterday. I experienced emotional overload, spiritual enrichment, and physical challenges. If, in fact, this safari would have been the one and only, I would still be the better for it.

Pierre told me early on in the planning stages, and I quote, "Mr. Donarski, do not come to Africa."

Spyker Joubert, at the first evening's dinner at Moreson, told me, and I quote again, "Mr. Donarski, you, sir, are a foolish man. You'll be back no matter what you say."

Yeah, yeah, right.

I should have been thinking, "Oh shit, what I have I done now?" One safari has turned into more than a few. I'm staring another three in the face as I write this. That first trip to Africa changed my life. I sold my boat to go on one. I sold stock to go on another. My disposable income has been and is being disposed of in Africa.

Doug told me that nothing would ever be the same after this first trip. I had no idea just how true that statement would turn out to be.

Some of the safaris took place with the same professional hunters that I was with on this one. Some safaris had others. As you would imagine, some were better than the rest.

I was quite lucky on this first safari. My buddy Doug set it up with someone he trusted and hunted with in Tanzania, Pierre van Tonder. PVT brought along a like-minded fellow in the form of Spyker Joubert. These two remarkable men are now my friends.

They have also, through a strange quirk, become business associates. It would be dishonest to tell you anything less. Just over a year ago, Hunter's Horn Adventures opened its doors. The company is a simple one. We book hunting and photo safaris to South Africa and Tanzania. We're looking at Swaziland and Botswana.

I agreed to play a part for one reason. I do not like being sold a bill of goods and then sent up the proverbial river. I have been on more than one occasion. You shouldn't. This little company wants to help people experience Africa in all its majesty and mystery and with no hidden costs or conditions.

All this means that more than my disposable income has found its way to Africa. Yeah, it may sound like a cool thing, but talk to me in ten years and see if I broke even. It is a huge risk as there are a lot of booking agencies and hunting consultants out there. Some are good, some are shysters.

Doug is still practicing law and hoping to someday get it right. Margaret is still launching rockets and watching for gamma ray bursts and other things I don't understand. Dave is still heavily involved in extremely high-tech optics and optics coating, which I also do not understand. Mary, after a rather intense medical scare, is now back on her feet, albeit still with a cane. The four of them are in the process of planning their next African adventure, a 21-day safari to the Selous Game Reserve in Tanzania. I dream of going along for the ride.

Right now I'm sitting at the dining table of our family's hunting cabin in the north woods of Marinette County, Wisconsin. It's a beautiful soft night. The woodcock danced on the western sky this spring evening. There's a glass of scotch sitting near the laptop. Condensation from the glass is creating a pool of liquid that is growing ever larger on the red and white checkerboard oilcloth. A half-finished issue of *Sports Afield* is opened to a Cape buffalo story on the couch.

Africa, always Africa. When I listen closely, I swear I can hear the laughing doves' final salute to another magnificent day. I hear the baboons roar in disgust at a disturbance. I hear the leopard's saw, the jackals' yip. I smell the blackjack and the aloe and the earth.

A small fire sends flickering shadow dancing through the window. I can hear muted voices and unrestrained laughter from the fire circle. Looking out I can see the shadows of my friends dancing across the pane, hail-fellows-well-met all.

Another piece of my soul has decided to return, and with it, another piece of Africa. It tells me that it is time go back. I leave in two weeks.

May 8, 2007
Donarski Rodzina Jelen Chalupa
Amberg, Wisconsin

If you'd like to see more photos from across southern Africa and see what Pierre, Spyker, and I are up to, check out www.huntershornadventures.com.

Safari Packing List

While on safari in South Africa, a variety of habitats and climates will be encountered. While the country has a very temperate climate, mornings and evening can be quite chilly, particularly in Free State province and KwaZulu-Natal. From May through August, expect daily high temperatures to reach the mid-70s to low 80s with very little humidity. Daily lows can reach the lower 30s with frost in the early morning. From March to April and September to October, temperatures range from the high 40s for the low, into the high 80s for the highs.

CLOTHING

2 pairs of comfortable and well-broken-in hunting boots

4 pairs of hunting socks and sock liners (I recommend Cabela's Outfitter series for both socks and liners. Mid-weight socks are preferred.)

1 pair of gaiters

3 to 4 pairs of underwear

1 pair of camp shoes (sandals, running shoes, etc.)

2 pairs of camp socks, something nice and comfy for after the day's hunt

3 pairs of hunting pants (I recommend Cabela's Trail Hikers.)

3 long-sleeve hunting shirts (I recommend Cabela's Serengeti Safari Shirt.)

1 or 2 sweaters

Fleece jacket (Cabela's Windstopper/Windshear series fleece works very well.)

Cabela's Safari jacket (This jacket, when worn over the sweater or fleece, will help prevent the thorns and seed pods from sticking to the sweater/fleece.)

Stocking cap

2 pairs of gloves (1 pair of lightweight shooting gloves, 1 pair of lightly insulated)

One set of "camp clothes" (sweatpants/sweatshirt or similar)

Swimsuit (Some camps have nice pools.)

PERSONAL EQUIPMENT

Toiletry kit

Medications as required (I would recommend having your doctor pre-
    scribe a broad spectrum antibiotic like Cipro, as well as a low-grade
    pain killer like Vicodin and possibly a muscle relaxer/inflamation
    reducer like Flexiril. You just never know.)

Sunglasses

Sunscreen

Lip balm

Medium-size daypack (for storing an extra sweater, safari coat, bullets,
    film, water, etc.)

Flashlight

Good quality binoculars

Pocketknife

Camera with extra batteries/film/memory cards (If using rechargeable
    batteries, make sure to purchase an international adapter.)

Gun Import Requirements

R equirements are constantly changing for flying and importing guns. Currently Air France requires advance notification that you are traveling with guns. They want to know the calibers/gauges, the action, the dimensions of the gun case or cases, and their weight. You or your travel agent must call them and give them the information a few weeks before you leave.

Flying through Amsterdam requires you to fax, and only fax, a special form that tells them you are in transit with guns. That goes even if you are only in the airport for an hour. You must fax this in, along with a statement of ownership like the US Customs Form 4457, at least four weeks before your flight. A couple of weeks later you will get a returned fax with the request approved. Though I have never been asked to show it to anyone in Amsterdam, I wouldn't recommend trying to fly through this city without it.

These are the only special requirements that I know of besides the simple stateside requirement of showing the TSA folks that your guns are unloaded and signing that foolish red tag stating so, and then slipping it into the case.

Once you land in Johannesburg you will clear your guns with a temporary import permit at the South African Police Office located inside the international terminal. This is a painless, although time-consuming, procedure.

You have two choices here. You can do it all yourself, or you can engage an "expediter." These expediters secure your temporary import permit before you arrive. They meet you at the SAP office with your permit in hand, and hustle you through the process. For this they charge anywhere from $90 to $120. Generally these services can save you time.

There are a number of companies that provide this service. Three that I am aware of and can recommend are www.phasa.co.za (This s a service provided by the Professional Hunters Association of South Africa.); www.riflepermits.com; and www.hunterssupport.com. (These last two are private companies.) Each supples a detailed instruction list and a timetable. Follow the instructions and abide by the timetable.

Doing it yourself isn't a hard thing to do; it just takes a little bit more time. In either case you are going to need a few documents. These are:

- SAP 520: Filled out in *black* ink, in *block* letters. DO NOT sign this form until one of the officers asks you to do so.
- Declaration/Statement of Ownership of Firearms (Customs Form 4457): This is a simple form that states the make, model, caliber/gauge, and serial number of the guns you are bringing. In lieu of this form, a letter from your local sheriff or chief of police stating the above will suffice.
- Letter of Invitation: This you get from your outfitter. It states the timeframe of your hunt, what you will be hunting, and generally where you will be hunting.
- Roundtrip Airline Ticket: Or a letterhead copy of your itinerary that states arrival and departure dates.
- Copy of Your Passport Title Page: This is the page with your picture on it.

Keep in mind that one gun per caliber/gauge may be brought in and that there are no semiautomatic firearms allowed.

Medical/Insurance Needs

et a physical! And be sure to bring any personal prescriptions and malarial prophylaxis if you'll be in a malarial zone.

MEDICAL INSURANCE

- Some U.S. insurance companies will cover you while traveling overseas; some do not. Be sure to find out if you're covered. If your insurance provider does cover you, ask for a letter attesting to that fact. If your company does not, a supplemental insurance rider is normally available.
- Be advised that some hospitals/clinics will require cash payment even if you're covered by insurance.
- MedJet Assist, a U.S. company, does provide evacuation insurance from a hospital to a hospital of your choice as long as you are more than 150 miles from your home of record. They can be reached at 800/963-3538 or www.medjetassist.com. Rates are very reasonable.
- Travel Guard, another insurance provider for evacuation/medical expenses, as well as trip cancellation, is highly regarded. Reach them at 800/826-1300 or www.travelguard.com. Rates with Travel Guard are also quite reasonable.

As an aside, on my third safari I had my own medical issue. I knew I was allergic to horses, cats, and white-tailed deer. On my first two trips I was careful to watch for symptoms when I handled the animals. I had no problem. Number three was not a charm.

After handling a kudu, I started to get itchy. Then I started to swell up around my face and neck. My eyes started to water. Soon they were almost swollen shut, and the swelling on my neck had grown so large that from my shoulders to my chin I looked like a triangle. My breathing wasn't labored, much. But I was in trouble.

Three hours later I made it to a clinic where a doctor gave me one shot, and when that didn't bring me around, gave me a second. Seems my allergies also now include kudu. After the shots I saw pink springbok, yellow kudu, and acacias of every color of the rainbow dancing through the haze that used to be my brain.

So, if you have allergies or other known issues, you should damn well be prepared to take care of them.

Taxidermy

o not wait until you're in Africa before thinking hard about taxidermy. You need to think well ahead. You need a well-thought-out plan.

There are two basic choices when it comes to taxidermy. You will either have the heads mounted and the skins tanned in Africa, or you will have them done back in the United States or your home country. There are pros and cons, and a lot of disagreements as to which is the wiser choice.

If you are going to have the work done in the United States or your home country, there is still some work that needs to be done in Africa. This process is called dip and pack. Dip and pack entails mainly an insecticide treatment of the head, horns, and capes. When these tasks are completed, the taxidermist calls you and requests payment, including the shipping charges. These must be shipped by air. Ocean freight does not accept raw skins. As of May 1, 2007, dip and pack trophies may be shipped air or ocean freight.

It is highly recommended that you engage the services of a customs broker to handle the shipment. Your trophies will be cleared by customs and U.S. Fish and Wildlife. There is a good deal of paperwork that needs to be done. These brokers are specialists. Find a good one and pay him for his services.

Once cleared, the broker or agent calls you and arranges shipping to the taxidermist of your choice. You pay the agent for the shipping to the taxidermist and off they go. I am most familiar with Fauna & Flora out of Jamaica, New York. Reach them at www.faunandflora.com or 718-977-7700. Quality service is what they deliver.

Dipping and packing and shipping of these trophies is much less expensive than the shipping of trophies completed in South Africa. We're talking only shipping now, not the taxidermy work. The dipping and packing service is quite reasonable as well.

There are a number of benefits in getting the work completed in the States. The first is time. You will get the trophies sent over to the States much quicker than if you have all the work done over there. Dip and pack should not take any longer than three months. Another is that you will be able to keep better track of the progress on your trophies. If money is an issue, and it probably will be, you can have the trophies done in batches and spread out the payments.

Another benefit is that you can visit a number of taxidermy studios and see who is doing the work you like best. Visit at least three or four. Look at their work. Do not trust a friend saying Acme Taxidermy is the best. Acme may be the best for him, but it doesn't mean that their work will trip your trigger.

Yet another benefit is that you may be able to have the taxidermist visit your home before the work is ever started. That way he can see for himself what space you have to work with and offer suggestions on how to best use that space. Legends Taxidermy of Ludington, Michigan, is five hours from my home. They offer this service to their clients at no extra charge with safari animals. They also deliver them to my home at no extra charge. If you are going to be handing over a few thousand dollars or more for your work, you should negotiate this into the bill, too.

And, finally, you can change your mind during the process. Say you want the ear cocked just so. You can have the taxidermist change it. Say you decide that you really want that kudu to hang on another wall, a wall where the thing just won't fit the way you thought you wanted. They can change it before the hide is fixed to the mannequin. Basically, when you have the work done here you will be at least in partial control. That is a big comfort.

So, what are the benefits of having the entire work done in South Africa? The first thing that comes to mind for most people is money. Taxidermy work is less expensive over there. Some say the work is substandard compared to the work done in the United States In some cases that is true. There are good taxidermists in Africa and there are not so good ones. The same holds true in the United States.

Some think that, as the work is being done in Africa, it will be more lifelike for the simple reason that the taxidermists see more of the real thing. That they see more is certainly true, whether it is more lifelike depends entirely on the taxidermist's skill.

If you get the work done over there, you will be pushed into what some call the black hole. Even the best and quickest of taxidermists won't get your completed trophies ready for shipment for at least a year. The standard is 14 to 16 months. That's a long time to wait and wonder.

Contact with the taxidermist will be hard. E-mails may or may not be answered in a day or two. Progress reports come all too seldom for a lot of people. You won't be able to change your mind as to how you want an animal mounted in any major way. And, chances are, the work will be done by a taxidermist you have never met. Don't expect to visit a few studios on your trip. Feel very lucky if you are able to visit more than one. Expect to pay a down payment of 50 percent before the work is started.

If you are having the work done in Africa, come prepared with a layout of where the animals will hang. Take your time with this. You will have these trophies for a long time, and you want to get it right. Decide if you want this one looking straight on, or left or right. How much of an angle left or right. Head tilted back, ears cocked. All of this needs to be decided before you leave for your safari.

When it comes time for shipping your completed trophies, the same rules apply as they did for the dip and pack work. Get a customs broker/shipping agent. The paperwork issues are still in effect. Now, however, you have a choice. Completed trophies can either go by air freight or ocean freight. Ocean freight is much cheaper and takes roughly 30 days to reach a port on the eastern U.S. seaboard. By air it takes a day and a half. Heck, you've waited so long, what will another 30 days mean?

Once in port, or at the airport, the trophies will be cleared. Your broker/agent will contact you and arrange shipping to your home. When they get there, kiss the box. Thank God for his providence. Admire.

Index